广东石油化工学院 2018 年度精品教材项目
广东石油化工学院教学团队（外语专业技能课程教学团队）资助项目（JXTD201924）

商务汉英翻译

Chinese-English Translation for Business Purpose

主　编　李太志
副主编　董　坤
编　委　李太志　董　坤　蒋　放

苏州大学出版社

图书在版编目(CIP)数据

商务汉英翻译 = Chinese-English Translation for Business Purpose / 李太志主编. —苏州:苏州大学出版社,2021.1
ISBN 978-7-5672-3371-3

Ⅰ.①商… Ⅱ.①李… Ⅲ.①商务-英语-翻译-教材 Ⅳ.①F7

中国版本图书馆 CIP 数据核字(2020)第 235948 号

书　　　名:	商务汉英翻译
	Chinese-English Translation for Business Purpose
主　　编:	李太志
责任编辑:	汤定军
助理编辑:	万才兰
策划编辑:	汤定军
封面设计:	刘　俊
出版发行:	苏州大学出版社(Soochow University Press)
社　　址:	苏州市十梓街1号　邮编:215006
印　　装:	镇江文苑制版印刷有限责任公司
网　　址:	www.sudapress.com
邮　　箱:	sdcbs@suda.edu.cn
邮购热线:	0512-67480030
销售热线:	0512-67481020
开　　本:	787 mm×1092 mm　1/16　印张:17.75　字数:366千
版　　次:	2021年1月第1版
印　　次:	2021年1月第1次印刷
书　　号:	ISBN 978-7-5672-3371-3
定　　价:	58.00 元

凡购本社图书发现印装错误,请与本社联系调换。服务热线:0512-67481020

前言

作为在商务语境或情景中使用的英语,商务英语不是一种独立的语言形式,而是一种社会功能语言变体。经过几十年的发展,商务英语在国外已经发展成为专门用途英语中最大的一个分支。国外学者对商务英语的定义、性质、范畴等进行了较为系统的研究。(王立非、李琳,2011)在我国,商务英语专业正在蓬勃发展,而同时商务英语研究也在不断深化,成果颇丰。

除学术论文之外,近年来以商务汉英翻译为专题进行研究的教材和专著越来越多。本教材的最大亮点就是以商务汉英翻译中出现的较为典型的问题为导向,以培养分析问题和解决问题的能力为目标。本教材从宏观和微观两个层面对比分析了商务汉英作为特殊用途的社会功能语言变体所表现出来的语言文化上的差异,并据此提出针对性较强的适用于商务汉英翻译的启示。

本教材的主要内容和总体框架如下:

第一,第一章以功能语境理论为指导,从宏观层面探讨商务英语作为商务汉英翻译译入语在语域之语场、语式和语旨三个方面的语言文化特征,继而分析功能语境对商务汉英翻译的制约作用。

第二,第二章以汉英对比分析理论为指导,分别从语言与文化两个宏观层面对比分析商务汉英作为特殊用途语言变体所表现出来的语言文化特征及其差异,并据此提出灵活而恰当的翻译方法和策略。

第三,第三章梳理并简述适用于商务汉英翻译的国内外翻译标准和原则,探讨分析商务汉英翻译标准的多样性以及商务汉英翻译中存在的问题。

第四,第四章和第九章以语体和文体为切入点,对比分析商务汉英在语体和文体方面表现出来的语言文化特征及其差异,在此基础上探讨语体和文体分析在商务汉英翻译中的作用,并据此分别统领和指导对词句段篇以及商标、商用名片、商务信函、商务合同、商业广告、商业说明书等几种主要文体中所表现出来的语言文化差异及其翻译的探讨。

第五,第五章至第八章以语体分析为引领,分别从词、句、段、篇等微观层面对比分析商务汉英语言文化差异,继而提出对商务汉英翻译针对性较强的启示与预防因受汉语负面影响而发生失误的警示。

第六,第十章至第十五章以文体分析为引领,分别对商标、商用名片、商务信函、商务合同、商业广告、商业说明书等几种具有代表性的应用文文体中表现出来的商务汉英语言文化差异进行比较系统的对比分析,继而提出对商务汉英翻译的启示与警示。

本教材分为概论、分论1(词句段篇)和分论2(几种主要商务汉英应用文文体)三部分。通过从不同层面、不同视角、不同切入点对商务汉英语言文化进行多维观照和对比分析,本教材旨在构建一个较为系统的商务汉英语言文化对比分析的框架体系,在对比分析商务汉英语言文化差异的基础上,有针对性地提出指导有效商务汉英翻译的启示。

本教材可供高等院校英语专业学生、翻译专业学生、商务英语专业学生、热心研究商务英语翻译与教学的高校教师、从事商务翻译实务的工作人员、翻译爱好者等使用。笔者相信,对商务汉英语言文化的对比分析将丰富我国商务汉英翻译教学内容,有助于商务汉英翻译水平和跨文化商务英语交际能力的提高,有益于我国对外商贸事业的繁荣发展。

本教材主编李太志负责编写第一章至第十二章,副主编董坤负责编写第十三章至第十五章。

由于时间仓促、编者水平有限,加上商务汉英翻译的研究有待深入和提高,本教材存在疏漏之处在所难免,请读者给予批评指正。

李太志

2020年9月

目 录

I. 概 论

■ 第一章 功能语境制约下的商务英语及其翻译 / 2
　第一节 功能语境制约下的商务英语语言文化特征 / 3
　　1.1 功能语境制约下的商务英语语言特征 / 3
　　1.2 功能语境制约下的商务英语文化特征 / 9
　第二节 功能语境对商务英语翻译的制约作用 / 11
　　2.1 功能语境与成功翻译的条件 / 11
　　2.2 功能语境与翻译表达 / 13

■ 第二章 商务汉英语言文化对比分析与翻译 / 17
　第一节 语言文化关联下的商务汉英对比分析 / 18
　　1.1 语言关联下的商务汉英对比分析 / 18
　　1.2 文化关联下的商务汉英对比分析 / 22
　第二节 以交际为目的的多"译"善"变" / 27
　　2.1 回译 / 28
　　2.2 套译 / 28
　　2.3 直译或音译加注 / 33
　　2.4 意译变"名" / 34
　　2.5 改译换"名" / 35
　　2.6 英译汉化 / 35
　　2.7 符合译语习惯的英译简化 / 36
　　2.8 解释性英译 / 36

■ 第三章 商务汉英翻译的标准及存在的问题 / 40
　第一节 适用于商务汉英翻译的标准 / 41
　　1.1 国外学者提出的翻译标准及其应用 / 42

1.2　国内学者提出的翻译标准及其应用　/45
第二节　商务汉英翻译中存在的问题　/48
　　2.1　翻译"不忠",误译较多　/48
　　2.2　翻译有失"准确",造成歧义　/49
　　2.3　翻译有失"统一",不地道,不规范　/50
　　2.4　翻译生硬,译文有翻译腔　/51
　　2.5　翻译"跑调",译文不得体　/52
　　2.6　死译硬译,搭配不当　/52

Ⅱ. 分 论（1）

第四章　商务汉英语体修辞对比分析与翻译　/56
第一节　多维度的商务汉英语体修辞对比分析与翻译　/57
　　1.1　语音层面上的商务汉英语体修辞对比分析与翻译　/57
　　1.2　词汇层面上的商务汉英语体修辞对比分析与翻译　/58
　　1.3　句子层面上的商务汉英语体修辞对比分析与翻译　/60
　　1.4　语篇层面上的商务汉英语体修辞对比分析与翻译　/61
第二节　对商务汉英语体翻译的启示与警示　/63
　　2.1　启示："斟词酌句"须有修辞眼光　/63
　　2.2　警示：不要文白夹杂,有失"体统"　/64

第五章　商务汉英词义对比分析与翻译　/67
第一节　"实"义与"虚"义、"增"译与"减"译　/68
　　1.1　商务汉英"虚"与"实"的词义差异对比分析　/68
　　1.2　对商务汉英词汇翻译的启示与警示　/69
第二节　商务汉英"普通词义"与"专业词义"对比分析与翻译　/71
　　2.1　商务汉英"普通词义"与"专业词义"的差异对比分析　/71
　　2.2　对商务汉英词汇翻译的启示与警示　/73
第三节　商务汉英褒贬词义对比分析与翻译　/75
　　3.1　商务汉英褒贬词义差异对比分析　/75
　　3.2　对商务汉英词汇翻译的启示与警示　/76
第四节　商务汉英正式与非正式语体词义对比分析与翻译　/77
　　4.1　商务汉英正式与非正式语体的词义差异对比分析　/77
　　4.2　对商务汉英词汇翻译的启示与警示　/79

第五节　商务汉英正反义对比分析与翻译　/ 82
　　　5.1　商务汉英正反义的差异对比分析　/ 82
　　　5.2　对商务汉英词汇翻译的启示与警示　/ 83

■ 第六章　商务汉英词类用法对比分析与翻译　/ 87
　　第一节　商务汉英动词与名词用法差异对比分析与翻译　/ 88
　　　1.1　商务汉英动词与名词用法的差异对比分析　/ 88
　　　1.2　对商务汉英词类翻译的启示与警示　/ 90
　　第二节　商务汉英动词与介词用法差异对比分析与翻译　/ 92
　　　2.1　商务汉英动词与介词用法的差异对比分析　/ 92
　　　2.2　对商务汉英词类翻译的启示与警示　/ 93

■ 第七章　商务汉英句法对比分析与翻译　/ 98
　　第一节　商务汉英意合与形合之间的句法差异对比分析与翻译　/ 99
　　　1.1　商务汉英意合与形合之间的句法差异对比分析　/ 99
　　　1.2　对商务汉英句法翻译的启示与警示　/ 101
　　第二节　商务汉英尾重与头重之间的信息结构差异对比分析与翻译　/ 105
　　　2.1　商务汉英尾重与头重之间的信息结构差异对比分析　/ 105
　　　2.2　对商务汉英句法翻译的启示与警示　/ 106
　　第三节　汉语突出话题与英语突出主语的句法结构差异对比分析与翻译　/ 109
　　　3.1　汉语突出话题与英语突出主语的句法结构差异对比分析　/ 109
　　　3.2　对商务汉英句法翻译的启示与警示　/ 110
　　第四节　商务汉英人称与物称之间的句法修辞差异对比分析与翻译　/ 111
　　　4.1　商务汉英人称与物称之间的句法修辞差异对比分析　/ 111
　　　4.2　对商务汉英句法翻译的启示与警示　/ 113
　　第五节　商务汉英主动语态与被动语态之间的句法修辞差异对比分析与翻译　/ 114
　　　5.1　商务汉英主动语态与被动语态之间的句法修辞差异对比分析　/ 114
　　　5.2　对商务汉英句法翻译的启示与警示　/ 115

■ 第八章　商务汉英语段语篇对比分析与翻译　/ 120
　　第一节　商务汉英语段差异对比分析与翻译　/ 121
　　　1.1　商务汉英语段差异对比分析　/ 121
　　　1.2　对商务汉英语段翻译的启示与警示　/ 127
　　第二节　商务汉英语篇差异对比分析与翻译　/ 131
　　　2.1　商务汉英语篇差异对比分析　/ 131
　　　2.2　对商务汉英语篇翻译的启示与警示　/ 133

Ⅲ. 分　论（2）

■ **第九章　商务汉英文体对比分析与翻译 / 138**

第一节　商务汉英文体特征对比分析与翻译 / 139

    1.1　商务信函的文体特征及其翻译 / 140

    1.2　商务合同的文体特征及其翻译 / 141

    1.3　商业说明书的文体特征及其翻译 / 142

    1.4　商业广告的文体特征及其翻译 / 143

第二节　对商务汉英文体翻译的启示与警示 / 145

    2.1　启示：分析与优化文体修辞，英译分"体"别类 / 145

    2.2　警示：切合原文文体，不能"跑调串体" / 145

■ **第十章　汉英商标对比分析与翻译 / 149**

第一节　汉英商标的语言文化差异对比分析 / 150

    1.1　以动植物命名的汉英商标文化现象 / 150

    1.2　使用溢美之词的汉英商标语言文化对比 / 152

    1.3　汉语商标仿造、自造"洋"名与英语商标创新词 / 152

第二节　对汉英商标翻译的启示与警示 / 153

    2.1　对汉英商标翻译的启示 / 153

    2.2　对汉英商标翻译的警示 / 155

■ **第十一章　汉英商用名片对比分析与翻译 / 160**

第一节　汉英商用名片的语言文化差异对比分析 / 160

    1.1　人名中的语言文化差异对比分析 / 161

    1.2　地名中的语言文化差异对比分析 / 161

    1.3　职务职称中的语言文化差异对比分析 / 162

第二节　对汉英商用名片翻译的启示与警示 / 163

    2.1　对汉英商用名片翻译的启示 / 163

    2.2　对汉英商用名片翻译的警示 / 164

■ **第十二章　商务汉英信函对比分析与翻译 / 170**

第一节　商务汉英信函语言文化差异的对比分析与翻译 / 171

    1.1　用词简练准确、行文专业规范上的汉英语言文化差异对比分析与翻译 / 172

    1.2　礼貌用语上的商务汉英语言文化差异对比分析与翻译 / 175

    1.3　语气和语态使用上的商务汉英语言文化差异对比分析与翻译 / 175

第二节　对商务汉英信函翻译的启示与警示　/ 177
　　　　2.1　对商务汉英信函翻译的启示　/ 177
　　　　2.2　对商务汉英信函翻译的警示　/ 178

第十三章　商务汉英合同对比分析与翻译　/ 186

　　第一节　商务汉英合同语言文化差异的对比分析与翻译　/ 187
　　　　1.1　商务合同都力求精确,但汉英各有其道　/ 187
　　　　1.2　商务合同都力求庄重典雅,但汉英各择手段　/ 189
　　　　1.3　商务合同都力求严谨,但汉英各有不同　/ 190
　　第二节　对商务汉英合同翻译的启示与警示　/ 191
　　　　2.1　对商务汉英合同翻译的启示　/ 191
　　　　2.2　对商务汉英合同翻译的警示　/ 192

第十四章　汉英商业广告对比分析与翻译　/ 201

　　第一节　汉英商业广告语言文化差异对比分析　/ 202
　　　　1.1　汉英商业广告语言及思维表达方式差异对比分析　/ 202
　　　　1.2　汉英商业广告语折射出的不同文化心理和价值观念对比分析　/ 204
　　第二节　对汉英商业广告翻译的启示与警示　/ 208
　　　　2.1　对汉英商业广告翻译的启示　/ 208
　　　　2.2　对汉英商业广告翻译的警示　/ 211

第十五章　汉英商业说明书对比分析与翻译　/ 217

　　第一节　汉英商业说明书语言文化差异对比分析与翻译　/ 218
　　　　1.1　力求客观准确,但汉英有别　/ 218
　　　　1.2　在说理与移情功能上的语言表现有异　/ 221
　　　　1.3　在专门性、行业性上各有表现　/ 222
　　第二节　对汉英商业说明书翻译的启示与警示　/ 223
　　　　2.1　对汉英商业说明书翻译的启示　/ 223
　　　　2.2　对汉英商业说明书翻译的警示　/ 226

思考与练习答案　/ 232
参考文献　/ 266

I. 概 论

> *Dynamic equivalence is therefore to be defined in terms of the degree to which the receptors of the message in the receptor language respond to it in substantially the same manner as the receptors in the source language. This response can never be identical, for the cultural and historical setting are too different, but there should be a high degree of equivalence of response, or the translation will have failed to accomplish its purpose.*
>
> ——*Nider & Taber*
>
> 翻译者必须是一个真正意义上的文化人。他处理的是个别词,他面对的则是两大片文化。
>
> ——王佐良

第一章

功能语境制约下的商务英语及其翻译

Identify the problems in the following translations

① 贵公司 2019 年 8 月 10 日的来函和所附文具报价单及另函寄来的样品已经收到。

英译：Your company's letter dated August 10, 2019 and the quotation sheet for stationery have been received. The samples you sent have also been received.

② 本协议由双方各自全权代表在上述首签之日起亲自签订,一式两份,双方各执一份,各自具有同等效力。立此为证。

英译：Two copies of the agreement shall be signed by the representatives of the parties hereto, duly authorized for the purpose, on the day and year first above written. Both of the agreement shall be authentic, each party retaining a copy thereof.

③ 中国粮油食品(集团)有限公司已经经历了五十多年的发展历史,五十多年来,我们与世界上一百二十多个国家和地区建立了良好的贸易合作关系,特别是近几年我们在国内组建了六十多个联营、合营企业,在国外建立了近十个海外企业。我们已经具有较强的经营能力,在国内外树立了良好的信誉。(李明,2007)

英译：China National Cereals, Oils and Foodstuffs Import and Export Corporation (COFCO), with a history of more than 50 years, has established trade links with more than 120 countries and regions in the world. In recent years, we have set up more than 60 joint ventures or cooperative enterprises at home and 10 overseas subsidiaries. We have greatly strengthened our capacity for handling our business and acquired good reputation at home and abroad.

商务英语是商务汉英翻译的目标语(target language)或译入语,我们有必要在本教材一开头就以韩礼德(Halliday)的系统功能语言学(systemic-functional grammar)为理论框架,分别探讨一下其语域的三个方面,即语场/话语范围、语式/话语方式和语旨/话语基调,并分析商务英语的语言文化特征及功能语境对商务英语翻译的制约作用,目的是熟悉并掌握商务英语的语域特征和文化语境特征,让我们在商务汉英翻译中避免犯"混淆不同语域"的错误。

第一节 功能语境制约下的商务英语语言文化特征

1.1 功能语境制约下的商务英语语言特征

作为英语的一种社会功能语言变体(a social variety of the English language),商务英语(business English; English for business purpose)是在商务情景(business situation)或商务语境(business context)中使用的英语。包括商务英语在内的特殊用途英语(ESP/English for specific purposes)并不是一种独立的语言形式,而是现代英语的一种社会功能语言变体(Hutchinson & Waters,1987),是专门供特定的社会文化群体所使用的一种语言范围。

1.1.1 商务英语的概念、定义和归属

"在我国,商务英语是一个动态的概念,有经贸英语、商贸英语、外贸英语等名目繁多的称谓。商务英语教学始于20世纪50年代。90年代以后,商务英语的教学和研究工作出现了欣欣向荣的局面。"(石春让、白艳,2012:80)

在国内外学术界,许多学者对"商务英语"这个学科概念给出了不同的定义和解释。Jones & Alexander(1989)把商务英语称为"商务用途英语"或"用于商务情景中的英语"。与其他特殊用途英语变体不同的地方是,商务英语常常融合(与某一职业或行业相关的)特殊内容和(与有效商务沟通能力相关的)普通内容。(Ellis & Johnson,2002)Jordan(1997)认为,作为特殊用途英语的一个分支的商务英语是以职业为目的的英语(English for occupation purpose),是指从事某一行业所使用的英语,它的实用性和专业性较强。Hutchinson & Waters(1987)则认为,商务英语不是一种独立的语言,它仍然是英语,是英语的一种社会功能变体,是特殊用途英语的一个分支,"是商务环境中应用的英语……也就是已在从事或将要从事商务行业的专业人才所学习或应用的专门用途英语"(王兴孙,1997:1-2)。或者说,它是一种包含了各种商务活动内容、适合商业需要

的标准英语。在当今世界,国际间的商贸往来越来越频繁,国际经济贸易越来越趋向于全球化和一体化。在经贸全球化和一体化进程中,英语的重要地位将越发显现出来。"据统计,全世界16亿以英语为第一语言、第二语言或外语的人群中,几乎90%的人每天都在与商贸英语打交道。"(刘法公,1999:37)可以说,人们在国际贸易、招商引资、技术引进等商务活动中,或在办理国际金融、对外劳务承包与合同、涉外保险、国际旅游、国际运输等商务领域的事务时所使用的英语就是商务英语。(刘法公,1999)

  因为商务英语是英语的一种社会功能变体,所以它的语言形式和内容与商务知识有着密切的关系。或者说,商务英语所承载的是商务理论、商务实践等方面的信息,没有承载商务理论和商务实践等方面信息的英语就不是商务英语。由此可见,商务英语是指以服务于商务活动为目标,集实用性、专业性和明确的目的性于一身,为广大从事国际商务活动的人们所认同和接受,并具备较强社会功能的一种英语语言变体。

  虽然商务英语源于普通英语并有普通英语的语言学特征,但由于其是特殊用途英语,所以它有固定的篇章建构模式和言语程式,即在斟词酌句、布局谋篇等方面具有与普通英语不同的语言特征。

  作为英语的一种语言变体,商务英语有着以下八个方面的显著特征:

  (1) 文体(style)多元化:商务英语"体中有体,类中有类";

  (2) 实用性(practicality)强:商务英语常使用信息型、呼唤型、表达型等具有不同功能的应用文文本;

  (3) 词汇再生力强:商务英语应用范围广,因而词类转换(conversion)、词语搭配(collocation)和词义引申(extension)现象普遍;

  (4) 行业术语/专业术语(technical terms)多:因涉及的行业众多,商务英语使用的专业术语繁多;

  (5) 缩略语(acronyms & abbreviations)多:商务英语较多采用经济省时的缩略语;

  (6) 句子结构较复杂:商务英语句式规范,文体正式,尤其在商贸合同中更是如此;

  (7) 套话、行话(conventional phrases & commercialese)多:商务应用文大多具有公文(officialese)的特征,所以行文较多采用老套的商业行话和惯用语(翁凤翔,2007b);

  (8) 行文客观精确、言简意明:商务英语"重纪实,少文饰",行文大多要求 ABC(accurate, brief, clear)或 ABCD(accurate, brief, clear, decisive)或 CLEAR(clear, logical, empathetic, accurate, right)或 Six Cs(correct, complete, concise, concrete, clear, courteous)或 KISS(keep it short and simple)。

1.1.2 商务语境制约下的商务英语语言特征

  商务语境的三个变项——话语范围、话语方式和话语基调自有其特点。商务英语的话语范围或语场(field of discourse)是商务,它涉及商贸活动的各个环节、各个场所。商贸活动牵涉面广,包括金融、运输、保险、法律等。信函、传真、电邮、备忘录、计划书、合同、报告等英语书面交流伴随着商贸活动的各个环节,贯穿商贸活动的全过程。商务英语的语篇大多简明扼要(concise and to-the-point)。撰写商务英语应用文旨在处理商务活动中的具体事务,牵涉到诸如询盘报盘、订货交货、索赔理赔等业务磋商环节和通知、报告、签约等语用功能,其最终目的是使商贸活动顺利进行。所以,商务英语应用文的文体"范围十分广泛、庞杂,在长期使用过程中,根据事务的性质和应用的场合逐渐形成了若干固定的篇章格式,即固定的篇章结构形式和言语程式"(王德春、陈晨,2001:113)。总体来说,商务英语应用文的文体"重纪实,少文饰",崇尚简洁直白的语言表达风格。上述这些便构成了商务英语的语式或话语方式(mode of discourse)。商务工作者在经商时需要有国际上接受的行事方式,以使来自不同文化、说不同母语的人们能很快地、更自如地相处(Ellis & Johnson,2002),因而他们注重商贸往来中的社交礼仪。这种意识、心态和行为准则要求或决定他们在商务英语书面交流与沟通中,往往采用"以您为先"(you-attitude)、积极主动的写作语气。这就是商务英语的语旨或话语基调(tenor of discourse)的具体表现。

商务英语因其使用语境不同而有着与其特殊语境密切联系在一起的语言特征(Hutchinson & Waters,2002)。换言之,商务英语在商务语境明显有着比在其他语境更常用的语言形式(Hutchinson & Waters,2002)和文体修辞特征。总的来说,商务英语的目的性强,选词恰当、精确,表达具体、明确,意思清晰,不含糊其词,行文简约(罗健,2002)。这就是商务语境对商务英语这种社会功能性语言变体及其写作翻译加以制约的结果。普通英语与商务英语的不同表达方法见表1.1。

表1.1 普通英语与商务英语的不同表达方法

普通英语	商务英语
in early October	within the first 10 days of October
before August 10	on or before August 10
after September 20	on and after September 20
in a week	in one week or less
till January 1	till and including January 1
the majority of the goods	74% of the goods
in the nearest future	next week
a slight increase	a 3% increase
reduce our price if your order is large enough	reduce our price by 3% if your order exceeds 6,000 pcs

1.1.2.1 话语范围制约下的商务英语语言特征

话语范围对词汇和话语结构选择的影响是显而易见的。在语言使用过程中,交际参与者需要根据所谈论的内容和所从事的社会活动在语言系统所提供的意义潜势中做出选择。因此,话语范围在一定程度上决定语言表达的引申意义。由此可见,"语言寓于行为之中,意义见于运用之中"(Language in action; Meaning as use)(Leech,1981)。所以,弗斯(Firth)指出"词本无义,义随境而生"(转引自马会娟,2004:91)。维特根斯坦(Wittgenstein)对意义与语境之间的关系的表述最为明确、直接。他在 *Philosophical Investigations* 中多次说到"… the meaning of a word is its use in the language"(一个词的意义要根据它在语言中的用法来定)。维特根斯坦所说的"in the language"就是语境。根据维特根斯坦的理论观点,词语一旦进入语篇生成过程,它们便不再是一个个孤立的词语,它们的意义也不再是词典上所罗列的孤立的、静态的意义。词语的意义是不同词语组合的结果,是受不同的上下文,或者说是受语境的制约而生成的。因此,语篇中的词语意义是相互支配或制约的。比如,在普通英语中,action, subject matter, acquisition 分别表示"行动""题材""吸收",而在商务这个话语范围或语境中,就有了半专业词义,即"诉讼""标的物""并购"。

请对比分析下列例子中加下划线的词语的半专业词义:

① With pledged investment of US $12 billion, the UK is acknowledged to be the leading European investor in China and the main EU (European Union) source of technology.(英国对中国的合同外资为120亿美元,被认为是中国最主要的欧洲投资国,同时还是最大的欧盟技术来源国。)(Wood,2002)

② The accelerated rate of globalization has left companies desperately seeking overseas acquisition in order to remain competitive.(不断加速的全球化迫使各公司千方百计地收购海外公司,以保持竞争力。)(Wood,2002)

③ It's already a long time since the United States broke out a white war against China.(美国早就打响了对中国的经济战争。)

④ It is an economical little car that doesn't use much fuel.(这是一种节省燃料、经济实惠的小汽车。)

⑤ The following offer is subject to our final confirmation.(以下报盘以我方最后确认为准。)

⑥ The local government is encouraged to build affordable houses to solve the housing problems of the low-income people.(大力提倡地方政府建设经济适用房,以解决低收入群体的住房问题。)

对比分析:pledge, acquire, white, economical, offer, affordable 在普通英语中分别表示"承诺""接受""白色的""经济的""提供""可以负担得起的",而在商务这个话语范围或语境中就有了自己的隐喻修辞引申义,即"协议/合同""收购""没有硝烟的""实惠的""报盘""经济适用的"。

1.1.2.2 话语基调制约下的商务英语语言特征

话语基调也影响交际参与者对语言手段的选择,特别是参与者的社会地位、角色、职业、相互关系等都会对言语表达和修辞手段的运用产生影响。针对不同交际对象,我们要选用不同的言语方式,以求达到最佳的言语交际效果。

首先,我们以商务合同为例,来分析、说明话语基调或语旨在商务英语这个特殊语境中的体现。商务合同的语旨是指参与者的性质以及身份与角色,即签订合同的双方建立了正式的法律约束关系,当事人必须承担法律责任和经济责任,因此当事人的角色关系是正式的、严肃的,语言行文要求逻辑严密、正式严谨、用词专业、表达精准。比如,"Both parties shall have the responsibility to keep this contract confidential and …"(当事人双方均有义务对本合同保密……)就充分表现出对当事人双方的权利与义务的严格规定。

其次,表1.2列举了几类不同语体的称呼与信尾客套语。从中我们可以看出,针对所选用的称呼语,写信人要选用合适的信尾客套语。一般来说,"关系亲密的程度越高,选用的商务英语称呼语和信尾客套语就越随便(less formal);关系亲密的程度越低,选用的商务英语称呼语和信尾客套语就越正式(formal)"(何维湘,1997:33)。

表1.2 不同语体的称呼与信尾客套语

语体	称呼	信尾客套语
Very formal	My dear Sir/Madam	Respectfully/Respectfully yours
Formal	Dear Sir/Madam Gentlemen/Sirs	Yours truly Yours faithfully (British usage)
Less formal	Dear Mr./Mrs. Smith	Sincerely yours (American usage)
Personal (implying personal relation)	Dear Mr./Mrs. Jefferson Dear John	Cordially Best regards (British usage)

1.1.2.3 话语方式制约下的商务英语语言特征

话语方式是对话语客体进行传导和交流的方法和形式。话语方式与符号现实相关。"对于一个语篇来说,它不仅要与语境发生联系,反映意义的社会交换,而且其词汇、语法的表现形式也要与语篇所表达的意义相匹配。"(朱永生等,2004:181)商务英语属于"公事公办的持重感"(businesslike poise)较浓的商用公文体(commercialese),在遣词造句、布局谋篇等方面均有其独特的言语和行文方式。

在遣词造句方面,商务英语常用书面词(learned words)、长词(long words)或古体词(archaisms)替代通俗词汇(popular words),如:正式的商务英语信函常用 forward(发送)、submit(提交,呈送)分别替代 send(寄)、give(给);合同常用 whereby, prior to, hereto, thereafter 分别替代 by which, before, to (what is said), after this or that。在句法结构上,语体庄重的英语句型结构"We would be much grateful to you if you could …"(如果……我们将不胜感激)就比口语化的"Please …"(请……)在一定场合更为得体,对于特定的交际对象来说就更符合商务英语的行文方式。在布局谋篇方面,商务英语除了有特定格式之外,还有固定的篇章模式和言语程式。

请观察分析下面的商务英语信函:

⑦ **THE EASTERN SEABOARD CORP**
350 Park Avenue, New York 10017
Telephone: 225 – 2780; Fax: 225 – 2711

Dear Mr. Brown,

　　Thank you very much for your order.

　　Unfortunately, in common with other suppliers, our prices have risen since you placed an order with us two years ago, but you will be pleased to hear that we will supply your current order at the old price.

　　Enclosed please find our new catalogue and price lists, which contain several exciting new products and our latest prices.

　　I will keep you fully informed about the progress of your order. If you would like to get in touch with me urgently, our new fax number is 225-2711 or, of course, you may prefer to phone me.

　　　　　　　　　　　　　　　　　　　　　Yours faithfully,
　　　　　　　　　　　　　　　　　　　　　A. Burke
　　　　　　　　　　　　　　　　　　　　　A. Burke
　　　　　　　　　　　　　　　　　　　　　Sales Director

　　分析:商务英语信函属于公函体,有固定的格式,包括信头、收信人的地址、称呼、正文、信尾客套语、签名等。商务英语信函的交流目的是磋商业务,因此它一般使用语体较正式的词语(如:unfortunately, risen),用词力求简洁、准确、庄重,避免空泛和文饰,讲求纪实(factual)。例示的商务信函没有华美的辞藻(flashy words),较少使用动听的形容词,偏爱使用介词短语和名词化结构(如:in common with other suppliers, at the old price);句式比较单一,多用陈述句和祈使句,很少使用感叹句和疑问句;句子有短有长,但以长句为主。此外,它还倾向于使用被动句(如:enclosed, informed),以求达到纪实、客观的修辞效果。

　　语域是由多种情景特征——特别是指话语范围(field)、话语方式(mode)和话语基调(tenor)——相联系的语言特征构成的(Halliday & Hason, 1976)。如果没有必要的语域或文体意识,那么就很可能选择错误的语域、混淆不同的语域(Halliday,1973),导致措辞不得体、不适合交际对象而有损交际效果。Halliday & Hason(1976)所说的"语域"(register)就是语境。语域的确定与遣词造句有着直接的联系。从某一方面讲,语域就是指词语的使用范畴,主要是指正式与非正式语体的等级(levels of speech)。狭义的语域也指词语使用的职业或行业领域。譬如,商务合同常使用古体词(如:whereby, hitherto, whencesoever 等)、介词短语和名词化结构,商务信函倾向于使用被动句(如:be appreciated, be placed)。斟词酌句正是商务这种特定语域的措辞或行文方式。

请对比分析以下商务汉英翻译实例:

⑧ Your close cooperation in this respect will be highly appreciated.(对于贵方的密切合作,我们将不胜感激。)

⑨ Should this trial order prove satisfactory to our customers, we can assure you that repeat orders in increased quantities will be placed.(假如我们的客户对这次试订货满意,我们可以保证以后还要订货,并且订货数量更多。)

⑩ The bank authorized by the holder to receive payment shall be liable only for crediting the sum on the bill to the holder's account according to the items specified in the bill.(受持票人委托进行收款的银行的责任限于按照汇票上记载的事项将汇票金额转入持票人账户。)(潘红,2004)

分析:例⑧⑨所用的正式词语(如:appreciated)、被动语态和虚拟语气(如:should this trial order prove)都显现出措辞正式、庄重、典雅的行文方式。例⑩属于商贸合同书面语体,所用句式较长、较正式,句型结构比较复杂,使用了过去分词短语和动名词短语。并且,措辞具有合同或法律专业色彩,使用的专业术语,如 shall(必须)、holder(持票人)、crediting(转入)等,体现正式语体和法律专业的行文风格。

1.2 功能语境制约下的商务英语文化特征

何谓文化?"文化"一词含义广泛,定义颇多。最简单而笼统的定义是:文化是一个民族的全部生活方式(ways of a people)(Newmark,1991)。任何一个语言使用者都是在一定的文化氛围中成长的。这就是他/她赖以生存的文化语境。他/她的一言一行、一举一动,包括他/她的行为习惯、思维模式、通常要说的话、要表达的意思,无一不受他/她所赖以生存的文化语境(文化背景)的影响。对于一个在非英语文化语境中成长起来的人(英语作为外语的学习者)来说,跨文化交际(包括商务汉英翻译)的成功不仅依赖对英语语言知识的掌握,更取决于对英语语言以外的文化知识的掌握,即"文化语境"。综合来说,"文化语境是指某种语言赖以根植的民族里人们的思想和行为准则的总和,即交际参与者所共有的背景知识,包括特定的社会传统习俗、历史文化知识、社会认知结构、社会心理、民族情感,以及交际个体之间的文化背景、认知结构和心理状态"(谢建平,2008:81)。

如上所述,文化语境对语言的影响至关重要,对商务英语同样有着十分重要的影响。在文化语境的影响下,作为用于商务语域的一种社会语言功能变体,商务英语有其独特的文化烙印：

第一，商务英语具有专业性与行业性特征。一方面，应用范围和领域十分广泛的商务英语在不同行业有着蕴含不同行业文化知识的专业术语。这些专业术语无不体现商务英语的文化内涵。比如，clean Bill of Lading 这个外贸专业术语中的 clean 一词是指货物或包装无破损或玷污等不良情况，"清洁提单"才是它准确而规范的对等翻译。再如，blue chip（蓝筹股）几乎成了"绩优股"或"值钱而热门的股票"的代名词，其中有个典故：美国人打牌下赌注，蓝色筹码为最高，红色筹码为中等，白色筹码为最低，后来人们就把股票市场上最有实力、最活跃的股票称为 blue chip。另一方面，商务英语的专业性与行业性还表现在对大量行话与套语的运用。比如，rock-bottom price 和 loan shark 属于非正式俚语用法，前者是指"最低价"（the lowest price），后者的意思是"放高利贷者"。再如，lemon market 不是"柠檬市场"而是"次品市场"；dry goods 不是"干货"而是"纺织品"（汪榕培、卢晓娟，1997）。又如，信函套语"Enclosed please find our order（PO No. V-576）for 100 each door hinges."，"At your request, we are pleased to make you an offer, which is effective until March 26."和合同套语"This Contract shall come into force from the date of execution hereof by the Buyer and the Builder."虽然陈腐，但人们还是照用不误。这充分反映出商务语言文化对商务英语交际的强大持久的影响力，同时也体现了商务合同、商务信函之类文本"格式固定、语言简洁、信息准确"（谢建平，2008：84）的语言文化特征。

第二，商务英语涵盖了丰富的商务文化习语熟语（idioms）。以习语 in the red 和 in the black 为例，in the red 是指"发生亏损""出现赤字""欠债"；"in the black"的意思正好相反，是指"有盈余"或"有存款"。又如，Black Friday（黑色星期五）是指感恩节过后的那个星期五（11月第4个星期五），通常标志着圣诞抢购季节（Christmas Shopping Season）的开始。在这天，美国的商店会提早营业、减价促销，美国人则纷纷上街抢购圣诞礼物。

第三，商务英语具有"简洁明了、用词具体客观"的语言文化特征。比如，宾馆、餐馆大堂的墙上常常有这样的牌匾——"Home from Home"（宾至如归）或"Booming Business"（生意兴隆）。又如，宾馆洗手间、道路施工现场或建筑工地有这样的标识语——"Caution: Wet Floor!"（地滑，小心摔倒!）、"Road Work Ahead!"（前方修路，请绕行!）或"Danger: Building Site"（工地危险，禁止入内!）。这些例子表明，不同的文化心理造就了不同的句子结构模式（彭增安，1998）。以上用词简洁、结构固化的语言背后具有以下特点：与汉民族"倾向于语言的浮夸和渲染"（蔡基刚，2003：336）和注重形象、概括性强的语言个性不同，西方人注重理性分析，语义细腻具体。

第四，商务英语体现出不同的商业社会文化心理和商业价值观。比如，"The employees/staff only."（闲人莫入）这句标识语的着眼点是自己，而不是他人。这就反映了有别于中国人的"群体取向"的西方人的"个人取向"价值观。又如,"Ask for a diamond brand watch, if every second counts for you."(出手不凡钻石表)这个广告语突出的是消费者,不是产品。这也反映出西方社会的"个人取向"价值观。

第五,商务英语具有特殊的语用功能。比如,"If you can offer us competitive prices and the delivery time is acceptable, we shall place a large order with you."表面上委婉,而实际上则是很老练的讨价还价用语。再如,"Please let me think it over. Let me have a word with my boss first."表面上是说"让我好好想一下,让我先跟老板谈一下",而实际上则是一种缓冲之策。上例表明,在商务英语文化语境中,已经约定俗成的一些委婉而老练的言辞反映出西方人性格含蓄的一面。这也是一种文化在商用语言中的表现。

第二节　功能语境对商务英语翻译的制约作用

在国际商贸交往的过程中,翻译起着重要的桥梁作用。作为跨语言、跨文化交流桥梁的翻译应包含两个层面,即语言与文化。所以,我国著名学者王佐良在谈到文化与翻译的关系时曾指出翻译者必须是一个真正意义上的文化人,因为翻译者处理的是个别词,面对的则是两大片文化。翻译是一种跨文化的活动。商务英语翻译(汉译英)的"翻译过程不仅是语言的转换过程,而且是反映不同社会文化特征的文化转化过程"(黄艺平,2010:34)。由此可见,商务英语翻译必然是在自觉或不自觉地对汉英两种不同语言与文化进行对比分析的基础之上进行的转换。

2.1　功能语境与成功翻译的条件

翻译时需要理解的难点不是"明说"的"字面意义",而是与功能语境有关的"指称""歧义辨别""修辞意义"等。英国翻译理论家彼得·纽马克(Newmark,1982)认为,语境在所有翻译中都是最重要的因素。他还指出,"语境的重要性大于任何法规、任何理论、任何基本词义"(转引自傅敬民、张顺梅、薛清,2005:169)。由此可见,交际的成功与否,在很大程度上取决于交际双方对"言内语境""情景语境""社会文化语境"因素的共享程度。语境因素的共享程度越高,交际的成功率越大;反之,交际的成功率越小。比如,如果对 Naderism 一词的社会文化语境不清楚的话,译者只会按表层信息将其直译成"纳德运动",汉语读者也会不知其所云;若对 Naderism 一词的社会文化语境因素有很高的共享程度,译者就会深入挖掘其背后的文化引申义(因批评政府和大公司、维护消费者权益而闻名的美国律师 Ralph Nader 的名字被引申喻指"客户第一"或"保护消费者权益者运动"),灵活对等地把它译成"客户至上"(冯志杰,1998)。这种功能对等的翻译转换是译者充分把握原文语境因素并对其文化语境意义进行灵活转换的结果。

由此可见,翻译这种跨文化、跨语言交际活动要想获得成功,在交际的全过程中译者和作者之间的语境共享程度应尽可能最大化。下面就让我们具体看一下怎样才能在翻译理解过程中提高语境的共享程度。

在翻译理解过程中,译者充当原文本的信息接收者,他要努力根据原文语境来实现原文语码和信息的理解,目的就是 $M_2 = M_1$。M_1、M_2 和语码、语境具有如下等式关系:

M_1 = 原文语码 + (原文言内语境 + 原文情景语境 + 原文社会文化语境)
　　　　　　└─作者创作的原文语境─┘

M_2 = 原文语码 + (原文言内语境 + 原文情景语境 + 原文社会文化语境)
　　　　　　└─译者理解的原文语境─┘

在翻译理解过程中,译者看到的语码与作者使用的语码是一样的,即原文语码。作者根据特定语境来传达意欲传达的语言文化信息。译者想要理解原文语码传达的语言文化信息,就必须共享与作者一样多的语境文化因素。因此,尽可能多地探索并把握原文的特定语境文化因素,是译者正确理解原文的关键。对原文的特定语境文化因素的把握出现任何偏差,都会导致翻译理解的语言文化信息与原文传达的语言文化信息发生偏离。对语境文化因素把握欠缺,会导致原文真正语言文化信息的丢失,或根本就得不到原文的真正语言文化信息;对语境文化因素把握过度,译者就会凭空臆造。只有原文的特定语境被译者完全共享,译者所理解的原文的语言文化信息才会与作者意欲传达的语言文化信息完全一致。

请对比分析以下商务汉英翻译实例:

① 我们公司一成立就来了个<u>开门红</u>:在开业后的第一周就得到了三笔大宗订单。

译文1:Our company <u>got off to a good start</u> when it opened to business:we got three big orders during the first week of opening.

译文2:Our company <u>got off to a flying start</u> when it opened to business:we got three big orders during the first week of opening.

对比分析:"开门红"这一商用汉语习语喻指生意在一开始就取得了显著的成绩。只有了解汉语"红"文化,才能真正把握其特有的民族文化内涵与生动用法。在理解并掌握了汉语原文的语言文化信息基础上,我们一般可以像译文1那样,把汉语原文通俗地英译成 make a good beginning 或 get off to a good start,而经过修辞分析与优化,在修辞意义上能够达到功能对等的英译则是译文2所用的比喻 get off to a flying start。get off to a flying start 属于比赛用语:在进行快艇或汽车比赛时,所有参加比赛的快艇或汽车发动时必须达到一定的速度,这种"助跑形式"在英语中叫 a flying start。后来人们将其喻指办事一开始的促动力,表示"有好的开端"(make a very good beginning)(萨默斯,2004:659),也就相当于汉语的"开门红"。

◆ 2.2 功能语境与翻译表达

翻译表达就是把原文语码在原文言内语境、情景语境与社会文化语境传达的语言文化信息改由译文语码和译文语境来传达,其目标就是使 M_3(译文传达的语言文化信息) $\cong M_2 = M_1$。在此使用"等于或约等于",因为"等于"一般说来只是译者追求的理想境界。下面,以具体实例来说明翻译表达应考虑的语境因素。

2.2.1 翻译表达应再现原文文体修辞情景

原文的情景语境是作者用风格不同的语言文字表现出的客观现实,译者作为作者的代言人,也应站在作者的立场上周旋于这些客观因素之中,作者的情景现实就是译者的情景现实。准确地再现作者的情景现实,不仅可以从客观上再现原文的风格,也为准确再现原文文体修辞意义提供了客观依据。

请对比分析以下商务汉英翻译实例:

② 本保险单<u>一经</u>涂改或无承保公司(指出单的分支机构)盖章及代理机构经办人签字<u>无效</u>。

英译:This policy <u>shall not be valid unless</u> all the particulars remain unamended and the policy is issued with the agent's signature or the seal of the branch of the issuing Company.

对比分析:此例是保险合同用语,原文的句型结构"一经……无效"和第一个用词"本"都是文体程度较高的法律正式用语。所以,在掌握了原文的文体修辞意义之后,译者就可以选用英语中具有同等文体程度的句型结构(如:shall not be valid … unless …)来再现原文的文体修辞情景和法律文体风格。

2.2.2 翻译表达应充分考虑译语言内语境,表达应符合译语习惯

翻译目的论认为,翻译是人类行为研究的范畴,人类交际受情境的制约,而情境又根植于文化习惯(Nord, 1997)。译语要让译语读者理解和接受,文字表达就必须以译语习惯为参照,接受译语言内语境的限制。超出译语言内语境的文字,要么令译语读者迷惑不解,要么会使译文读者产生误解。换言之,我们在直译或异化不通的情况下,就要采用意译或归化的策略。例如,把"经济作物"译作 economic crops,就令人费解,而采用意译或归化翻译所做的正确翻译应是 ready-money crops 或 cash crops;将"摇钱树"翻译成 shake-money tree,就是死译硬译,正确的应是意译为 cash cow。又如,将"亚洲四小龙"简单地直译成 the Four Asian Dragons,就有可能使译文读者产生不好的消极联想,所以

我们最好采纳已被广泛接受的意译或归化翻译,将其译为 the Four Asian Tigers。

2.2.3　翻译表达应照顾译语文化语境,忌不顾译语读者理解力的限度

"存异"不是保存"不可理解"的东西,而是在如实保存不同之处的同时,处理得让读者能够理解"异"之所在及其含义。如果"存异"让读者难明其义或者使意义发生改变,变更表达方式就是有必要的。

请对比分析以下商务汉英翻译实例:

③ 尽管他多年来对他老板阿谀奉承、拍马溜须,但是他们没有给他加薪。

英译:They didn't give him a raise, though he had licked his boss's boots for years.

对比分析:汉语表达"奉承某人"的通俗说法有"拍马屁""给某人提鞋子""做哈巴狗"等,如果直译成 pat a horse on its buttock,译文读者就不可能理解其文化喻指意义。所以,为了功能对等地传译出原文的文化意义,我们不妨把汉语习语"拍马屁"套译成英语中同样生动而通俗的习语 lick one's boots(安亚中、张健,2008)。

2.2.4　翻译表达应尽量照顾原文文化语境,忌过于归化

照顾原文文化语境,既是对原文文化的尊重,也是对译语读者拥有的对原语文化理解力的充分信任,以"存异"的原则进行翻译,可以增进不同文化间的交流,提高不同文化在不同读者心目中的可理解性。

请对比分析以下商务汉英翻译实例:

④ 手艺是个正道,是铁饭碗,砸不破!

英译:Technical skill is a proper thing—it's an iron rice bowl that cannot be broken!

对比分析:汉语"铁饭碗"属于比喻性说法,可以采用归化翻译将其译成 a lifelong job(安亚中、张健,2008)。但是,为了保持汉语的文化特色,不妨将其直译成 iron rice bowl,附加"打不破"的说明;或者,把"铁饭碗"采用异化加注法译成 an iron rice bowl—a secure job,这样就更加容易理解。

由上述分析可以看出,在商务英语翻译过程中,语境起着非常关键的作用。译者依据各种语境因素所理解的语言文化意义或效果,可以被称为语言文化语境。对于译者在翻译表达时要考虑的语境因素,我们称之为"翻译语境"。翻译语境是原文本所有语境因素与译者解读原文本时由原文本的语码和语境激活的相关语境因素的总和,是两种语言和文化对比融合的结果。Shaw(1987)对语境与翻译问题做了极具启发性的论述,他认为翻译语境是翻译过程中聚合起来的文化互动的总和,从而揭示了语境在文化互动中的调和与连接作用。

思考与练习

1. 思考题
(1) 语境制约下的商务英语有什么语言文化特征?
(2) 功能语境对商务英语翻译有什么制约作用?

2. 句子翻译
(1) 如果由于他方的违约行为或疏忽而使本合同任何一方遭受损失,其索赔通过协议或仲裁予以理算。
(2) 厄瓜多尔银行将通知其在美国的代理银行开立信用证。价格为:成本、保险加运费到拉格斯,每码30元人民币,包括5%的佣金。付款方式为:使用保兑的、不可撤销的即期信用证支付。信用证应于装运期前30天开出。
(3) 承蒙格林豪先生介绍,我们得知在贵国你们是中国化工产品和药品的主要进口商之一。
(4) 恭候佳音。
(5) 敬请早日答复,将不胜感激。
(6) 文化搭台,经贸唱戏。
(7) 这条步行街拥有近10个主题商业平台,将集餐饮、娱乐、旅游观光、休闲、购物于一体。
(8) 烦请贵方尽快报伦敦离岸最低价。
(9) 这是卡森公司在波兰新收购的工厂。
(10) 1990年共批准"三资"企业99家,全省"三资"企业已达284家。

3. 语篇翻译

● 语篇1

合资企业是指由两个或两个以上的公司共同拥有和经营的企业。许多公司通过和当地公司合资的方式渗透到国外市场。在多数合资企业中,两个公司都能在特定的项目中发挥各自的比较优势。例如,通用磨坊公司和雀巢公司合资,使得通用磨坊公司生产出的谷类食物可以在雀巢公司建立的海外销售分布网点进行销售。

美国施乐公司和日本富士公司合资,使得施乐公司渗透到日本市场,并同时使得富士公司进入影印行业。美国莎莉公司和西南贝尔公司都与墨西哥的公司合资,从而进入墨西哥市场。在汽车制造业有相当多的合资企业,其中每个制造商都能提供其技术优势。通用汽车公司则在匈牙利等不同国家与汽车制造商共同经营合资企业。

- 语篇 2

耐克是当今商界最有影响的销售公司之一,但它起步时却是微不足道的。这家全球巨人公司在20世纪60年代靠推销廉价日本运动鞋起家。公司的创始人将运动鞋放在自己的小汽车里,带到美国高中田径运动会上向运动员兜售。

- 语篇 3

投资者必须了解当今世界经济地理、财富以及地缘政治力量的变化,理解地缘政治在带来高风险的同时也为新兴经济体提供了巨大的机遇。他们是空想社会主义理论消亡、便捷即时通信、高效交通运输以及美国宽松货币政策的直接受益人。投资者可以在那些类似于泰国、马来西亚、越南、新加坡等不同的国家取得举足轻重的地位。在未来的几年内,这些国家的经济表现很可能将远远超过美国。

第二章

商务汉英语言文化对比分析与翻译

Identify the problems in the following translations

① 竭诚欢迎国内外新老客户来公司洽谈指导！

英译：Wholeheartedly welcome all new and old clients domestic and abroad to our company!

② 重庆主城区南部新城是商家置业的黄金口岸。

英译：The New Town in the southern section of the City of Chongqing proper is a port promising unrivaled opportunities for commercial and real estate investments.

③ 中国煤炭工业进出口总公司（简称"中煤总公司"）是中国煤炭行业从事对外经济和贸易的国家支柱企业。中煤总公司实行工贸结合、技贸结合，统一经营全国煤炭进出口，经营煤炭技术和机电设备及矿产品的进出口，经营利用外资开发煤矿，经营煤炭系统对外承包工程和劳务输出及海外开发等业务。中煤总公司的宗旨是"信誉第一，质量第一，服务第一"。中煤总公司热诚欢迎海内外各界人士前来洽谈、投资和进行经济技术合作。

英译：China National Coal Industry Imp. & Exp. Corp. (CNCIEC) is a national mainstay enterprise in China's coal industry specializing in foreign trade and economic cooperation. With a comprehensive advantage of combination of industry, technology and trade, CNCIEC is authorized to import and export coal in a unified way for China. Besides import and export of coal mining technology, machinery, electrical equipment and other mineral products, its business scope covers coalmine development and cooperation at home and abroad, international engineering projects and manpower supply for overseas projects and works. Abiding by the enterprise principle of "reputation first, quality first and service first", CNCIEC awaits with great enthusiasm people from all walks of life both at home and abroad coming for talks over business, investment, technical and economic cooperation.

随着经济全球化和国际经贸往来的不断发展,中外商务交流越来越多。在进行商务汉英翻译时,我们发现,汉英两种语言有着极大的差异。这种差异必然涉及汉英两种文化。萨丕尔(Sapir,1921)认为语言的背后是有东西的,而且语言不能离开文化而存在。所谓文化,就是社会遗传下来的习惯和信仰的总和。帕默(Palmer,1936)认为,语言的历史和文化的历史是相辅而行的,它们可以互相协助和启发。由此可见,翻译应包含两个层面才完整,即语言与文化。"对真正成功的翻译来说,双文化能力甚至比双语能力还要重要,因为词语只是在其发挥功能的文化中才具有意义。"(Nida,1998:308)商务汉英翻译更是如此。

除了语言文化上的差异之外,商务汉英两种不同的语言文化变体也有其突出鲜明的特征。作为翻译工作者,我们要跨越语言文化差异,采用归化(domestication)的翻译策略。归化的手段就是"变",目的就是"通",即符合汉英各自语言习惯和文化传统的语言表达,也就是追求不同语言文化之间的顺利交流。此外,我们在传播不同文化特色时也要采用异化(foreignization)的翻译策略。异化的目的是存"异",以便实现不同文化特色的保存与传播。

第一节 语言文化关联下的商务汉英对比分析

商务汉英翻译体现出来的语言文化具有不同于普通汉英语言文化的独特专业和行业特征,这些独特的专业和行业特征则带有明显的商务英语或商务汉语语域属性。

◆ 1.1 语言关联下的商务汉英对比分析

1.1.1 汉英两种语言之间的普遍差异

有比较才有鉴别。汉英两种语言分属两大不同语系。汉语属于汉藏语系,而英语属于印欧语系的日耳曼语族的西日耳曼语支。汉语是象形文字、表意文字,而英语则是拼音文字。汉语是语义型意合语言(paratactic language),而英语则是形态型形合语言(hypotactic language)。这是汉英之间最大的差异,也是最本质的不同。汉语不像形态型形合语言那样通过语言本身的形态变化来表达,而是通过语序(word order)、使用虚词或形式词(form words or function words)等手段来建构,"汉语造句少用甚至不用形式连接手段,注重隐性连贯(covert coherence),注重逻辑事理顺序,注重功能、意义,注重以神统形"(连淑能,1993:53)。汉语的形合手段,即连接用语(connectives)或关联词(linking words and expressions),比英语少得多。汉语没有英语常用的那些关系代词/副词、连接代词/副词,其介词只有 30 个左右,并且大多是从动词"借"来的。在汉语中,介词、连词等虚词往往可以省略不用,这是因为一句话中的词语之间的关系常常尽在不言之中,语法意义和逻辑联系常隐含在字里行间。与汉语相比,英语常用各种各样的关系代词/副词、连接代词/副词、介词、非谓语动词等形式手段来连词成句、组句成篇。英语造句"注重显性接应(overt coherence),注重句子形式,注重结构完整,注重以形显义"(连淑能,1993:48)。正是因为上述差异,汉语不受形态约束,没有主谓形式协调一致的关系,也就没有这种关系可以驾驭全句,因而句式松散,呈流散型(diffusiveness),流水句(serial clauses)居多,并且句式量大繁杂,如话题句、施事句、关系句、呼叹句、存现句、有无句等;英语则多用名词化短语、分词、动词不定式、介词短语等结构和各种各样的从句,句子主次分明,严密规范,句式呈聚散型(compactness)。

请对比分析以下商务汉英翻译实例:

① 承蒙早日回复,不胜感激。

英译:Your early reply is highly appreciated.

对比分析:此例英译采用了变"态"的处理方法,即汉语原句使用了主动语态,而英译句则转换成了英语所偏爱的被动语态。此外,汉语的无主句隐去了可以意会的主语"我们",而按照英语句法,英译时采用被动语态而译成了有主语句。

② 青岛海旺花园家具有限公司的主要产品为"海旺"花园家具和"金华"木制太阳伞。我公司设备齐全,管理体系完善,已有几十年的加工、生产、销售历史,从而积累了丰富的出口经验。目前在国内设生产加工基地近 10 处,并由公司质量控制中心随时做巡回检查。

我公司生产的两个系列产品有 200 多个品种,设计美观,款式考究,深受国内外客人喜爱。目前已销往欧美等十几个国家和地区。本公司以"信誉为本,质量上乘,开拓创新"为宗旨。

恭请各界朋友光临!

英译:Qingdao Hivigor Garden Furniture Co., Ltd. is a plant manufacturing "Hivigor" brand garden furniture and "Jinhua" brand wooden umbrella as its main products. Our company has complete equipment with good management. In the past decades of manufacturing, processing and marketing, our company has accumulated rich experience in exportation. Up to now, nearly ten production bases have been set up nationwide, which is under timely supervision by the quality control centre of the headquarters.

The plant has formed two products categories with more than two hundred different varieties. They are novel in design, exquisite in pattern and are well received in Europe, the U. S. A. and some other regions in the world.

Our motto is: Reputation First, Quality First and Constant Innovation.

You are sincerely welcome for visit and business negotiation with us.

对比分析：此例汉语原句有无主句"目前在国内设生产加工基地近10处"、流水句"我公司生产的两个系列产品有200多个品种,设计美观,款式考究,深受国内外客人喜爱"等汉语特有的句式。在对汉语无主句进行处理时,英译采用了变"态"翻译法进行灵活的转换,补充英语句式中必要的主语"ten production bases have been set up";而在对汉语流水句进行处理时,英译采用了合译法译成"They are novel in design, exquisite in pattern and are well received in Europe, the U.S.A. and some other regions in the world.",使得英译的句式紧凑,结构严密。

③ 这批货我们急用,请立即装运。

英译：We need the goods urgently, so prompt delivery will be most appreciated.（谭硕,2008）

对比分析：此例汉语句子为话题句,"这批货"用作话题,作主语,而作谓语的则是"我们急用"这个主谓词组。与英语句式相比,汉语句式松散,注重语义贯通,但"强调"的修辞意图得到突显。如果使用类似的英译句式,汉语原句可被改写为"我们急需此货"。相比之下,英语更注重句法和形态结构。

由此可见,汉英两种语言之间既有相同或类似的地方,又有特性与差异,或者说其个性远大于共性：共性是相对的,而个性与差异则是绝对的。就翻译而言,译者应熟悉语言之间的共性特征,这将有助于我们避开诸多不必要的周折,从而将主要精力投注于语言的差异性化解,因为后者才是引发并致使种种翻译问题的诱因与渊薮（冯庆华、刘全福,2011）。

1.1.2 商务汉英两种语言变体之间的显著差异

商务汉英两种语言在实现其社会功能的过程中自然而然地表现出其特有的语言文化上的显著差异。这些差异仍然属于汉英两种语言文化之间的差异,只不过在商务语境中的表现比较突出罢了。

1.1.2.1 商务汉英用词正式严肃,但措辞不同

商务汉英的用词正式严肃、庄重典雅。比如,商务汉语为了塑造正式、严谨、庄重、典雅的修辞效果,往往采用文言词和半文言词（如"本""惠请""盼复""启者""谨启""贵公司""贵函收悉"）、四字结构（如"欢迎惠顾""随函附寄""悉听尊便""如蒙答复,不胜感激"）等书面语汇。相比之下,商务英语信函、合同、报告等正式文体常采用诸如ameliorate, promulgate之类的长词和书面词（long & learned words）、像whereby和hereto这样的古体词（archaisms）,以确保文体的正式性和严肃性;特别是商务英语合同协议之类的法律文体往往使用 fulfill or perform, rights or obligations 等并置词语（juxtapositions）,以产生庄重、典雅和严谨的文体效果。

1.1.2.2 商务汉英用词专业,因词义范围不同而半专业语汇的生成手段有别

商务汉英专业性强,所以专业术语和半专业语汇十分丰富。这些专业术语和半专业语汇的语言形式已经固定,其词义也已约定俗成。汉语所用专业术语和半专业语汇包括诸如"老板椅"(exec chair)、"赤字"(red figure)和"一揽子交易"(package deal)之类的外来词,像"唛头"(shipping mark)、"土纸"(handmade paper)和"小康"(a relatively comfortable living for all)这种中国特有的已经固定的名称和有待统一的新生术语,通过增加修饰限定词而形成的像"转账"(transfer)和"赔偿费"(damages)这样的语汇等;英语的专业术语和半专业语汇包括诸如"FOB"(船上交货价)和"D/P"(付款交单)这样的固定缩略词、像"brown goods"(茶色商品:电视机、音响设备、放像机等)和"OEM"(贴牌)这样的汉语缺失而有待俗成的语汇等。就词义范围而言,"汉语词义严谨固定,词的含义范围比较窄,词义对上下文的依赖性比较小。英语词义灵活多变,词的含义范围较宽,词义对上下文的依赖性比较大"(潘红,2004:51)。比如,policy 和 inquiry 在普通英语中的词义分别是"政策"和"询问",而用于保险业和贸易中的词义分别是"保单"(insurance policy)和"询价,询盘"。由此可见,汉语半专业语汇生成的手段主要是另用他词,而英语半专业语汇主要是通过词义引申。

1.1.2.3 商务汉英实义词密度高:汉语动词使用频率高,英语名词化程度高

商务语篇的信息量大,主要依靠实义词(notional words)来体现。商务语篇对实义词的依赖程度非常高,因此语篇所负载的信息量就很大。为了传递大量的信息,"重纪实、少文饰"的商务汉英语篇因汉英之间的句法差异而采用不同的词类:汉语较多采用动词短语,而英语较多采用名词化短语。以商务信函结尾段常用的"盼复"一句为例:汉语只有短短一句,两个词都是动词,而其英译就不能像汉语这样不做任何形式上的变化就连用动词,它需要将第二个动词译成动名词(非谓语动词形式),如"We are looking forward to hearing from you."。

1.1.2.4 商务汉英语句简明、结构严密,但句法不同

一般来说,商务汉英语句结构严谨,简练准确,但各有句法。"意合型"汉语短句多,流水句多。相比之下,"形合型"英语长句多,复合句多。例如,"不管怎样,从贵方闻悉发生这一不幸事件,我们深表遗憾。如有必要,我们将很乐意代贵公司向船方提出交涉。"这一汉语句群有两个完整的语句,但是,其英译"At any rate, we deeply regret to learn from you about this unfortunate incident and should it be necessary we shall be pleased to take the matter up on your behalf with the shipping company concerned."就用了一个小小的连词 and 将汉语两句合成了一个并列复合句。由此可见,汉英之间的这种差异在商务汉英信函、合同、报告、计划书等文体中比较常见,特别是在协议合同之类的法律文件中更为突出。

1.1.2.5 商务汉英句法不同,主动语态与被动语态、人称与物称的句法有别

汉语偏爱采用人或类似于人的有生命的东西作主语,而英语则较多采用无生命的事

物作主语。鉴于汉语人称与英语物称之间的差异,英语被动语态在应用文体、科技文体中用得极为普遍。相比之下,汉语对被动语态使用较少。比如,"人们认为,营销就是为某个公司的产品寻找买主,并鼓励购买"(邹力,2005:39)。这句汉语用的是以"人们"为主语的主动句,而英译"marketing is seen as the task of finding and stimulating buyers for the firm's output."用的却是以 Marketing(营销)为主语的被动句。由此可见,汉语略显主观,而英语较显客观。

1.1.2.6 商务汉英篇章格式化,但建构模式有别

商务汉英语篇大多不长,其篇章模式约定俗成,不能有较大的改变。汉英在信息结构、思维表达模式、逻辑推理方式等方面都有一些区别,所以商务汉英语篇建构模式自然有自己的特征。比如,汉语偏爱间接式的篇章布局,而英语喜欢直接式的篇章布局,因此汉语使用圆周段较多,而英语中松散段较为常见。

1.2 文化关联下的商务汉英对比分析

语言学家萨丕尔(Sapir)认为,隐含在一种语言中的差异不可能在另一种语言中体现出来。因为"一个民族的人民总是以同样的独特方式理解词的一般意义,把同样的附带意义和情感色彩添加到词上,朝同一方向联结观念、组织思想"(威廉·冯·洪堡特,1997:204)。著名翻译理论家纽马克(Newmark,1988)认为,语言有普通语言、个人语言和文化语言之分;当交际中出现文化焦点(cultural focus)时,就会由于文化差异而造成翻译问题(translation problem)。由此可见,汉英翻译既是汉英语言的转换,也是汉英双语文化的交流。汉英翻译除了要通晓两种语言文字之外,还要了解两种文化,深入理解两种文化之间的差异。正如王佐良先生所说,翻译者必须是一个真正意义上的文化人。文化包罗万象,涵盖面很广。因此,要对文化下一个准确的定义很难。但有一点是明确的,即语言与文化密不可分。语言是文化的载体,语言反映文化。每一种语言都有着自己不同的文化痕迹,处处可见文化的影响。

文化是"某一人群及其生存环境中所特有的各种活动、思想及其在物体和活动过程中所表现出来的物质形式的总和"(Newmark,1991:73)。美国著名翻译理论家奈达(Eugene Nida)将语言中的文化因素分为五类:① 生态文化(Ecological Culture);② 物质文化(Material Culture);③ 社会语用文化(Social Pragmatic Culture);④ 宗教文化(Religious Culture);⑤ 习语文化(Idiomatic Culture)。

由于文化的范围很广、意义很复杂,下文就从五类文化出发,对商务汉英的文化差异做概括性的对比分析。

1.2.1 生态文化

中国虽有漫长的海岸线,但在历史上是一个幅员广阔、以农耕文化为主的大陆国家。

中国经历了漫长的自给自足的封建农业社会，"重农主义"（agrarianism）盛行，对外贸易较少，长期"重农抑商"，富足安逸的农业社会的生活方式长久以来大受推崇。比如，"三十亩地一头牛，老婆孩子热炕头"这句十分流行的俗语描绘的是令人羡慕的乡村田园生活。相比之下，商品经济和商业向来不被人重视，商人始终不被人看重，经商甚至被认为是不务正业，汉语习语"无商不奸"便是有力佐证。

英国是一个岛国，历史上航海业十分发达。因此，英国的资本主义兴起最早，也最发达。资本主义社会的一个主要特征就是商品经济取代自然经济。所以，商业备受人们青睐，"重商主义"（mercantilism）大行其道；汉语"奸商"的英译 profiteer 就无汉语中刻薄狠毒的"奸"词之意。为了积累原始资本，欧美等西方国家在历史上跨洋过海，极力推崇自由贸易，大肆对外掠夺扩张，实行"炮舰外交"（gunboat diplomacy），持剑经商。英语谚语"Trade follows the flag."（意为"资本主义向外扩张时，国家的政治军事力量扩展到什么地方，其商业贸易就紧跟其后蜂拥而至"）就是最好的诠释。

汉英两种语言有着迥然不同的俗语表达。比如，汉语中的"土布"（handmade cloth）、"土纸"（handmade paper）等俗语和英语中的 watered-down stocks（掺水股票）、keep one's head above water（摆脱困境或债务，不负债）等俗语则表明，大多数长期生活繁衍在中国的人与"土"有着十分密切的关系，而 water 一词在英语中十分常见，因为英国四面环水。汉语"水货"（smuggled goods）一词也是源于广东方言，其词源与英语 smuggled goods（走私货）的定义与渊源密切相关。在英语中，smuggled goods 是指早期走私者为逃避关税，将从海上船运过来的商品用塑料袋等密封好后投入约定的浅海中，再从陆上坐小船到该地点将货物取走偷运入关。

1.2.2 物质文化

说汉英语言的不同民族的衣食住行大不相同。这些必然会在汉英两种不同语言中有所表现。在衣着上，中国清朝的官员戴红顶官帽，所以官商（government merchant）就被称作"红顶商人"；英国的上层男士在过去甚至现在还习惯戴圆顶帽（bowler hat），商人、成熟的男人也常戴圆顶帽，所以圆顶帽常被用来象征英国的商人和成功的男人。此外，中国有"长袍马褂"（long gowns and mandarin jackets），英美等西方国家则有他们的"西装革履"（suits and leather shoes）。

在餐饮上，中国有着富有特色的中餐（Chinese food），而英美等西方国家有他们别具一格的西餐（Western food）。饺子（jiaozi/dumpling）、豆腐（tofu）、炒面（Chaomian）、馄饨（wonton）、元宵（yuanxiao）、锅贴（guotie）、北京烤鸭（Roasted Peking Duck/Beijing Roast Duck）、酱油（soy sauce）、工夫茶（congou）、茅台（Maotai）、白菜（Chinese cabbage）、猕猴桃（Chinese gooseberry）等在西方早已家喻户晓。同样，热狗（hot dog）、汉堡包（hamburger）、巧克力（chocolate）、三明治（sandwich）、威士忌（whiskey）、白兰地（brandy）、咖啡（coffee）、啤酒（beer）、奶昔（milkshake）、圣代（sundae）等西式饮食备受

中国年轻人青睐。有些餐饮食品的名称作为比喻词,常被用于商贸汉英之中。比如,汉语有"豆腐渣工程"(jerry-built project)之说,英语有 goods that sell like hot cakes(热门货)之辞。

在"住"的方面,两个不同民族都有丰富的文化遗产。比如,中国有"四合院"(courtyard houses; siheyuan, a compound with houses around a square courtyard);西方有"双拼别墅"(twin houses)和"四拼别墅"(quadruplet houses)。

在"行"的方面,汉英文化更是丰富多彩。中国人有"八抬大轿"(a sedan chair carried by eight men),西方人有"三驾马车"(troika)。出口、消费、投资就常被比喻成拉动经济增长的"三驾马车"。汉语中,与"行"有关的习语"火车头"喻指"起带头作用或领导作用的人或事物";英语中,与"行"有关的习语 in the van 喻指"先锋;在……前列"。此外,商用英语有一个很形象的习惯用语 living out of a suitcase,其翻译不能用其字面意思"从旅行箱里出来",而要用其引申比喻意义"老是出差在外"。

1.2.3 社会语用文化

在汉语中,人们交往除了采用"先生""太太""老爷爷""老奶奶""大妈""大娘""大叔""大嫂""大哥""大姐""小姐""阿姨""师傅""同志"等称呼语之外,陌生人越来越多地在非生意场,所以生意场上常用的"老板"或"老板娘"相称(特别是在广东),熟悉的人有时也以"张老板""刘老板""万老板"相呼。硕士生、博士生甚至也把有许多项目和经费的大学教授们称为"老板"(甚至不分男女),这可能是老师有时会因他们为自己所干的活儿酬劳或宴请犒劳他们一番。比如,在广东菜市场买东西时经常听到有摊主招呼说:"老板,请问想买什么?"(What can I do for you, sir?)由此可见,与汉语"老板"这个通称相对应的英译就是泛称的 sir。再如,在商务信函用语方面,商务汉语信函常用称呼语"敬启者"和信尾客套语"谨启/敬上",而商务英语信函则习惯采用"Dear Sir or Madam/Dear Sirs/Gentlemen"和"Sincerely yours/Faithfully yours/Best regards"。又如,在公共商务场所标识语方面,汉语常用"闲人免进!""男士止步!",而英语惯用"Staff Only!""Women Only!"。这些表明商务汉英语用交际文化存在"语言形式不同而语用交际意图相同"(赵彦春,2005:181)的现象。

不同的社会文化中,颜色词的商用联想引申义有所不同。红色对于汉民族来说就意味着幸福、喜庆、吉祥、欢乐、热烈等,并由此引申出"兴旺""发达""顺利""受人欢迎""成功""运气好""福利""成就"等含义。在中国,以"红"为语素的商标名称不计其数,如"红双喜""红牛""红高粱""红梅"等。此外,汉语形容生意兴旺常说"红红火火的生意"(brisk/flourishing/prosperous business),说开业生意好是"开门红"。与红色不同的是,黑色这一商用颜色词对于汉民族来说意味着"黑暗""邪恶""阴险"等贬义,如"黑货"(smuggled goods)、"黑车"(unlicensed vehicle)、"黑店"(an inn run by brigands)、"黑作坊"(underground workshop)等。相比之下,red 这个英语颜色词在英美等西方国家象征着"热烈""刺激""兴奋""勇敢"。英美等西方国家的色情业场所 red-light district(红灯区,花街柳巷)常用这种刺激性色彩来招揽生意。在经济贸易等商务领域,red 一词常被用于表示"赤字""亏损""负债"等,如 red letter/red figure(赤字)、in the red(亏损,有赤字)、get out of the red(不再亏损,扭亏为盈)。与 red 一词有着相反联想引申义的 black 的商用文化含义则积极正面,如 in the black(有盈余)。

1.2.4 宗教文化

绝大多数民族都有自己的宗教信仰。佛教、道教、儒教影响深远,因此汉族人民有很多与上述宗教相关的思想和价值观念。比如,"修身齐家治国平天下"构成一种以"家国天下"为内核的伦理道德精神。这种伦理道德精神在商业思想上的体现就是"衣食父母论"。在旧时,商人往往把照顾自己买卖的顾客视作父母,比如,中国商人常说"买主买主,衣食父母"。而在英美等西方国家,人们普遍信仰基督教。基督教的一些思想价值观念在英语中广为传播,如"Customers are God."(顾客就是上帝)、"God helps those who help themselves."(自助者天助之)等。

中西方宗教文化的影响在中外翻译家杨宪益夫妇和霍克斯(David Hawkes)对《红楼梦》的不同英译中就有所反映。

请对比分析以下汉英翻译实例:

④ 谋事在人,成事在天。

杨译:Man proposes, Heaven disposes.

霍译:Man proposes, God disposes.

对比分析:杨宪益夫妇把"天"视作自然界的主宰,所以就把"天"译成了 Heaven,保持了原作的佛教色彩。而霍克斯则把"天"译成了 God,是基于译语读者的基督教背景和文化接受心理(邵志洪,2005:287)。

1.2.5 习语文化

"语言之所以被看作文化的一个组成部分,是因为它具备文化的特点。"(李发根,2004:142)汉英两种语言在习语(idioms)中有着生动的文化表现与特征。作为语言的重要组成部分,习语是人们从社会活动中经过长期使用而提炼出来的固定的短语或短句。从广义上说,习语"通常包括成语(set phrases)、谚语(proverbs)、格言(sayings)、俗语(colloquialisms)、典故(allusions)和俚语(slangs),在汉语中还包括歇后语"(包惠南,2001:148)。它们凝聚着丰富的民族文化信息和聪明才智,蕴含着独特的民族文化特征和文化背景,具有鲜明的形象和地域色彩。比如,汉语"生意场上无父子""买卖无亲戚"就与英语"Business is business."(在商言商)蕴含着同样的商业文化思想。再如,汉语"货物是草,顾客是宝"与英语"Customers are God."(顾客就是上帝)有着不谋而合的"顾客至上"(Customers First; Customer care is our top priority.)的商业思想。

汉语习语的结构稳定，主要以四字结构为主，也有五字、七字结构。这种已经固化的语言形式具有明显的汉语言文化特征。例如：

一本万利（a small investment that brings big profits / make big profits with a small capital）（安亚中、张健，2008）

薄利多销（small profits but quick returns / small profits and quick returns / small profits, large sales volumes / small profit margins, big sales / small profits but quick turnover）（危东亚，1997）

一手交钱，一手交货。（Cash and carry. / Cash on delivery. / Give me the case, and I'll give you the goods.）（安亚中、张健，2008）

王婆卖瓜，自卖自夸。（Wangpo selling melons praises her own goods. / Every ass loves to hear himself bray.）

挂羊头卖狗肉（cry up wine and sell vinegar / sell horsemeat as beefsteak / pass off fish-eyes as pearls）（尹帮彦，2006）

漫天要价，就地还钱。（The seller can ask a sky-high price; the buyer can make a rock-bottom offer.）（尹帮彦，2006）

物以稀为贵（Rare things are dear, plenty brings disaster. / That thing which is rare is dear. / When a thing is scarce, it is precious.）（尹帮彦，2006）

酒好不怕巷子深。（Good wine praises or sells itself. / Good wine needs no bush or crier.）（周锡卿，1987）

三百六十行，行行出状元。（Every trade has its master. / Every profession produces its own leading authority.）（尹帮彦，2006）

不怕不识货，只怕货比货。（Comparisons are odious. / Just compare them and you'll see which is better. / Don't worry about not knowing much about the goods.）（尹帮彦，2006）

便宜无好货，好货不便宜。（Cheapest is dearest. / Cheap things are not good, good things are not cheap. / A bargain usually costs you more in the end.）（周锡卿，1987）

货有高低三等价，客无远近一般看。（Your tariffs may be low, your tariffs may be dear, but treat us all the same, who come from far or near.）（尹帮彦，2006）

（某度假村）环境优美、功能齐全、服务到位，理想选择。（The holiday resort, nestled in a locale endowed with wonderful landscape and equipped with full facilities, offers quality services for your holiday stay.）

相比之下，英语习语的结构就无严格的格式要求，词数不一，但讲究排比，讲究平衡，常用押韵。这就是英语语言体现出来的文化特征。例如：

  value for money（物有所值）
  more value for the money（物超所值）
  Honesty is the best policy.（诚信是上策。）（周锡卿，1987）
  Buy in the cheapest market and sell in the dearest.（贱买贵卖。）（周锡卿，1987）
  No customer, no business.（没有客户，就没有生意。）
  No checkee, no shirtee.（一手交钱，一手交货。）（周锡卿，1987）
  cash and carry（一手交钱，一手交货）
  booming business（生意兴隆）
  high street fashion trends（大众时尚流行趋势）

  诚如萨丕尔所言，分属于两种不同文化的语言"在表述同一社会现实时是不可能完全一致的"（Sapir, 1970）。再者，"文化差异注定了作为文化载体的语言之间的翻译转换不可能走直线"（张传彪，2012：42）。鉴于文化差异，英译只能"绕道"以求变通。

第二节 以交际为目的的多"译"善"变"

  "萨丕尔-沃尔夫假设"（Sapir-Whorf Hypothesis）的"语言相对论"（Linguistic Relativity）认为，人的语言不同，思维也不同；语言不仅为其使用者所使用，也在相当程度上影响着使用者的思维与表达。沃尔夫（Whorf）认为，"语言是思维的工具，语言对于思维的整体建构起着必不可少的作用：每一种语言的语言系统的背景（即语法）不仅仅是表达思想的再创造性工具，其本身就是思想的塑造者，也是个体思维活动的程序和向导——思想的构造不是过去严格意义上所讲的独立过程，而是特定语法的一部分，在不同的语言之间或多或少有所不同"（转引自杨景萍，2011：118）。

  由于汉英两种语言的本质性差异，加之汉英两个民族在自然环境、社会制度、宗教信仰、哲学传统等方面的巨大差异，汉英语际间的翻译几乎就是在异质语言与文化的"不可通约"（incommensurability）中寻求沟通。从这个意义上来说，翻译根本无法做到完全对应或对等；但从另一方面讲，由于人类具有的情感、思维和生活经验又是基本相通的，所以严格意义上的不可译性又是有限度的。"无论译者翻译的对象是什么，变通总不可避免，因为翻译所涉及的诸如语言形式、文化内涵、作者意图、民族心理以及读者期待、可接受程度等都是随时必须考虑和妥善应对的。"（张传彪，2012：44）毕竟，"不同民族的语言棱镜所折射的世界是很不相同的"（申小龙，2000：4）。

鉴于汉英两种语言在商务这个特殊语域或社会功能中的差异，商务汉英翻译就需要采用套译（corresponding）、回译（back translation）、直译或音译加注（literal translation or transliteration plus annotation）、语意翻译（semantic translation）、改译（adaptation/modification plus translation）、符合语言习惯的翻译（idiomatic translation）、传意翻译（communicative translation）、解释性翻译（translation plus explanation）等方法，以求进行功能对等（functional equivalence）或信息灵活对等（dynamic message equivalence）（Nida, 2001）的跨文化有效交际活动。

2.1 回 译

在国际贸易中，有很多具有西方语言文化特色的商标、品名、企业机构名称、专业术语等。对这些带有浓厚西方语言文化色彩的商标、品名、企业机构名称、专业术语等进行英译，我们可以采用回译法。例如，"福特"（汽车品牌）、"万宝路"（香烟品牌）、"固特异"（汽车轮胎品牌）、"的士"、"酒吧"、"咖啡伴侣"、"炸薯条"、"芭比娃娃"（玩具）、"奶昔"（饮品）、"微软"、"麦当劳"（快餐店）、"沃尔玛"（超市）、"辛迪加"（财团）等名称原本就是英语名称，英译就可以直接回译成英语原来的名称，即 Ford, Marlboro, Goodyear, taxi, bar, coffee mate, French fries, Barbie doll, milk shake, Microsoft, McDonald, Wal-Mart, syndicate 等。再如，"傻瓜照相机""老板椅""蛇皮袋""总厂""条形码""通用汽车""离岸价""光票信用证""欧元区""首席执行官""一揽子交易""交钥匙工程""没有硝烟的战争"等名称原本就是汉语从英语借来的外来词（loan words），因此英译就可回译，恢复其本来的面目，即 fool-proof camera（automatic camera）, exec chair, poly sack, headquarters（factory）, bar code, General Moters, FOB（Free on Board）, clean L/C, Eurozone, CEO（Chief Executive Officer）, package deal, turn-key project, white war 等（许建忠，2002）。

此外，中国很多商家在命名商店商标时纷纷采用带有"洋味"的名称，先选定一个英语名称，如 Higher, Youngor, Safeguard, Nice, Gree, Longlife, Bird, Aux, Magic 等，再用汉字去拟写这些名字，将其"英化"（戴卫平、裴文斌，2008），如"海尔"（电器）、"雅戈尔"（西服）、"舒肤佳"（香皂）、"纳爱斯"（洗衣粉）、"格力"（空调）、"隆力奇"（保健品）、"波导"（手机）、"奥克斯"（空调）、"玛奇卡"（神奇扑克牌）等。英译这些"英化"汉语商标时就要回译，即使其变回原来的英语名称。

2.2 套 译

汉英分属两大不同的语言体系，它们的语言外显形态在表达同样的语义时会有所不同,甚至完全相反。所以,在进行汉英翻译时,我们对于商务语域比较突出的语言形态就要做变"型"、变"态"、变"序"、变"性"、变"色"的翻译转换。

2.2.1 套译变"型"

汉英两种语言所用的一些句型或句式是对应的,而有些句型则是不同的甚至完全相反的。这也表明,有着不同文化背景的汉英两种语言在进行广告、标识语等文体的翻译转换时,必须从受众的角度出发,充分考虑受众的生活习惯、思维方式、对事物的喜好等方面的文化适应性,灵活运用汉英各自语言的优势,使汉英翻译达到功能对等的效果。鉴于此,商务汉英翻译就应采用套译法,将汉语原文译成符合英语语言习惯的句型结构。

请对比分析以下汉英翻译实例:

① 浴室地滑,小心摔倒!

英译:Caution:Wet floor!

对比分析:此例汉语商用标识语使用了两个分句,套用的英译句型将两个分句合在一起,变成一个句式。

② 茂名是我家,清洁靠大家。

英译:Keep Our City Clean!

对比分析:此例汉语商用标识语使用的是陈述句,套用的英译句型则是一个祈使句。

③ 楼内禁止拍照、录像!

英译:The Use of Cameras or Video Equipment Is Prohibited!

对比分析:此例汉语原文使用的是命令口气的祈使句,而英译则采用了比较温和的陈述句。

④ 严禁酒后驾车!

英译:If you drive, don't drink. If you drink, don't drive.

对比分析:汉语公益广告使用的语气具有强制性,而英译则采用了比较人性化的劝说口吻。这就表明汉语读者习惯于强制性语言表达。

⑤ 商场拥挤,注意钱包!

英译1:Watch your personal belongings while shopping.

英译2:Thieves love crowds; watch your wallet, bag and camera.

对比分析:此例汉语原文使用了两个分句。英译1发挥英语形合语言的优势,采用合译法把两个分句并在了一起;英译2套用的英语句型不是与汉语原文对应的祈使句,而是陈述句。

2.2.2 套译变"态"

汉语不太使用被动句,因"主体意识"(潘文国,1997:366)而较多使用主动句。在英语中,被动语态是人们比较喜欢使用的一种语态表现形式。刘宓庆(1998)认为,英语被动语态在应用文体、科技文体中用得极为普遍。汉语句子在形式上多使用主动语态,因而需要转换为英语被动语态的句子大约占句子总数的三分之一,这个比例是相当大的。这种变"态"的处理方式在商务汉英翻译中十分常见。

请对比分析以下商务汉英翻译实例:

⑥ 我方将按所发货物发票价值的110% 办理综合险和破损险。

英译:Insurance will be covered against All Risks and Breakage Risk for the amount of 110% of the invoice value of the consignment.

对比分析:译文做了语态的转换,既贴切、自然地再现了汉语原文的意思,又符合英语表达习惯。如果不变"态"而直译成"We'll cover the consignment against All Risks and Breakage Risk for the amount of 110% of the invoice value.",尽管在形式上与原文很对应,但语句表达生硬,主语与状语前后不呼应。直译强调的是保险的办理方式;we 并非特指办理保险的具体当事人,而是泛指办理保险的义务人,即"我方"。由此可见,语态的变通再现了原文语义,达到了语义上的忠实。

⑦ 要发展经济应当组织使用各种各样的人才,对那些真正有本事的人在工资级别上可以破格提高。

英译:To develop economy, different kinds of talented people should be organized. People of real ability should be especially promoted and given raise.

⑧ 任何企业都可以以合伙的方式经营。

英译:Any business may be operated as a partnership.

⑨ 结论是,投资举办文化比较课程对于公司和职工来说,将是一件双赢的事情。

英译:It is concluded that a win-win situation for both the company and staff would be achieved by investing in culture-comparative courses.

对比分析:汉语例句用的都是主动语态。例⑦⑨是无主句,英译采用的变"态"处理方法突显了商务英语信函和报告"重纪实"的客观而精确的文体修辞特征。

2.2.3 套译变"序"

汉语是左分叉(left-branching)语言:状语成分,包括状语从句,一般都被放在主句前表达;定语成分,包括各种修饰语都被放在所修饰的中心词前面,可以按其数量无限地向左伸展,如"中国将接待的第一位澳大利亚贸易代表团团长""所用的各种材料的样品"等。相比之下,英语属于右分叉(right-branching)语言:中心词在前,状语、定语可以向右无限伸展,如"the first head of the Trade Delegation of Australia to be received in China""samples of the different qualities of material used"等。汉英定语修饰语的位置要颠倒过来才符合汉英各自的表达习惯。

上述例子中的定语修饰语都是短语。即便是一个单词,汉英互译也需要将定语修饰语颠倒,如"可利用的货币资金"(the money funds available)、"所需设备"(equipment required)、"由此造成的损失"(the loss sustained)、"上述商品"(the kind mentioned)、"支付的利息"(the interest rate charged)、"所用的材料"(the materials used)、"一个在国外的佣金商或代理人"(a commission representative or agent abroad)等。

此外,汉英翻译一定要注意汉英惯用语的固定词序,如"总计"(the sum total)、"市价"(price current)、"法人团体"(body corporate)等。

当然,汉语的状语从句一般在主句前面,而汉英翻译就需要变"序",将状语从句后置。

请对比分析以下商务汉英翻译实例:

⑩ 除非另有要求,他不会增加数量。

英译:He will not increase the quantity unless requested.

⑪ 要不是下大雨,货物早该装运完毕了。

英译:The goods would have been shipped but for the heavy rain.

对比分析:这两个汉语例句中的状语从句都在主句之前,而英译就把主从句做了前后对调。

2.2.4 套译变"性"

汉英两种语言在表达方式和用词习惯上存在差异,特别是在名词与动词、介词与动词等词性使用方面有很大不同。首先,由于汉语具有连动结构和兼语结构的特点,动词在汉语句中用得较多;而英语倾向于多用名词或名词化短语来表达动作、行为概念。因此,汉英翻译就要变"性"。

请对比分析以下商务汉英翻译实例:

⑫ 感谢您挑选在西格奈连锁酒店用餐。

英译:Thank you for choosing to eat at a Signet House Restaurant. (Wood, 2002)

对比分析:汉语使用了兼语结构"感谢您挑选"和连动结构"挑选在西格奈连锁酒店用餐"。而对应的英译却用了两个名词化短语:一个是动名词choosing,另一个是动词不定式to eat at a Signet House Restaurant。

⑬ 正如您可从我方1月份所寄产品目录中了解到的那样,我们的毯子暖和、柔软,并易于保管,它集中了所有上述优点。

英译:As you realized from the catalogue we had sent in January, our blanket is a perfect combination of warmth, softness, and easy care.

对比分析:汉语连用了几个动词,而英译使用了由动词派生而来的动名词

combination、零派生名词化短语 easy care，以及由形容词派生而来的名词 warmth 和 softness。

其次，汉英两种语言用词的词性差异还表现在：英语中介词的使用非常频繁，介词的搭配能力很强，含义也很丰富；汉语的介词多从动词演变而来，没有形态变化，介词与动词很难被区分开，两者经常被互换使用。

请对比分析以下商务汉英翻译实例：

⑭ 这是一艘<u>开往</u>美国旧金山的货船。

英译：This is a freight <u>for</u> San Francisco.

对比分析：汉语使用的动词"开往"被转换成了英语介词 for。与汉语相比，商务英语较多地使用介词或介词短语，力求表达简洁、经济与客观，如 cash on delivery（现钱现货）、small profits with quick returns（薄利多销）等。

2.2.5 套译变"色"、减"色"或添"色"

表示物质的一个重要属性的颜色词在商务汉英中除了具有相同或相似的文化联想义外，还有各自独特的民族文化引申义。中国哲学讲"虚"，中国文化注重神似，如中国画追求托物寄意、物我两化，多模糊曲笔，以达形神兼备；而西方哲学讲"实"，西方文化讲究科学精确，如西洋画十分注意保证描写对象的比例准确以给人真实的感觉。这种文化气质就反映在颜色词中，如"红糖"体现了红色在汉文化中的重要性和影响。红色是喜庆、成功的颜色，故汉族人民习惯于将接近红色的事物统称为"红"。既然深颜色的糖有助于补血养身，人们就褒称之为"红糖"，其实这种糖的颜色更接近棕色，英语将其译为 brown sugar（棕色糖）就比较精确。又如，"红茶"也不真是红色的，若跟"绿茶"一起考虑，这"红""绿"相对的茶名，充分展现了汉文化讲究、追求对称美的传统。而英语称"红茶"为 black tea（黑茶），黑色确实更接近此茶深浓的颜色。由此可见，汉语对颜色词的使用比较模糊却传神；英语使用颜色词倾向于精确，比较真实。正是这种虚、实、神、形方面的文化差异，造就了汉英颜色词的"不对应"，甚至"词汇空缺"（谭载喜，1997：128）。因此，商用颜色词的汉英翻译就可采用套译法进行变"色"、减"色"或添"色"处理。例如，汉语"黑面包"应变"色"套译成 brown bread（棕色面包），而不是 black bread；汉语"红木家具"的功能对等英译应是 blackwood furniture（黑木家具）。汉英翻译减"色"的例子有白米（rice）、白酒（liquor）、红酒（wine）、红利（divident）、绿色食品（health food）、绿宝石（emerald）、黄豆（beans）、黄麻（jute）、黄油（butter）、黑车（unlicensed vehicle）、黑交易（a shady deal /transaction）等；汉英翻译添"色"的例子有牛皮纸（brown paper）、温室（green house）、蔬菜水果商（green grocer）、大型家用电器（white goods）等。

2.3 直译或音译加注

汉语有着丰富而独特的民族文化。为了传播并帮助译文读者理解我国的民族文化，英译就需要采用直译或音译附加注释的方法。一些汉语商贸谚语、习语、行话等词语的英译就需要采用直译加注法。比如，汉语"三通"一词就可以被译成 three links：link of trade, travel and post。此外，在商贸领域，若出口中国土特产品或者对外接待时向外国客商介绍中餐菜名，我们就不妨采用直译或音译加注的方法。

请对比分析以下商务汉英翻译实例：

⑮ 一锤子买卖

英译1："once for all" deal：the one and only business deal to be made with sb. (from which the greatest possible advantage is to be derived)（安亚中、张健，2006）

英译2：a one-shot deal（Used metaphorically to mean that a thing is done just once, no matter how good or bad）（尹帮彦，2006）

⑯ 挂羊头卖狗肉

英译：hang up a sheep's head and sell dogmeat—try to palm off sth. inferior to what it purports to be（安亚中、张健，2008）

对比分析："一锤子买卖"和"挂羊头卖狗肉"作为源自生意场上的汉语习语或熟语，表义形象生动。如果只是直译不加注，英语读者理解起来就会比较困难。因此，为了便于读者理解，英译就需要加注，对原汉语习语进行解释说明。

⑰ 叫花子鸡

英译：beggar's chicken—There's a legendary story connected to it. Long long ago there was a beggar. One day, he stole a chicken and was pursued by the owner. He was almost caught when he suddenly hit upon a good idea. He smeared the chicken all over with clay, which he found nearby and threw it into the fire he had built to cook it. After a long while the beggar removed the mud-coated chicken from the fire. When he cracked open the the clay he found, to his astonishment, that the clay together with the feather had formed a hard shell in which the chicken had been baked into a delicious dish with wonderful flavour. That night he had a very enjoyable meal. Hence the name of the dish.（顾维勇，2005）

对比分析：对于汉语菜名，直译很难体现其中的文化内涵与历史渊源。所以，为了便于英语读者了解中国的饮食文化，直译加注法就成了不二选择。

⑱ 佛跳墙

英译：Fotiaoqiang（assorted meat and vegetables cooked in embers）（翁凤翔，

2002)

对比分析：此例也是一个中餐菜名。音译加注能帮助英语读者了解这个菜的原料和烹饪工艺，这样也有利于传播中国传统饮食文化。

2.4 意译变"名"

汉语有很多承载浓厚民族文化色彩的词汇，其中涉及一些地名、人名、动物名称、品名、企业名称和商标名称，这些名称的英译不能一对一地逐字转换。比如，不能简单地将汉语"牛饮"硬译成 drink like a cow，而要跨越文字表层进行深层次的文化信息的转换，即意译成 drink like a fish。由此可见，为了便于译文读者理解，上述这些名称的英译宜常用意译法，进行变"名"处理。

请对比分析以下汉英翻译实例：

⑲ 杜康

英译：Bacchus

对比分析："杜康"是传说中中国酿酒的鼻祖，以此给白酒命名，足见其用意就是表明其名酒的身份与地位。如果直译为 Dukang 就完全失去了其汉语文化信息（王月峰、胡登勇，2007），所以有人建议意译成 Bacchus（希腊酒神）。这在很大程度上传译出了中国博大精深的酒文化，算得上是异曲同工之笔（黄艺平，2010）。

⑳ 鱼米之乡

英译：land of milk and honey

对比分析：有人直接把汉语"鱼米之乡"硬译成 land of fish and rice，这种译法对英语读者来说就有些难懂了。英语习语 land of milk and honey (a place where life is pleasant and easy and people are very happy) 是指"富饶之地"，其表达的意思接近汉语习语"鱼米之乡"，只不过因文化习俗差异，所用象征之物不同而已。鉴于上述缘由，汉语"鱼米之乡"最好被改译成 land of milk and honey。

㉑ 龙头企业

英译：bellwether

对比分析：在汉语中，"龙头企业"是指在某个行业或领域处于领先地位的企业。若直译成 dragon-head enterprise 则显然不通，所以意译之一是 leading enterprise 或 enterprise playing a leading role。若为了保持与汉语同样的生动形象，英译可采用另一种意译而转换成 bellwether（领头羊、领头企业）。

2.5 改译换"名"

为达到预期的翻译目的,译者在翻译时可对原文的形式或/和内容做一定程度的修改,以适应译入语国家或读者的政治语境、文化背景或技术规范。改译可在小到词语、大到语段的范围内进行。(方梦之,2003)改译有时会在商标、名片、说明书、广告等商用汉英应用文文体翻译中被用到。

请对比分析以下商务汉英翻译实例:

㉒ "飞鸽"牌自行车

原译:"Flying Pigeon" Bike

改译:"Flying Dove" Bike

对比分析:在汉语商标名称中,"飞鸽"中的"飞"字暗示其产品性能,"鸽"字表示人们爱好和平。其原译 Flying Pigeon 中的 Pigeon 一词在英语中表示猎人打来食用的(又小又弱的)鸽子,而 Dove 一词象征和平。由此可见,原汉语商标所追求的效果没有被译出来,改译为 Flying Dove 更合适。(金惠康,2003)

㉓ "帆船"牌皮鞋

原译:"Junk" Leather Shoes

改译1:"Junco" Leather Shoes

改译2:"Yacht" Leather Shoes

对比分析:"帆船"牌皮鞋是中国传统出口产品,原先被直译成了 Junk 一词。因 Junk 一词在英语中有"废旧杂物"之意,所以这种牌子的皮鞋在国际市场上的销售不太好。改译用创新词 Junco 来译,从而避免了出现消极的文化联想。当然,用 Yacht 替换 Junk 来译"帆船"也可解此忧。因为国际帆船比赛中的"帆船"一词也是用 Yacht,所以 Yacht 这个皮鞋品牌的英译也就名正言顺了。(顾维勇,2005)

㉔ 2012年6月15日,丝的价格从每斤14元降至每斤12元。

英译:The price of silk has dropped from US $1.1095 a kilogram to US $0.9510 a kilogram on June 15, 2012.

对比分析:为了便于进口商更好地理解丝产品的出口价格,英译按照当日的汇率把人民币换算成了美元,把市斤也换算成了公斤。

2.6 英译汉化

一些汉语词语是汉语特有的语言表达,其英译可能带有中国特色。比如,"红包""小康""一刀切""菜篮子工程"等汉语习惯表达是英语没有的,其英译就不免多多少少带有中国特色,如:money-contained red envelope, a relatively comfortable living for all, impose uniformity, Vegetable Basket Project/shopping basket program (a program for increasing food production)。上述"英译汉化"现象在中国对外语言文化交流中的出现是不可避免的,关键在于无论是翻译汉语中具有悠久文化传统的习语,还是翻译中国特有的新生术语,英译都要参照《中国日报》《北京周报》等英文报刊上出现的译名,或《中国翻译》的封底上提供的译名。

2.7 符合译语习惯的英译简化

汉语偏爱语言的渲染,喜欢"堆砌大量的并无多少实际内容的修饰词"(程镇球,2002:69),重复使用一些渲染之词。中国人喜爱使用四字词语,但一些汉语广告中的四字结构词语纯属堆砌,言之无物。直译就会给读者冗余之感,不符合译入语的语言表达习惯。所以,此类浮夸渲染之词的英译就需要进行简化处理,以便译文符合英语的表达习惯。

请对比分析以下商务汉英翻译实例:

㉕ 这套设备价格昂贵,这限制了它的批量生产。

英译:The price limited the production of the equipment.

对比分析:汉语"价格昂贵"被英译成了price,这种简化实际上隐含了原义。这一点是可以通过上下文推测判断出来的。

㉖ 它保持了酱香浓郁、典雅细致、协调丰满、回味悠长等贵州茅台的特点。

英译:It possesses unique style and flavor and is an extremely enjoyable drink.

对比分析:中国人常用"酱香浓郁""典雅细致""协调丰满""回味悠长""醇和协调""绵甜甘冽""落口净爽"等四字结构词语来形容白酒的好口感,但西方人很少喝白酒,更没有这种对白酒的口感描写得非常具体的印象式表达。如果将其直译出来,西方读者很可能会感到别扭,无法接受。所以,英译将原文中这种既具体又特殊的中国说法概括化,并做笼统性描述,译为 unique style and flavor and is an extremely enjoyable drink,既传达了原文的基本信息,让读者可以理解原文的意思,又使译文更加简练。

2.8 解释性英译

许多汉语特色语汇的翻译是直译、音译加注、套译加注等翻译方法解决不了的。唯一的解决方法就是采用解释性英译转换,即对原文进行补充说明。具体来说,就是在翻译中补充一些背景信息,通常是加几个词或一两句话,但不一定是字典"释义"性的(常玉田,2002)。

请对比分析以下商务汉英翻译实例:

㉗ 深圳特区发挥了很好的<u>窗口作用</u>和辐射作用。

原译:Shenzhen Special Economic Zone(SEZ)has served the nation well as <u>a showcase of opening-up</u> and a powerhouse of economic growth.

改译:Shenzhen Special Economic Zone(SEZ)has served the nation well as <u>a showcase of opening-up</u>,<u>a gateway of international exchange</u>,and a powerhouse of economic growth.

对比分析:汉语原句中的"窗口作用"是一个比喻性说法,如果只是简单地将其译成 a showcase of opening-up,那么读者理解起译文来就会有困难。因此,改译补充了一个简洁明了的解释,这样读者理解起来就容易多了。

㉘ 一<u>钉子户</u>的房子像个孤岛耸立在工地中央。

原译:<u>The recalcitrant's</u> house is looking just like an island on the construction site.

改译:<u>A household refuses to move and bargains for unreasonably high compensation when the land is requisitioned for a construction project</u>,so his house is looking just like an island on the construction site.

对比分析:"钉子户"也是汉语中非常形象的一个比喻性俗语,原译所做的简单的意译 recalcitrant 对于英译读者来说理解起来有困难。改译所做的解释性翻译提供了补充信息和说明,读者理解起来就不会那么困难了。

汉英两种语言在语言文化上千差万别,而通过翻译实现语言文化之间转换的方法与技巧林林总总。由于以后的章节对此都将有所涉及,在此就不一一叙述。

思考与练习

1. 思考题

(1) 商务汉英两种社会功能语言变体在语言层面上有什么差异?

(2) 商务汉英两种社会功能语言变体在文化层面上有什么差异?

(3) 跨越语言文化之间的障碍,商务汉英翻译可以采取什么策略?具体的翻译方法包括哪些?

2. 请将以下汉语外来词译成英语,并做适当的解释说明

(1) 盎司

(2) 芭比娃娃

(3) 玻璃天花板

(4) 西红柿

(5) 洗钱

3. 句子翻译

(1) 你会发现从我们这里拿货是有益的,因为我们的产品质量远远超过了你们区域内其他外国制造商的产品质量。

(2) 据估计,他们的股票价格在一个月后每股会超过 15 美元。

(3) 我们的商品价格公道、品质优良。

(4) 在餐桌上做成的生意的数量并不亚于谈判桌上做成的生意的数量。

(5) 此房报价两百万元人民币,价格面议。

(6) 本公司的产品远销英国、美国、日本、意大利和东南亚,深受消费者欢迎。

(7) 海河边的天津,"三绝"之一是桂发祥的十八街大麻花。

(8) 小草微微笑,请走人行道。

(9) 为了您的安全,请勿在床上吸烟。

(10) 热烈欢迎国内外嘉宾参加贸易洽谈会!

(11) 不得退换,过期无效。

(12) 他们以外商为对象,通过各种形式,调查研究国外市场的需求情况以及他们对我国出口商品的反应,从而弄清我国出口商品哪些可发展,哪些宜控制,哪些该提高质量、增加花色品种、改进包装装潢以及如何扩大推销等,并制订计划、拟定措施,使我国生产出更多的适销对路的出口商品,换取更多的外汇。

(13) 创建于 1982 年的广州服装厂是产销量和出口量均居广东第一的服装生产专业厂,其独特的设计使其"新星"牌夹克产品远销世界 30 多个国家和地区,深受国内外用户的广泛欢迎。

(14) 最近 20 多年来,中国实行改革开放,综合国力大大提升,与中国打交道,对中华文化感兴趣的国家、国际组织和人员日益增多。

4. 语篇翻译

● 语篇 1

副主席先生,

美国朋友们,

同事们,

女士们,先生们:

我谨代表我们代表团的所有成员,为邀请我们参加这个盛大的圣诞晚会表示衷心的感谢!

我们享受了美酒佳肴,聆听了美妙的音乐。我很高兴能有机会和大家共聚一堂,共同度过这美好的夜晚。俗话说:"好的开端是成功的一半。"我希望我们能够保持这种良好的关系,在新的一年里更加精诚合作。

再次感谢邀请,感谢你们使我们度过了欢乐的时光。

最后,请各位与我一起举杯

为副主席先生的健康,

为美国朋友们的健康,

为我的同事们的健康,

为在座所有的女士们、先生们,

干杯!

- 语篇2

商务谈判压力很大,有时似乎劳而无功。首席谈判官必须具备很强的幽默感才能熬过各种难关。谈判拖延、会务安排出错、恶劣的会谈环境等都会像是无理取闹。而在商务旅途中遭罪,简直是自贬身份。但若能用幽默的眼光来看待这一切,不过于较真,那就一切都不同了,谈判就能顺利地进行下去。

- 语篇3

逶迤秦岭,气象峥嵘;潺潺山泉,峭壁奇峰。蓝天白云,鸟唱蜂鸣。走进秦岭,你就像回归了远古,走进了童话般的境界。这里是中国南北的分界线,是长江、黄河两大水系的分水岭。这里资源丰富,动植物种类繁多,单种子植物就有1 988种,药用植物有510种,闻名世界的蜂蜜——上品山花蜜就出产在这崇山峻岭中。

在秦岭山脉北坡,关中平原西端,闻名遐迩的山西省宝鸡市高新技术开发区,坐落着一家专门研究蜂乳生物科学、生产"锥老大"牌系列蜂乳蜜酒的生产厂家——陕西黑马蜂乳生物技术发展有限公司。

第三章

商务汉英翻译的标准及存在的问题

Identify the problems in the following translations

① 请勿践踏草坪!

英译:Please do not step on the grass!

② 你11月15日的订单上所说的那种货,我这儿现在没有,抱歉。

英译:In reply to your order of November 15, we regret to say that we do not have in stock any such articles as you described.

③ 为了开好本次大会,邮联大会中国组委会全力以赴做了大量的准备工作。中国政府和北京市政府均对本次大会的筹备给予了大力支持。很多国家政府和邮政主管部门也为中国筹备本次大会提供了有益的帮助。在此,我谨向所有支持本次大会筹备工作的国家、部门和朋友们表示最衷心的感谢!

英译:The Chinese Organizing Committee of the Postal Union Congress has gone all out to make preparations in order to make the Congress a success. The Central Government and the Beijing Municipal Government of China have given unfailing support to the preparatory work of the Congress. The governments and competent postal departments of many countries have provided kind assistance to China's preparatory work for the Congress. Here I'd like to express my most sincere thanks to all the countries, departments and friends that have given us support to the preparatory work for the Congress.

商务汉英翻译比普通汉英翻译复杂得多。这是因为商务汉英翻译的译者既要熟悉汉英两种语言文化及翻译技巧,又要掌握商务知识、商务理论,还要了解商务汉英作为专门用途语言变体的语言文化特征。国内外现有的翻译标准和原则很多,对商务汉英翻译具有一定的借鉴与参考价值。但是,不同文体、不同体裁的翻译标准不必苛求全面统一,可以视不同文体而定；若用"信、达、雅"三字翻译标准来衡量，则应有区别地有所侧重（王永泰，2002）。

严复在100多年前提出的"信、达、雅"三字翻译标准在我国翻译历史上起到了很好的指导作用，至今翻译界人士在制定翻译标准时仍没有跳出其设定的框架。比如，林语堂提出的"忠实、通顺、美"、瞿秋白提出的"信顺统一"以及刘重德提出的"信、达、切"等翻译标准无一不以"忠实"为核心标准。但是，这些翻译标准过于笼统，一般适用于文学翻译，另外一个不足之处就在于，它们没有将翻译这种社会交际行为置于社会文化的背景之下进行考察。所以，把这些翻译标准拿来指导商务英语翻译就会有其局限性。

随着国际化、全球化的加快发展，我国对外翻译的数量庞大、类别繁多。时至今日，翻译标准也应趋向于多元化（multiplicity）和多样化（diversity），不同文体的翻译标准也应有所不同。就"信、达、雅"而言，"重纪实、少文饰"的商务英语的翻译就与文学翻译不同；商业广告的翻译与其他类别的商务英语文体的翻译也不同。商务英语的涵盖面比较广，它涉及许多不同的领域。正如刘法公教授所说，凡是在国际贸易、国际金融、国际旅游、国际投资、国际运输等国际商务活动中使用的英语都可以被称为国际商务英语。因此，商务英语的翻译标准有其特殊性，即翻译标准的多重性。多重性就是指不同文体的翻译标准应按照不同文体的语言特征分"体"别类，有所差异，灵活处理。

商务汉英"体中有体、类中有类"，包括商务信函、商务报告、商贸合同、商业广告、产品说明书、企业简介、商业计划书、招商简介等。商务汉英涉及商法、保险、金融、投资、运输、广告等。商法的语言特点与广告的语言特点大相径庭：法律具有规定性、约束性，法律语言庄重，措辞严谨，很少有模糊语言；商业广告的目的在于宣传推销产品，建立产品和企业的良好形象，所以广告用词新颖别致，语言简洁明了、生动形象，文字具有渲染力。由此可见，从不同文体的语言社会功能角度来看，翻译是在一定社会语境下发生的交际过程（Hatim & Mason，2001），是一种跨语言、跨文化的交流活动（沈苏儒，1998）。那么，商务汉英翻译标准就应根据商务语言的社会功能、商务语境、跨语言跨文化商务英语交际活动的本质特征与要求而更具针对性、多样性、应用性、职业性等。

第一节　适用于商务汉英翻译的标准

翻译标准是长期以来各派争论的焦点之一，可以说是百家争鸣、各抒己见。比如，国外有英国著名学者泰特勒（Alexander Fraser Tytler）提出的翻译"三原则"、功能学派提出的"目的论"（Skopostheorie）、美国翻译理论家奈达提出的"功能对等"翻译理论；国内有严复提出的"信、达、雅"翻译原则、钱锺书提出的"化境"之说、刘重德提出的"信、达、切"

翻译原则、刘法公教授提出的"忠实、准确、统一"。

1.1 国外学者提出的翻译标准及其应用

1.1.1 泰特勒提出的翻译"三原则"及其应用

英国法学家、历史学家泰特勒在1791年出版的《论翻译的原则》(*Essay on the Principles of Translation*)一书中提出了翻译"三原则":

(1) The translation should give a complete transcript of the ideas of the original work.(译文应完全复写出原作的思想。)

(2) The style and manner of writing should be of the same character with that of the original work.(译文的风格和笔调应与原文的性质相同。)

(3) The translation should have all the ease of the original composition.(译文应与原作同样流畅。)

以上三原则类似于严复提出的"信、达、雅"翻译原则:第一条相当于"信",第二条相当于经过重新解释的"雅",第三条相当于"达"。虽然泰特勒提出的"三原则"主要是指文艺翻译尤其是诗歌的翻译,但从广义上来说,他的"三原则"适用于所有的翻译。这是因为泰特勒强调的是原文读者和译文读者的反应一致。他的翻译标准对国际商务英汉互译具有指导意义(翁凤翔,2007b)。

1.1.2 翻译的"目的论"及其应用

"目的论"是功能翻译理论中最重要的理论,"是西方翻译理论中的一支劲旅"(杨晓荣,2001:14),是20世纪70年代以来德国最具影响力的翻译学派(谭载喜,2004)。以德国翻译理论家汉斯·弗米尔(Hans J. Vermeer)、凯瑟琳娜·赖斯(Katharina Reiss)、曼塔莉(Justa Holz-Manttari)和诺德(Christiane Nord)为主要代表的功能主义"目的论","以目的为总则,把翻译放在行为理论和跨文化交际的框架中进行考察,为世界翻译理论界开辟了一条崭新的道路"(李长栓,2004:11)。"目的论"的另外两个原则就是语篇内连贯(intratextual coherence)和语篇间连贯(intertextual coherence)。语篇内连贯也称"连贯原则"(the coherence rule),是指译文必须符合逻辑,符合译入语的表达习惯,能够让译文读者理解,并在目的语文化以及使用译文的交际环境中有意义。语篇间连贯又称"忠实原则"(the fidelity rule)。在"目的论"中,忠实原则是指译文不违背原文,译文和原文存在某种联系,并不要求译文和原文在内容上一字不差。忠实的程度和形式是由译文的目的和译者对原文的理解来决定的。

"目的论"的核心概念是"决定翻译过程的最主要因素是整个翻译行为的目的"(文月娥,2008:92)。汉斯·弗米尔指出,翻译是在目的语情景中为某种目的及目的受众而产生的语篇。"目的论"不仅认为翻译是一种跨文化的交际行为,还认为翻译是两种文化的比较。由此可见,以目的为导向、以译语为中心、重视译语文化语境与读者反应的"目的论"对商务汉英翻译这种应用性翻译来说具有重大的实际指导意义。

请对比分析以下商务汉英翻译实例:

① 小心地滑!

英译:Caution:Wet Floor!

对比分析:有人直译、硬译,把原文译成了 Careful Slippery Floor,岂不是滑稽可笑!根据"目的论"翻译理论,就要究其内涵,采用意译,把原文的"提示"目的在目的语中传译出来。

1.1.3 "4Es"翻译标准及其应用

传统翻译往往把翻译仅仅看作语言框架内的双语转换(transformation or shift),而在社会功能语言学指导下的翻译则强调"功能对等"(functional equivalence)原则,把视点拓宽到语用、文化、文体、语篇功能、译文读者反应等层面。奈达在《翻译科学探索》一书中首次提出了"动态对等"翻译观。所谓动态对等就是"译文接受者和译文信息之间的关系,应该与原文接受者和原文信息之间的关系基本上相同"(Nida,1964:159),就是"信息灵活对等"或"信息动态对等"(dynamic message equivalence),即"4Es"。

- Equivalence of semantic message of source language and target language(原文的语义信息与译文语义信息对等)
- Equivalence of stylistic message of source language and target language(原文的风格信息与译文风格信息对等)
- Equivalence of cultural message of source language and target language(原文的文化信息与译文文化信息对等)
- Equivalence of response of source language readers and target language readers(原文的读者反应与译文的读者反应对等)

第一,翻译要做到语义信息对等。语义信息对等包括表层和深层语义信息对等(equivalence of surface and deep structure semantic message)。表层语义就是话语或语篇的字面意义(literal meaning);深层语义则是透过字面意义推测出来的意思,是原文所蕴含的深层结构语义。

商务汉英应用文所传达的大多为表层结构语义,极少蕴含深层结构语义。因此,商务汉英翻译更多的是传译原文的表层结构语义。例如:

② 我方经营多种轻工业产品,详见附表。

英译:We deal in a wide range of light industrial products as per list enclosed. (邵志洪,2005)

当然,在传译表层结构语义的过程中有一个顾及汉英两种不同语言差异的问题,即遣词酌句以求通达。比如,有人将"蛇皮袋"和"宫娟扇"分别译成了 snake-skin bag 和 palace silk fans。这种翻译只顾及表层结构上的对应而没有实现其深层语义的对等转换。其实,英语中有现成的对等语 poly sacks 和 mandarin fans。

第二,在文体/语体风格上,翻译也要力求对等,特别是在风格信息非常突出时更要如此。语义信息对等和风格信息对等是商务汉英翻译中最基本的要求。商务汉英应用文"体中有体,类中有类"。不同文体需要用不同风格的词语、句式与篇章模式来表现。这是一个文体/语体修辞问题。

请对比分析下例中风格信息的对等传译:

③ a. 请速报产品最低价。

英译:Please quote us your lowest product prices as soon as possible.

b. 如能速报你方产品最低价,我方将不胜感激。

英译:We shall be obliged if you will quote us your rock-bottom prices for your products at your earliest convenience.

对比分析:这两个例句属于外贸信函语句。句子传达了同样的语义信息,但是因贸易双方之间的关系不同而采用了不同语体等级。因交际双方之间的关系比较亲密,例③a 所用的语体不是那么正式;在例③b 中,因交际双方彼此之间不熟悉,写信人所用语体非常正式。

第三,在语义和风格信息对等的基础上,如果原文承载了文化信息,尤其是当文化信息特别浓的时候,译文应尽量把文化信息加以恰当地传递。例如,汉语商标"紫罗兰"在汉语文化中有着"浪漫""高雅"等文化联想意义,而直译的 Pansy 一词在英语文化里是个带有贬义的俗语词(colloquialism),其内涵之义为 effeminate man(女人气的男人)或 male homosexual(同性恋男子)。可想而知,以 Pansy 冠名的男装在英美等西方国家的销路是不会好的。如果换一种创新译法——Violetex,效果将大为改观。Violetex 这个创新词是由 violet(紫罗兰)和 texture(织物)两个词合并而来的,这种译法既在一定程度上保留了原貌,又弱化了 Pansy 一词的不雅色彩(顾维勇,2005)。

请对比分析以下商务汉英翻译实例:

④ 这笔买卖最后一刻<u>黄了</u>。

英译:The deal <u>fell through</u> at the last minute.

对比分析:如果把原文"黄了"直译成 yellow,岂不是滑稽可笑! 旧时代做生意,开张的那天,门外要贴上写着"开张大吉"的大红纸喜报一张。春节休息,正月十六开始营业,开门那天,也要在门外贴上写着"开市大吉"的大红纸喜报。相反,如果一家商店经营不善,没法支撑下去了,店铺关门,就用一张黄纸,写上"收市大吉",贴在门上。由此,人们就将一家店铺的关门,说是"黄了"(That business has closed down for good.),避讳"关门"这两个不吉利的字眼儿。现在,"黄了"的词义范围大大拓展了,凡是没有办成的事情通通可以说成"黄了"。比如,"有人想承包一项工程,没有办成,也说'黄了'"(王垂基,2008:62)。

最后一个对等是以前三个对等为条件的。若前三个对等有一个做得不够,那么译文读者的反应与原文读者的反应就不可能做到对等。

请对比分析以下商务汉英翻译实例:

⑤ 天津国际经济贸易展览中心是由中国、德国、日本合资经营的综合性现代化大型国际展览与经济贸易中心,它坐落在中国天津国际经济、贸易、旅游中心,是举办各种规模和类型的国际展览会、博览会及国际会议的理想场所。"中心"附设三星级酒店及公寓,娱乐消遣设施俱全,<u>是客商来华拓展贸易的最佳选择</u>。

英译:Tianjin World Economy Trade & Exhibition Centre is a first-class modern comprehensive exhibition and trade center jointly operated by China, Germany and Japan. Located in the central part of the international economy, trade and tour area, the Centre offers you the most ideal place for various kinds of international exhibitions, trade fairs and conventions. It is the best facility for customers worldwide to promote business in China. The three-star hotel and apartments with complete recreational facilities available in the Centre can give you pleasure after traveling and negotiations.

对比分析:汉语原文的最后一句"是客商来华拓展贸易的最佳选择"过于自夸,这种字眼在汉语简介中十分常见,属于典型的自我渲染性言辞,带有明显的个人主观色彩(邵志洪,2005)。为了避免使英译读者产生反感,译者灵活地删减了最后一句话。这样才可能保持原文的初衷和表达原意。

◆ 1.2 国内学者提出的翻译标准及其应用

"对商务文本的翻译来说,国内外翻译史上的翻译标准大多笼统,现有翻译原则难以完全适用于商贸汉英翻译。"(石春让、白艳,2012:81)刘法公(2002)在《商贸汉英翻译的原则探索》一文中率先提出了商贸翻译"忠实、准确、统一"的六字翻译原则,并详细阐述了该原则的实质内容,强调了商贸专业知识和语言特点决定翻译原则的变异。此外,其他学者也对商务翻译的原则进行了广泛的探讨。恒齐、隋云(2003:74)认为,商务翻译要"做到'达意(习惯的表达方法)、传神(恰当的语言风格)和表形(通用的规范格式)',要按照'入乡随俗'的原则,用英语中'约定俗成'的语言和形式来进行创造性的翻译"。彭萍(2004)认为,商务文本翻译的具体尺度应该是意思准确、术语规范、语气贴切。李明清(2009)指出,商务英语有其自身的特点和规律,在翻译中需要通过"变通"来完善和促进"等效"。下面将分别对两种影响较大、适用性较强的商务汉英翻译标准和原则做简单介绍。

1.2.1 "忠实""准确""地道""通顺""统一"等翻译标准及其应用

除上述翻译标准以外,刘法公(1999)在《商贸汉英翻译专论》一书中提出了商贸汉英翻译的标准——"忠实、通顺、统一"。张新红等(2003)则提出了与之类似的商务英语翻译标准——"忠实、地道和统一"。2004年,刘法公在他的《商贸汉英翻译评论》一书中进一步完善并提出了适用于商贸汉英翻译的"忠实"(faithfulness)、"准确"(exactness)、"统一"(consistency)的标准或原则。

(1) 忠实:译文信息与原文信息对等,即正确地将原文语言的信息用译文语言表达出来;

(2) 准确:译者在商贸汉英翻译过程中选词准确,概念表达确切,物与名所指正确,数码与单位精确(刘法公,2004);

(3) 统一:商贸汉英翻译过程中所选用的译名、概念、术语等在任何时候都应该保持统一,不允许随意变换同一概念或术语的译名(刘法公,1999)。

在上述翻译标准中,"忠实"是核心标准,其他标准或原则都是围绕"忠实"展开的。"忠实"强调的是"信息等值",而不单纯是"语义等值"。

请对比分析以下商务汉英翻译实例:

⑥ 客商从开发区企业分得的<u>利润</u>在汇出境外时,免征<u>所得税</u>。

英译:<u>Dividends</u> for the investors and businessmen from their Development Zone enterprises <u>will be exempted</u> from <u>personal income tax</u> if remitted out of China.

⑦ 但是由于要求收货人是托运人,并要求托运人空白背书提单,提单就成为<u>可转让的票据</u>,货物的所有权随持有者而转移。

英译:However, by requiring that the <u>consignee</u> be the <u>shipper</u> and by requiring the shipper to <u>endorse the bills of lading in blank</u>, the document becomes <u>a negotiable instrument</u> wherein the <u>title to the merchandise</u> goes with possession of the bills of lading.

对比分析:这两例译文都忠实地再现了原文的语义、风格、文化等信息。比如,专业术语 dividends 和 personal income tax 对等转换了原汉语专业术语"利润"和"所得税";再如,译文所用语态 will be exempted,remitted out of China 和名词化短语 requiring that …都传译出原文的正式语体风格。此外,英译所用专业术语 negotiable instrument, consignee, title 等都是国际贸易惯用语。

"准确"和"统一"都是从"忠实"这一首要标准引发出来的。

翻译准确与否,与译者的商贸专业知识和对汉英双语词汇的深刻理解密切相关。例如,"保税区"的英译是 bonded zone,而"保税卡车"的英译是 customs bonded vehicle。由此可见,翻译应按照词语内涵准确地选用英译词语,这样才能保证信息与概念的对应转换。此外,商贸翻译涉及许多数字、名称的英译问题。数字的英译要准确,名称的英译更应统一。经过商贸工作人员多年的共同努力,许多中国的对外贸易商品基本上都已经有了固定的英译名称。这些英译名称虽然略显汉化,但在国际上通用已久,若随便用另一种英译法,势必造成物名分家。这些中国特有的商品的英语名称在国际商贸英语中不易找到,所以我们只能查找到一些中国外贸领域约定俗成的译法,见表3.1。

表3.1 中国外贸领域约定俗成的译法示例

汉语商品名称	约定俗成的英译名称
皮蛋	preserved eggs
咸腊肉	salt preserved meat
花茶	scented tea
乌龙茶	oolong tea
哈密瓜	Hami melon
阿胶	ass-skin glue
榨菜	hot pickled mustard tuber
清凉油	essential balm
膏药	dog-skin plaster
豆腐乳	salted bean curd
小磨香油	sesame oil

1.2.2 "四达"翻译标准及其应用

自20世纪80年代,我国开始引进西方翻译理论,诸如"等值""等效""等同""对等"等翻译新概念不断涌现。但这些翻译标准或原则均是基于语言文化习惯非常接近的西方语言文字之间的翻译而提出的,若将它们直接用作语言文化差异较大的汉英之间的翻译标准显然不合适(李明,2007)。

当代哲学的发展为我们提供了进行翻译研究的不同视角。德国哲学家哈贝马斯(Habermas)认为,交往行为就是以符号、语言、意识、文化等方式表现出来的人与人之间的相互关系和相互作用,或者说是主体之间借助语言符号,通过对话而达到相互理解、信任与和谐的过程(李彬,2003)。"针对语用学的三项功能,即呈现事实、建立关系和表达意向,哈贝马斯提出了三点要求,即相应于事实的真实性、相应于关系的正确性和相应于表达的真诚性。"(李明,2006:268)李明等据此在《商务英语翻译:汉译英》一书中提出了与奈达"4Es"十分类似且同等重要的"四达"翻译标准:

- "达意"(conveyance of semantic meaning):译文必须传达源语文本的语义。
- "达旨"(conveyance of intention):译文必须传达原文作者的写作意图。

- "达趣"（conveyance of charm）：译文必须传达源语文本的神韵和语趣。
- "达效"（conveyance of effects）：译文必须取得同原文一样的效果。

其中，"达意""达旨""达效"更适合非文学翻译的商务英语翻译标准（李明，2006），而"达意"尤其重要。

第二节　商务汉英翻译中存在的问题

由于不懂汉英两种语言之间的普通语言文化差异，特别是不熟悉商务汉英作为特殊用途的社会功能语言变体之间的特殊差异，商务汉英翻译中就会出现翻译"不准确"、翻译"不忠"等问题。另外，因为违背翻译原则或者其他原因，翻译"不统一"、翻译"跑调""胡翻乱译"、"死译硬译"等问题在商务汉英翻译中也是司空见惯。

2.1　翻译"不忠"，误译较多

商贸活动涉及很多实用信息，特别是一些经济利益，所以商务汉英翻译首先应该做到"忠实"，即"信息等值"。否则，翻译"不忠"或不"达意"，就会造成许多错译、误译。造成错译、误译的原因有二：一是译者想当然胡翻乱译；二是疏忽所致。如果肯勤查词典，又能结合上下文来理解原文，这样的错误是可以避免的。

请对比分析以下商务汉英翻译实例：

① 纽约 ECO 集团拥有五个控股子公司。

误译：New York ECO Group has 5 share-holding companies.

改译：New York ECO Group is a holding company of 5 subsidiary companies. ／
New York ECO Group holds shares of 5 subsidiary companies.

对比分析：在误译中，译者所译 share-holding companies 是指控制或持有某公司股权的股东公司，其意思是 5 个公司持有纽约 ECO 集团的股份，这不符合汉语原义。正确的英译应该是带有一个修饰限定语——介词短语，即 a holding company of 5 subsidiary companies。

② 日本人甚至使用从中国进口的<u>一次性筷子</u>制造高级纸张，卖给中国人。

误译：The Japanese even make high-grade paper with <u>once only chopsticks</u> imported from China and sell it to the Chinese.

改译：The Japanese even make high-grade paper with <u>disposable chopsticks</u> imported from China and sell it to the Chinese.

对比分析:"一次性筷子"的英译 once only chopsticks 显然有悖于原词的深层语义,即"用过这一次之后就扔掉"。所以,忠实的英译应该是 disposable chopsticks 或 throwaway chopsticks。(安亚中、张健,2008)

③ 你方必须用铁桶包装货物。

误译:You must wrap the goods in iron drums.

改译:You must pack the goods in iron drums.

对比分析:汉语的"包装"通常是指将物品打包,放在箱子、袋子等里面捆扎起来,以便于运输和携带。这种包装方式适用于大件或大宗物品的运输包装,其英译为 pack。由此可见,pack 一般指外包装。然而,wrap 虽然也表示"包"或"打包",但有别于 pack。wrap 是指用纸、布等材料把小件物品包起来。比如,商店售货员用纸等可卷的或柔软的材料把小商品包裹起来。wrap 一般指内包装。(翁凤翔,2007a)

◆ 2.2 翻译有失"准确",造成歧义

翻译欠准确,或译文易产生歧义,在表面上看来似乎不是什么大问题,实际上却严重违背了商务翻译准确传递原文信息的基本原则,致使翻译不能传译深层语义。其原因主要有两个:一是译者懂得原文的意思,但表达得不准确;二是译者不够谨慎,没有弄清原文的意思就匆忙下笔。

请对比分析以下商务汉英翻译实例:

④ 这块手表的保修期是一年。

误译:This watch is warranted for one year.

改译:This watch is guaranteed for one year.

对比分析:guarantee 和 warrant 都可表示"保证"或"担保",但 guarantee 的主要意思是"许诺做某事,提供或更换某物",所以常表示"保修"。而 warrant 的主要意思是"保证某物是真品或正品",如"All the spare parts are warranted."(所有备用零件都是保证质量的。)。

⑤ 买方须预付100万美元,占货款总额的60%。货款付清后,卖方交货。

误译:The Buyer shall pay in advance US $1,000,000.00, that is 60% of the total value of the goods. The Seller is to make shipment of the contracted goods when the payment is made.

改译:The Buyer shall pay in advance US $1,000,000.00, that is 60% of the total value of the goods. The Seller is to make shipment of the contracted goods when the down payment is made.

对比分析:因为对"货款"的所指不够明确,误译就不够准确地将其翻译成了泛

泛而谈的 payment，而不是根据上下文译成准确的 down payment（预付款，定金）。结果，交易双方发生了经济纠纷而各执一词，买方因此而遭受了巨大的经济损失。

2.3 翻译有失"统一"，不地道，不规范

商务汉英翻译所遵循的另一个重要原则是：术语翻译应符合商业惯例，译名、概念、术语应始终保持统一，同一概念或术语不能随意变换译名。

请对比分析以下商务汉英翻译实例：

⑥ 如贵方能将尿素报价降至<u>每吨1 200 美元</u>，我们可订购150～180 <u>吨</u>。

误译：If you can reduce your price of urea to <u>1,200 dollars per ton</u>, we may be able to place an order of 150 −180 <u>tons</u>.

改译：If you can reduce your price of urea to <u>1,200 US dollars per metric ton</u>, we may be able to place an order of 150 −180 <u>metric tons</u>.

对比分析：误译中有三处有失准确：第一，作为重量单位，吨在不同的度量制中有不同的解释。美制中分长吨（long ton）（1 长吨 =1.016 05 公吨）和短吨（short ton）（1 短吨 =0.907 2 公吨）。英制中，1 长吨 =2 240（英）磅（pounds）。在公制重量单位中，1 公吨（metric ton）= 1 000 千克（kilograms）。经过核准，原文中的"吨"宜译为 metric ton，以免造成误解。第二，在中国的一般读者眼中，美元就是美国的货币单位，就是英语 dollar，但 dollar 在英语中并不仅仅表示"美元"，加元、澳元、新元等货币都以 dollar 为单位。为了避免混乱，译者若译"美元"，就应写为 US dollar，缩写是 USD/US $。（刘法公，2004）

⑦ 同时，我国政府已同瑞典、罗马尼亚、联邦德国、丹麦、荷兰签订了<u>相互促进和保护投资协定</u>，同加拿大、美国、法国、比利时-卢森堡经济联盟、芬兰、挪威、泰国、意大利、奥地利签订了<u>投资保护协定</u>，还同日本、美国、法国、联邦德国、英国、比利时等国签订了<u>避免双重征税协定</u>。我国还参加了<u>保护工业产权</u>（包括<u>技术转让</u>）的《巴黎公约》。

误译：The Chinese Government in the meantime, has signed <u>agreements of investment promotion and protection</u> with Sweden, Romania, Federal Germany, Denmark, the Netherlands; <u>agreements on investment protection</u> with Canada, the USA, Belgium-Luxembourg Economic Alliance, Finland, Norway, Thailand, Italy, and Australia; <u>agreements of double tax prevention</u> with Japan, the USA, France, Federal Germany, Britain, Belgium and other countries. China is a member of the <u>Paris Convention on Industrial Property Protection</u> (including <u>assignment of technology</u>).

改译：The Chinese Government in the meantime, has signed <u>agreements on mutual</u>

promotion and protection of investment with Sweden, Romania, Federal Germany, Denmark, the Netherlands; agreement on protection of investment with Canada, the USA, Belgium-Luxembourg Economic Union (BLEU), Finland, Norway, Thailand, Italy, and Australia; double taxation relief treaty with Japan, the USA, France, Federal Germany, Britain, Belgium and other countries. China is a member of the Paris Convention for the Protection of Industrial Property (including technology transfer).

对比分析：原文涉及的许多商贸术语在英语中已有固定译名，若任意译出，则难以让英语读者对描述的内容产生共识。译者自编的这些译名有的与通用译名相似，有的差别很大，足以让商贸领域的英语读者感到莫名其妙。（刘法公，2004）

◆ 2.4 翻译生硬，译文有翻译腔

好的翻译没有翻译腔，这可以说是商务汉英翻译应遵循的一个基本原则。但是，如果译文中生硬牵强的痕迹随处可见，这就是翻译没有跨越表层结构上的差异而表达有失地道或不符合语言表达习惯的问题，主要是死译、硬译的中式英语（Chinglish）问题。

请对比分析以下商务汉英翻译实例：

⑧ 妥善保存，遗失不补。

误译1：Please safekeeping, lose no reissue.

误译2：Please keep it safe. No replacement if lost.

改译：Please keep this voucher in a safe place. It will not be replaced if lost.（李长栓，2004）

对比分析：这些标识语常见于宾馆、酒店等商贸场所。诸如误译1之类的胡翻乱译现象在商贸场所屡见不鲜。误译2大有改进，但这种字面翻译仍带有很浓的汉语腔。

⑨ （各位）辛苦了！

误译1：You're tired!

误译2：You're hard-working!

改译：Thank you very much for your good job! / You've done a very good job. Thank you very much!

对比分析：以上客套语常见于上级在特定场合对下级工作的肯定与慰问，而不是真正地说"你累了"。误译1完全是不问青红皂白的死译；误译2也是背离汉语原文的语用功能和社会语用意图的乱译，是完全不符合英语社交语境的汉语式英译。

2.5 翻译"跑调",译文不得体

因对汉语原文的文体等级把握不当,英译经常"跑调",出现(译)文不对"体"的情况。

请对比分析以下汉英翻译实例:

⑩ 由于交货日期临近,谨请贵方尽早开立信用证。

误译:As the date of delivery is approaching, we request you to expedite the establishment of the L/C.

改译:As the date of delivery is approaching, you are requested to expedite the establishment of the L/C. (余富林等,2003)

对比分析:汉语原文使用了语体正式的词汇,如"谨请""贵方",以彰显作者庄重的语体修辞立意。按照文体/语体对应性原则,译文也使用了主动语态,在表层结构上与原文对应,但在文体/语体修辞功效上有些失误。通过对比分析,可以发现使用文体/语体正式的被动语态可达到与原文正式文体/语体基本对应的文体/语体修辞效果,如改译后的译文。

⑪ 如果你的打字机还没有卖的话,请告知价格。

误译:I was informed that you had a typewriter for sale and would like to know if it is still on sale; if so, please advise me as to the price.

改译:If you still have the typewriter which you offered for sale, please inform me of the price.

对比分析:汉语原文的文体等级属于中等,第一句英译的用词过于正式,有些陈腐老套;第二句英译通俗自然,与当代文体风格相吻合,具有时代感。

2.6 死译硬译,搭配不当

汉英两种语言的词汇在搭配能力和使用习惯上存在着许多差异,这就给汉英之间跨语言、跨文化的交流活动造成了许多难以逾越的障碍。稍不注意,英译中就会出现中式英语。

请对比分析以下汉英翻译实例:

⑫ 价格太贵,我方不能接受你方报盘。

误译:We are not in a position to accept your offer for your price is too expensive.

改译:We are not in a position to accept your offer for your price is too high.

对比分析： 汉译英不能照本宣科，不能死译、硬译。"太贵"就不能被死译成 too expensive，否则就会出现搭配不符合英语语言习惯的错译、误译。其他类似的例子还有："恢复经济"就不能被硬译成 recover the economy，而应该被译成地道的 reconstruct the economy。

思考与练习

1. 思考题

（1）适用于商务汉英翻译的标准有哪些？请举例说明在商务汉英翻译实践中如何采用奈达的"功能对等"翻译标准。

（2）商务汉英翻译中存在哪些问题？你能举例说明其他一些问题吗？

2. 句子翻译

（1）为了获得数量上的快速增长，国内许多开展特许经营的企业跑马圈地，往往不收取任何特许经营费用，这样就必然导致投资洋品牌的人在心理上承受较大的不悦。

（2）由于经济结构的调整，我国现有较多的下岗职工。

（3）随着中国人财富的不断增多，他们将越来越多地下馆子。

（4）改革开放之后，很多人都下了海，发了大财。

（5）忠实的朋友有三：老妻、老狗、现款。

（6）通常，小包装货比散装货要贵。

（7）据披露，他还有小金库，藏有至少 60 万元现金。他至今不能就这些钱的来路给出令人满意的解释。

（8）在中国，排量不到 1.0 升的汽车被定为小排量汽车。

（9）交换是营销的核心概念。为使交换发生，必须满足几个条件：第一，必须存在交换的双方；第二，每方都拥有对方所需要的有价值的物品；第三，每方都想要与对方交换；第四，双方都能自主地接受或拒绝对方的报价；第五，双方都有能力进行沟通和交货。

（10）西欧受到的经济影响要比美国、日本大。经济衰退至今只在一定程度上影响到了诸如马来西亚、泰国这样的国家。

3. 语篇翻译

- 语篇 1

消费者行为领域涵盖了众多方面：它研究一些涉及个人或团体为满足其需要和欲望而选择、购买、使用或处理产品、服务、理念或经历的过程。消费者包含了多种人，从向母亲乞求口袋怪兽卡片的 8 岁幼童，到一家大公司中决定价值几百万美元的计算机系统的主管。而消费品则包括从罐装豌豆、按摩服务、民主概念、嘻哈音乐到"花花太岁"丹尼斯·罗德曼的任何事物。亟待满足的需要和欲望包含饥饿、对爱的渴望、社会地位甚至精神上的满足。我们对日常商品的依恋可以以我们与可乐类饮料的情缘为例。拉斯维加斯的可口可乐大世界每年都会吸引上百万的游客。那儿的展览品上都有一个问题:"可口可乐对你来说意味着什么?"许多的反馈都说起与品牌之间强烈的情感联系。

- 语篇2

信息技术和互联网的发展加快了经济全球化的步伐,打破了国与国之间、地区与地区之间的界限,带来了资本、商品和技术在国际范围内的流动和合理配置,各国贸易、金融、服务等越来越紧密地联系在一起,国际合作和国际化经营十分普遍,地区经济甚至全球经济牵一发而动全身,正日益成为一个不可分割的整体。

- 语篇3

今天的南京大学包括鼓楼、浦口两个校区,风景优美,建筑规模宏大,教学、科研设施先进,已发展成为综合实力位居全国高校前列的一流大学。

校园内小桥流水,绿树成荫,环境优雅,空气清新,是陶冶情操、求学、授业的理想之地。

Ⅱ. 分论(1)

> *From a translator's point of view, I think the main descriptive units are a hierarchy: text, paragraph, sentence, clause, group, word, morpheme.*
>
> ——Peter Newmark
>
> 只要原文承载意义、具有语言交际功能、有翻译价值、有交流传播目的，在翻译中就必然存在一个遣词酌句的审美问题……有人认为，翻译文艺小说要审美，翻译科技论文、法律条文、合同契约等非文艺文体不要审美，就是因为他们没有看到翻译中不分文本、一律要求遣词酌句等文字优化工作本身就是审美活动。
>
> ——刘宓庆

第四章

商务汉英语体修辞对比分析与翻译

Identify the problems in the following translations

① 兹证明张明(男,1946年4月1日出生)于1993年1月7日来到我处,在我面前,在其本人所立的遗嘱上签名。

英译:This is to show that Zhang Ming, male, born on April 1, 1946, came to my office on January 7, 1993. And right before me, he signed his name to his own dying words, which are attached here to this certificate.

② 在特殊情况下,公司可在原定的投标有效期满之前向投标人提出投标有效期延长到另行规定时间的要求。

英译:In exceptional circumstances, before the expiry of the original tender validity period, the company may ask the tenderers to make a specified extension of the period of validity.

③ 欣寄我方目录,以介绍我方各类产品的详细情况。

英译:We are sending our catalogue, which gives full information about our various products.

语言是在选择性的纵聚合轴和组合性的横组合轴上组合起来的。(陆国强,1983;徐烈炯,1990)语言符号以线性序列呈链形横向组合,构成横组合关系(syntagmatic relationship)(Happ, 1985);而横组合轴上的语言成分在纵聚合轴上有着潜在的、可替换或可选择的、呈纵聚合关系(paradigmatic relationship)的一串词,瑞士语言学家索绪尔把纵聚合关系称为"联想关系"(associative relationship)。根据索绪尔的联想关系说,"各个有某种共同点的词会在人们的记忆里联系起来,构成具有各种关系的聚合,它们是属于个人的语言内部宝藏的一部分"(索绪尔,1980)。有某种共同点的词可根据上下义关系或同义与近义关系组成一个个语义场(Grandy, 1987)。在此,我们所关注的是后一种

"同义场或近义场"。按照不同的交际目的和语境,我们可从中"斟词酌句,布局谋篇",以求达到最有效的语言交际效果或审美功效。由此可见,从"同义场或近义场"中选词(包括词、词组和个别语法结构)是有修辞立意的。按照不同的修辞意图斟词酌句、布局谋篇的修辞优化过程可以说是一个动态过程。但是,从修辞功效来说,"斟词酌句,布局谋篇"是有选择限制的(selection restriction)。因此,在商务汉英翻译中,我们要注意这种限制,要有比较修辞意识及同义场或近义词的分级性(gradability)语体修辞差异的观念。

彼得·纽马克(Peter Newmark,1988)认为,篇章翻译大多是在词、词汇单位、搭配、词组、小句及句这些层次上操作,很少在段落,从不在篇章上操作,其顺序也大概如此。但有时翻译也对语音(音素)进行比较选择,以求美感。鉴于此,下面就从语音、词汇、句子和语篇层面来观照商务汉英翻译中"斟词酌句,布局谋篇"的修辞优化过程,主要是从词、句两个层面对商务汉英的语言文化差异进行对比分析,继而探讨翻译转换的问题。

第一节 多维度的商务汉英语体修辞对比分析与翻译

◆1.1 语音层面上的商务汉英语体修辞对比分析与翻译

语音揭示语言的发音构造、发音变化及发音规律,规范读音标准(刘继超、高月丽,2002),而修辞并不具体研究这些语音问题,它所研究或关注的是如何利用语音条件和规律构成各种不同的表达手段,进而提高语言的表达效果。

语音修辞主要涉及词语的选用。词语是声音和意义的结合体:声音是词语的形式,意义是词语的内容。好的语言,从内容上说要准确、贴切、生动,从声音上说要念得上口、听得悦耳,给人以美的享受。例如,在"His soul swooned slowly as he heard the snow."这个句子中,詹姆斯·乔伊斯(James Joyce)连用五个"/s/"音,以徐缓的语流渲染了作家的漫漫悠思。

语音可以表达特定的意义,因此语音的选择有着特定的修辞意图。比如,单音节词(monosyllable)、同音异义词(homonym)、重叠词(reduplication)、拟声词(onomatopoeia)、押头韵(alliteration)、押尾韵(end-rhyming)、韵律节奏(rhythm)等都可以被用来创造或表达特定修辞意义。

请对比分析以下商务汉英翻译实例:

① 要买房,到建行。(中国建设银行房贷广告)

英译:Wanna house of your own? Buy one with our loan.(谢建平,2008)

② 穿上"双星"鞋,潇洒走世界。("双星"鞋广告)

英译:Double Star takes you afar.(谢建平,2008)

对比分析:在以上两个例子中,原汉语广告的两个分句前后对称、互相押韵,看上去对称工整,读起来朗朗上口。第一个汉语广告的英译也从词数和押韵两方面保持对应,读起来同样朗朗上口;"双星"鞋广告因 Star 与 afar 相互押韵,读起来韵味十足。

此外,汉语有着偏爱押尾韵的民族修辞情结。相比之下,英语则有着使用押头韵的民族修辞情结。比如,英语中许多商业广告、商品名等都会注意头韵的使用,如 A Simple Solution for a Healthy Home(洗涤用品广告)、A Smooth Silky Skin(化妆品广告)、Sweet, Smart & Sassy(美国 Sunkist 柑橘公司的广告)、Mickey Mouse(米老鼠)、Donald Duck(唐老鸭)、French Fries(炸薯条)等。

◼ 1.2 词汇层面上的商务汉英语体修辞对比分析与翻译

"相对同义与语义近似表示相同或相近的语义概念,组成一个'语义同义场'(semantically synonymous field)。"(王逢鑫,2001:11)在商务英语中,同义词十分丰富,同义词或同义词组用得很多。例如,"公司"有二三十种英译,如 company, corporation, incorporation, firm, agency, industry, products, enterprise, store, service, agency, line, system, group, holdings, laboratory, insurance, assurance, office, proprietary, associate, alliance, union, united, limited(Ltd.)等。它们在国别上〔如:company(英), corporation(美)〕、规模上〔如:firm(小公司或商号), company(较小的公司), corporation(较大的公司); group(集团公司), holdings(控股集团公司)〕、行业类别上(如:agency, industries, products, enterprise, store, service, line, system, laboratory, insurance, assurance)、组合方式上(如:incorporation, proprietary, associate, alliance, union or united)、管理层次上(如:headquarter, office, subsidiary, branch)有所差异。这些同义词貌似同义,但它们在指称意义上有着细微差异(shades of meaning)。我们在斟词酌句时需要注意语境与语义的要求与差别,努力做到选词准确、用词得当。

请对比分析以下例句中"货物"一词的英语对应词:

③ No firm can affect the price of that good.(没有一家公司能够影响那种商品的价格。)

④ The quality of the goods is better than that of the last shipment.(这批货的质量比上批货的质量好。)

⑤ The cargo was damaged in transit.（货物在运输途中受损。）

⑥ Our product sells very well in the international market.（我们的产品在国际市场上销路很好。）

⑦ We have sold many parcels on this basis.（我们已经按照这种方式售出多批商品货物。）

⑧ Eight thousand tons of freight have been landed.（已经卸货八千吨。）

⑨ Those commodities shall be delivered soon after all necessary documents are submitted to the vendor.（在将一切必要的单据提交给买方后，应立即发送这批商品。）

⑩ When shall we take the delivery?（我们什么时候提货？）

对比分析： 在商务英语中，goods 一词最常用，往往用于统称"货物"（things or possessions that are movable）；cargo 则被限制指称"运货"（the goods carried by a ship, plane, or vehicle）；product 一般是指"产品"，特别是"工业制造品"（thing or substance produced, especially by manufacture），它与 produce（农产品）一词相对；parcel 特指"一批所交易的货物"（quantity dealt with in one commercial transaction）；freight 是指"运货"（goods transported），与 cargo 一词的意思几乎相同，但比 cargo 常用；commodity 是指"商品，货物"（article of trade, esp. a raw material or product as opposed to a service），其含义是"可用来进行买卖的与服务相对的一切商品"；而 delivery 则仅指"交付的货物"（goods delivered），其使用范围大大缩小了。（翁凤翔，2007a）

除了要注意同义词或近义词的指称意义之外，我们还要注意斟词酌句是有修辞立意的。人们使用同义词或近义词时可能带有表明"态度、立场、感情、正式程度"等修辞色彩。下面我们来对比分析如何选用不同词语来创造不同的语体修辞效果：

⑪

Dear Mrs. Denton,

Thank you / **Thanks** for your letter dated 21 October.

As I am sure you will appreciate / **understand**, I am most upset / **very sorry** to learn / **hear** that you were unable to / **couldn't** locate my suitcase. As I indicated / **pointed out** in my original letter, the suitcase contained many / **a lot of** documents that I require / **need** for my work / **job**. I have had been obliged / **had to** contact / **get in touch with** my publishers to obtain / **get hold of** copies of documents that your airline mislaid / **lost**.

Naturally / **Of course**, I will complete / **fill in** the claim form, but it is not easy / **I find it difficult** to estimate / **guess** the value of the documents. Approximately /

About half of them are irreplaceable.

I trust / **hope** that in the meantime you will continue to look / **are still looking** for my case. Should you find / **If you find it**, please contact me immediately / **straight away**.

I look / **am looking** forward to hearing from you.

             Yours sincerely,
             Philip Buik

对比分析：在以上商务英语信函中，表达相似意义的画线单词或词组中，粗体部分语体色彩淡一些。如果使用斜线后的粗体词语，如 thanks, understand, very sorry,这封书信的正式语体修辞的韵味就没有了。

由此可见，词语的语体修辞色彩对于恰当而得体地传达修辞意义至关重要。在商务汉英翻译中，如果对语域或语体修辞色彩不加注意，就很有可能产生修辞失误。

请对比分析以下商务汉英翻译实例：

⑫ 这家工厂每月都要采购大量原料。

误译：This factory buys a large quantity of raw materials every month.

改译：This factory purchases a large quantity of raw materials every month.

对比分析：通过比较 buy 与 purchase 这两个同义词，就可辨别语体修辞失误所在，并获知应该用语体较正式的 purchase 一词。这样，译文才能"语随境、文适体"。语域与语体修辞密不可分，因为语域是词语的使用范畴，主要是指正式与非正式语体的等级（levels of speech）。

◆ 1.3 句子层面上的商务汉英语体修辞对比分析与翻译

汉英两种语言中，句子成分之间与分句之间的连接方式截然不同。"汉语的方块字在结构上是孤立的，字与字的结合没有形态上的变化，而是直接连缀拼接，从结构形式上是单层面的、线性的。汉语中几个名词或名词短语、几个动词连用都可以分别连缀成句，没有主谓框架的限制，不用区别谓语动词和非谓语动词。汉语没有动词不定式、分词、动名词等所谓的非限定动词形式，表面上短语与短语、分句与分句甚至句子与句子都可以并列、排比下去，都用逗号来标点，成为很长的一串。汉语句子较短，一个短句接一个短句地如流水一般往下叙述，逐步展开，信息内容像竹竿子一样一节节地通下去，很少有叠床架屋的结构，因而有人称之为'竹竿型'结构。汉语的语法关系直接依赖于语义、语序和逻辑来表达。英语语法讲究句型，主谓结构是全句的框架，所有修饰、限制、补充成分归于附属，借助各种连词、介词、关系词与主框架连接。句子的 SV 结构是大树的主干，各个从属部分是大树的枝丫,枝丫与大树的连接点是关联词。如果说汉语句子是大红灯笼一串串,那么英语句子就是枝形吊灯一大盏。"(王大来,2005:42)

以上只是对汉英两种语言在语法结构上的对比分析。除此之外,语句建构还有修辞上的考虑。一个句子可以使用肯定的说法,把意思准确明白地表述出来,也可以采用否定或双重否定的说法,把意思委婉或强烈地表达出来;可以使用主动句式,突出施事者的动作,也可以采用被动句式,强化受事者所遭受的动作;可以写得长些,意思表达得更完备,也可以写得短些,意思表达得更简短有力;可以使用大致整齐的结构,形成一种整齐美,也可以采用松散有致的结构,形成一种错综美;可以按照正常的语序组织,符合人们的心理,也可以将正常的语序加以变通,造成一种特殊的效果。这些都属于句式的选择和锤炼问题。一句话来说,句子的修辞好坏与语体恰当与否,都得以表达或交际效果来定。所以,进行商务汉英语体翻译时,我们必须比较分析同义或近义的句式,选用最有效的句式进行汉英语体意义的对等转换。

请对比分析以下商务汉英翻译实例:

⑬ 本合同由买卖双方订立,双方同意按照下面规定的条款购买以下商品。

误译:This contract is made between the buyers and the sellers, who agree to buy and sell the under-mentioned commodity according to the terms set forth below.

改译:This contract is made and entered into by and between the buyers and the sellers, whereby the buyers agree to buy and the sellers agree to sell the under-mentioned commodity according to the terms and conditions stipulated below.

对比分析:通过对比,我们发现,第一个译句虽与第二个译句相比较为简短,但有以下不足:没用古体词(如:whereby),用词不够庄重典雅,不符合商务合同文体修辞的要求;用词(如:set forth)过于通俗,语体不够正式;没用并置词语(如:by and between, terms and conditions),不符合同行文规范;过于简短,行文不够严谨。相比之下,改译虽显"啰唆,却是商务合同的特点使然"(潘红,2004:273)。

⑭ 敬请函告。

误译:Please give us a reply by letter.

改译:We should be grateful to you if you could inform us by letter.

对比分析:汉语原句语体正式、庄重,第一个译文十分不正式,原文的韵味、风味顿失。第二个译句选用的句式"We should be grateful to you if..."就非常正式,译得十分得体。

1.4 语篇层面上的商务汉英语体修辞对比分析与翻译

不同语言的语篇建构方式是在不同的民族文化背景下进行的,并且与不同民族的思维方式有着密切的关系。正因为民族文化和民族思维方式不同,"一种语言中的词语的组合不同于另一种语言。也许更重要的是,一种语言中意思的黏合也不同于另一种语言"(胡曙中,1993:161)。与汉语典型的"螺旋型"修辞模式不同的是,英语语篇一般按照一条直线展开,呈"直线型"修辞模式。汉语之所以有着"螺旋型"修辞模式,是因为汉语的语篇发展采用的是"意合法"。英语之所以有着典型的"直线型"修辞模式,是因为英语的语篇发展往往采用"形合法"。英语有着丰富无比的连词、关系代词或副词、介词等衔接词语或手段,这些连词、关系代词或副词、介词等可以被充分用来连接词与词、句与句、句群与句群、段与段甚至篇与篇。这种"形合"的修辞衔接方式足以使英语语篇达到行文流畅、上下文连贯而浑然一体的修辞效果。所以,进行商务汉英翻译时,我们应该注意汉英语篇衔接上的差异,分别选用汉英各自恰当的语篇衔接手段,进行有效的"布局谋篇"。

请对比分析以下商务汉英信函的不同语篇衔接手段及其转换:

⑮
尊敬的史密斯先生:

  我们通过汉堡 Swanson & Bros. 公司的 A. G. TopWorth 先生的介绍获知贵方行名、地址。A. G. TopWorth 先生是我们的一个老客户。敬告贵方,我们专营出口瓷器,并想与贵方建立业务关系。

  如果贵方要求与我方要求一致,请告知,并说明具体询价要求,以便我方能即时给贵方寄发附有图示的产品目录和价目表,以供贵方参考。

  同时,在做成第一笔生意之前,贵方若能把贵方开户银行的行名告诉我方,我方将不胜感激。

  我方期待贵方询价。

谨启

英译:
Dear Mr. Smith,

  We have your name and address through the introduction of Mr. A. G. TopWorth of Swanson & Bros., of Hamburg, <u>who</u> is one of our old clients. We wish to inform you <u>that</u> we specialize in exporting chinaware and shall be pleased to enter into business relations with you.

  <u>If</u> our above desire coincides with yours, please let us know and also keep us informed of your specific inquiries <u>so that</u> we can send our illustrated catalogue and price list for your reference without delay.

  In the meantime, we shall appreciate it very much <u>if</u> you will furnish us with the name of your bank prior to the conclusion of an initial transaction between us.

We are looking forward to receiving your first inquiry.

Sincerely yours,

Prince Lee

对比分析：汉语重复使用上句中提到的名词"A. G. TopWorth 先生"，把它用作下一句的主语（已知信息），从而引出新信息。汉语常用这种语篇扩展（textual development）方法，使行文呈现"螺旋型"发展模式。相比之下，英语使用了关系代词 who，将从句依附在主句上。

无论是"意合"型语言的汉语，还是"形合"型语言的英语，它们都需要运用多种不同的语篇组合方式。语篇组合或构合方式与修辞意图或修辞立意有着密不可分的关系。如果在语篇组合或构合方式中忽视了语篇的修辞意图，可能就会出现语篇构合方式不当的修辞模式失误。

第二节　对商务汉英语体翻译的启示与警示

2.1　启示："斟词酌句"须有修辞眼光

汉英两种语言的同义词丰富多彩，句式变化多样，篇章发展模式异彩纷呈。因此，在进行汉英翻译时，"斟词酌句"就要用修辞的眼光来上下求索，进行修辞考虑与选择。稍有不慎，就会有修辞闪失。例如，在正式文体中，若使用诸如 go on, make up 10%, go through the procedure 此类非正式语体的短语动词（phrasal verbs），而不用语体较正式的单个动词 continue, constitute 10%, undergo the procedure，就会有修辞失误的问题。这是因为在英语中短语动词的语体不如单个动词（single verbs）的语体正式，它们常用于口语。

请对比分析下面两例中不同语体修辞立意的传译，以此来观察比较、分析、甄别、遴选等方法在语体修辞翻译中的重要性。

① a. 请尽快发货。

英译：Could you please send us the goods as soon as possible?

b. 若及时发货，我方将不胜感激。

英译：We would be grateful if you could send us the goods without delay. / We would appreciate it if you could send us the goods immediately.

对比分析：以上两个汉语原句表达了同样的意思，但因选词、用词及选用句式不同，所蕴含的修辞立意大不相同。

② a. 很抱歉地告诉你们，我们不能按时交货。

英译：I am sorry to tell you that we cannot deliver the goods on time.

b. 我方不能按时交货，甚是遗憾。

英译：I regret to advise you that we will not be able to deliver the goods on time.

对比分析：②a 句的语体为中性，既可用于口语体，也可用于书面体，所以英译选用了语体色彩不浓不淡的小词 tell 和系表结构 am sorry 进行对等转换。相比之下，②b 句的语体正式，所以就选用了语体色彩较浓的大词 regret 和 advise 进行翻译。

2.2 警示：不要文白夹杂，有失"体统"

为了准确、恰当而得体地表达思想感情，翻译与写作一样有着对许多同义的语言手段进行筛选和修辞抉择的过程。在这个筛选与抉择的过程中，我们首先要对原文的文体（genre）进行准确定位，然后量体裁衣式地选用恰当而准确的语音、词汇、句式、篇章模式等进行译文的语篇重构，从而实现与原文的语体修辞对接。

请对比分析以下商务汉英翻译实例：

③ 谈到中美贸易问题，首先要看到一个最基本的事实，这就是 25 年来我们两国之间的贸易有了巨大的发展。（张春柏，2009：43）

误译：When talking about China-US trade, we should not overlook one fundamental fact, that is, in the past 25 years, two-way trade has expanded enormously.

改译：Regarding / Concerning / With regard to / With respect to / On the issue of China-US trade, we should not overlook one fundamental fact, that is, in the past 25 years, two-way trade has expanded enormously.

对比分析：第一句英译所用的 When talking about China-US trade 较口语化。根据汉语原文的正式文体特征，第二句英译将其译成介词短语 Regarding / Concerning / With regard to / With respect to / On the issue of China-US trade。

思考与练习

1. **思考题**
   (1) 在词法、句法、语篇等层面,商务汉英有着什么样的语体修辞特征?
   (2) 商务汉英语体修辞的对比分析对商务汉英翻译有什么启示与警示?
2. **句子翻译**
   (1) 若因买房的延迟,CAE公司保留每月获得1.5%延付费的权利。
   (2) 饮立顿红茶,品独到风味。
   (3) 谢天谢地,星期五到了!我走了。周末愉快!
   (4) 欲知详情,请索取广告单。
   (5) 质量上乘,价格公道。
   (6) 质量完全以卖方2008年2月15日提供的样品为准。
3. **语篇翻译**
   - 语篇1

   新闻稿
   2020年3月16日
   发布日期:2020年3月22日

   ABC公司重组

   正如一个人做更复杂的工作需要学习新的技术一样,一家公司有时随着工作量的增大不得不寻找出完成工作的新方法。这是件很好的事情。

   为了处理好随着良好服务和快捷反应而迅速增长的专营权和账户数,ABC公司正在重组其地区销售力量,并于2020年4月1日生效。ABC公司把全国划分成四个市场区域,即东部市场、南部市场、中部市场和西部市场,并将各设一名区域经理:Margaret Olson(东部市场)、Harry Baines(南部市场)、Rolf Johnson(中部市场)和Barry Jones(西部市场)。为协调全国整体销售工作,Mark Vinson将出任公司的全国销售经理。5月前,整个公司系统内的工作会准备就绪,并且这四个区域的工作会步入正轨。公司相信在未来几个月里更大的销售量中可以看出所做出的努力是完全值得的。

   ——结束——

   联系人:G. L. Sender先生,公共关系部经理
   电　　话:6654388

• 语篇2

尊敬的李先生:

4月15日有关付款条件的来函已经收悉。

本公司同意贵公司如下建议:

(1) 以见票即付的保兑不可撤销信用证付款,而非见票直接付款。

(2) 贵公司的报盘不会有折扣。

以上建议获本公司总经理批准,今后将如述执行。

现正拟订有关订单,10日内将送达贵公司。

另外,本公司代表约翰·格林先生将参加即将举行的广州交易会,并会于不日以书面形式与贵公司联络。

诚望今后两公司之间的会谈能促进双方的业务发展。

敬复

丹尼斯·索普

• 语篇3

位于福州市中心的榕山宾馆环境优美、交通便利、装潢典雅、设施豪华,是理想的商旅之家。

宾馆拥有豪华套房300多间,环境清洁、幽静。6个装饰精美的餐厅提供各式中西饮食,服务周到,气氛舒适。全套休闲健身设施使您白日驰骋商场的紧张神经得以放松,并让您享受锻炼的乐趣。

宾馆拥有现代化商务中心。先进的通信设备和多功能会议厅使您即使远离办公室,也能事半功倍。

不管您的事业遍及何处,宾馆提供的国际电脑网络服务将使您与世界紧密连接。

第五章

商务汉英词义对比分析与翻译

Identify the problems in the following translations

① 由于柔软而耐用的品质,我们的全棉床单及枕套很快成了畅销产品。你们在研究了我方价格之后,对我方为什么甚难满足需求这一事实就不难理解了。

英译:Because of their soft and durable quality, our all-cotton bed sheets and pillowcases are rapidly becoming popular products and after studying our prices you will learn the fact that we are finding it difficult to meet the demand.

② 由于贵公司信誉一直良好,我方可以同意D/P付款。

英译:Owing to your consistently good credibility, we can accept payment by D/P.

③ 定价之前,你必须了解自己的产品市场、分销成本和竞争情况。

英译:Before settling your prices, you must understand your product's market, distribution costs and competition situation.

商务语篇用词严格规范、专业性强,同时一词多义的情况非常普遍。词义的发展是一个从单义到多义、从概念义到引申义的过程。一个单义词会从同一词源出发,在不改变词形的前提下,被赋予新义,接着就有了第二个、第三个甚至更多的意义。汉英两种语言都是富有多义词的语言。20世纪70年代,英国著名语言学家杰弗里·N. 利奇(Geoffrey N. Leech)在他的《语义学》(Semantics)中把词的意义归纳为七种类型:① 概念或理性意义(conceptual meaning),即语言交际中所表达的最基本的意义。② 内涵意义(connotative meaning),即概念意义之外暗含的意义。③ 风格意义(stylistic meaning),即词语在言语交际中表现出的风格意义。④ 情感意义(affective meaning),即说话者的感情或态度。⑤ 联想意义(reflected meaning),即引起联想的意义。也就是说,当读到某一个词时,马上会联想起别的事情来。⑥ 搭配意义(collocative meaning),即通过联想词语的常用搭配而传达的意义。因为大部分词汇有一词多义(polysemy)的现象,所以同一个词能与多个对象搭配,形成不同的搭配意义。⑦ 主题意义(thematic meaning），即通过改变句子语法结构或词序所表现出来的意义。杰弗里·N. 利奇还把其中第②③④⑤⑥五种意义统称为"联想意义"。词语的联想意义在很大程度上就是指文化意义。词语的文化意义往往因文化、时间和个人经历的不同而变化，内容是不稳定的。

　　同一个词既然可能有上述如此多的意义，就可能引起歧义，使读者产生误解。但是，同一个词在不同的语境中有不同的词义，而语境能够帮助排除歧义。我们要在商务汉英词汇翻译中做到词义掌握准确、用词得当，在斟词酌句时就一定要弄清楚汉英两种语言之间的词义差异，力求避免汉语对商务英语词汇表达的负面干扰。一般来说，汉语用词的词义较具体，常常以实的形式表达虚的概念，以具体的形象表达抽象的内容。这主要是因为汉语缺乏英语的词缀虚化手段。现代汉语词语的含义范围较窄，词义较精确、固定、严谨，其伸缩性和对上下文的依赖性较小，具有很强的独立性。与汉语相比，英语词语的词义内涵较为宽泛，词语用法比较灵活，一词多义、一词多用的现象十分普遍，这有助于表达比较概括、抽象的意义。但是，这也造成因汉英词义混淆而误译、错译的情况。

　　汉英词语的"具体与模糊""实与虚""普通与专业""褒与贬""正式与非正式""正与反"等词义差异，要求我们在商务汉英词汇翻译中要掌握分寸，进行"实与虚""正与反"的灵活转换，做好"普通与专业""正式与非正式""褒与贬"的词义选用和把握。

第一节　"实"义与"虚"义、"增"译与"减"译

◆1.1　商务汉英"虚"与"实"的词义差异对比分析

　　汉语是以分析型（analytic）为主的语言，英语是从综合型（synthetic）向分析型发展的语言，属"综合—分析语"（synthetic-analytic language）。汉英两种语言之间的这种本质差异反映在词汇上表现为汉语趋向于具体（concrete），而英语趋向于抽象（abstract）。比如，对于同样一个意思，汉语说的"不怕不识货，只怕货比货"实有所指；而英语说的"Comparisons are odious"无实指。汉语往往将具体或抽象的事物度量化、单位化。与汉语相比，英语词义通常比汉语词义"虚"。商务汉英词汇与普通汉英词汇一样具有上述差异。比如，商务英语常使用一些内涵比较空泛的名词、副词、形容词等。这类词语的词义抽象、概括、笼统，词义范畴宽泛；而汉语则倾向于使用所指较具体的表示类属的词语。

　　请对比分析汉英"实"与"虚"的词义差异与转换：

① 难怪跨国公司一直以惊人的速度发展并且控制了国际市场的许多领域。

英译:No wonder the multinational corporations have been growing fantastically and now dominate many sectors of the international market.(张新红等,2003)

② 出口物资不得超过限制范围。

英译:The export is not permitted to exceed its limitation.(叶玉龙、王文翰、段云礼,1998)

③ 除非这些问题作为当务之急得到及时解决,否则员工中随之出现的消极怠工情绪无疑将对公司的整个运营业绩产生负面影响。

英译:Unless these issues are addressed as a matter of urgency, the consequent demotivation of staff will undoubtedly have a negative impact on the performance of the company.(潘红,2004)

对比分析:以上例句表明,汉英两种语言都有表达抽象词义的名词、副词、形容词等,但表达抽象词义的程度不同。英语名词、副词、形容词所表达的是抽象的,汉语名词、副词、形容词所表达的就较具体。

1.2 对商务汉英词汇翻译的启示与警示

1.2.1 启示:"实"与"虚"相互转化

在进行商务汉英词汇翻译时,我们会遇到某些词,在词典里找不到其恰当的译文;或者说,词典里的翻译不能恰当准确地表达出原文的含义。遇到这种情况时,我们应该按照一定的语境和逻辑关系,对词义做引申处理,选择恰当而准确的译词来表达。引申分为四种,即逻辑引申、语用引申、修辞性引申和概念范围的引申。这种引申的翻译法也可以说是根据汉英两种语言在词义和表达上的差异,对汉英词语做"实"与"虚"的转化,即从汉语用词的"实"向英语用词的"虚"转化;反过来就是,从英语用词的"虚"向汉语用词的"实"转化。具体来说,我们应根据汉英两种语言的表达习惯在翻译时做到该增就增、该减则减。

1.2.1.1 英译"虚"化

汉语有许多所指较具体的名词、形容词、副词等,英译时需要进行"虚"化处理,也就是按照英语的语言表达习惯与要求使用抽象名词或词义较抽象的形容词、副词等。

请对比分析以下汉英翻译实例:

④ 无论在哪里,只要出现效率不高和浪费现象,都必须一概加以反对。同时,一些非必需的项目也要迅速下马。

英译:Wherever they occur, inefficiency and waste must be attacked and nonessential projects be brought swiftly to an end.

⑤ 在民主国家中，征收哪些税是各级政府要做的一项最困难的决策。

英译：In a <u>democracy</u>, one of the most difficult discretions governments have to make is what kinds of taxes to levy.（叶玉龙、王文翰、段云礼，1998）

对比分析：汉语"效率不高和浪费现象"和"民主国家"与英语名词 inefficiency and waste 和 democracy 相比，词义就较具体，而对应的英语名词就较抽象、模糊。汉英翻译需要根据汉英语言的表达习惯做必要的删减。

⑥ 访问北京的澳大利亚商务代表团将在最近动身。

英译：The Australian <u>commercial trip</u> to Beijing will leave in the near future.（叶玉龙、王文翰、段云礼，1998）

⑦ 美国已大量增加从中国进口玩具和鞋袜的数量。

英译：The greatest increase in US imports of China goods have been registered in toys and <u>foot-wear</u>.（叶玉龙、王文翰、段云礼，1998）

对比分析：英译中的 trip 与 foot-wear 两词比汉语原文所用的"商务代表团"和"鞋袜"抽象宽泛多了。

1.2.1.2　英译减词

根据英语的表达习惯与修辞要求，我们在汉译英中要删减一些表示具体范畴的词语，使语言表达更简练、更明快。

请对比分析以下汉英翻译实例：

⑧ 根据一般加工工业生产能力普遍过剩的<u>现实状况</u>，把国债投资重点放在基础设施建设<u>方面</u>。

英译：In view of the over-productivity in the general processing industries, investments from national bonds were mainly put into infrastructure development.

⑨ 我们对南非的<u>市场情况</u>了解不够多。

英译：We do not know much about the South African <u>market</u>.

⑩ 本电扇<u>款式</u>新颖，<u>造型</u>大方，<u>色彩</u>鲜艳，色泽调和，是炎炎夏日消暑纳凉之家电精品。

英译：The fan, with its <u>modern</u>, <u>elegant</u>, <u>bright</u>, and harmoniously colored design, is an excellent electrical household appliance for cooling purposes on hot summer days.

对比分析：在以上例句中，英译省去了汉语原句里表示属性或范畴的具体化用词，如"现实状况""市场情况""方面"等。最后一句英译减掉了形容词的实指名词"款式""造型""色彩"。

1.2.2　警示："虚""实"不可过度

汉语用词较"实"，英语用词较"虚"。因此，在进行商务汉英翻译时，我们应有意识地把握商务汉英用词的"虚""实"之度,避免出现受汉语负面影响或干扰而发生的"画蛇添足"式的修辞失误。下面就让我们来分析一些受汉语修辞表达习惯的影响所译的商务英语错句,并按照英语的修辞表达习惯加以修改,使其符合英语的修辞要求。

⑪ 随着日本<u>泡沫经济</u>的破灭,对这个位居第三的资本主义经济大国的期望值正在下降。

误译:As Japan's <u>bubble economy</u> bursts, a downsizing of expectations is taking place for the world's third-largest capitalist economy.

改译:As Japan's <u>bubble</u> bursts, a downsizing of expectations is taking place for the world's third-largest capitalist economy.(叶玉龙、王文翰、段云礼,1998)

⑫ 中国政府历来重视对外贸易<u>工作</u>。

误译:The Chinese government has always attached great importance to <u>foreign trade work</u>.

改译:The Chinese government has always attached great importance to <u>foreign trade</u>.

对比分析:在以上例句中,误译属于一字一字的对译、死译,有悖于英语的修辞习惯。为了使英译更地道、更符合英语表达习惯,改译省掉了汉语中表示状况或类属的名词"经济"和"工作"。

第二节 商务汉英"普通词义"与"专业词义"对比分析与翻译

◆ 2.1 商务汉英"普通词义"与"专业词义"的差异对比分析

商务英语是英语在商务语域中的运用,是英语的社会功能语言变体,因此许多普通英语词语在商务这个特殊用途的英语变体中经引申获得了特殊词义,逐渐固定下来而变成了专业、半专业词汇。另外,值得注意的是,商务英语有大量的语义已经约定俗成的专业缩略术语(technical acronyms),而商务汉语则往往是从英语中直接借用过来。与商务英语相比,商务汉语词语的表意范围较窄。例如,除了是常用的价格术语外,FAS还可以表示商品的等级,意为"一等品和二等品"(firsts and seconds),还可以是"农产品外销局"(Foreign Agricultural Service)的缩写。因此,对应的商务汉语常用修饰限定语、范畴词、两个甚至更多的词语,来确保语言表达的准确性;有时,商务汉语就直接从英语借用词语。

"有人曾经对部分商贸文献中的专业术语和行话进行过统计,发现其中相关术语的数量占总字数的9.1%,这么高的术语使用率在其他文体里并不多见"(转引自张新红等,2003:166-167)。这显然是商务英语写作力求语言规范专业和表达准确经济的客观反映。夸克认为,不管在任何特定情况中人们关于最清楚的表达持有什么样的理由,一般总是强烈地倾向于采用最经济的变体,即那种表现最大程度缩约的变体。在其他情况相同时,语言使用者总是遵循"尽量缩约"的准则。(Quirk,1972)

请对比分析以下商务汉英翻译实例:

① 工业股票的平均价格在上涨。

英译:Industrial averages were up.(叶玉龙、王文翰、段云礼,1998)

② 海损有两种:一种是共同海损,另一种是单独海损。

英译:Average is of two kinds: General Average and Particular Average.

对比分析:average在不同专业领域具有截然不同的专业引申义。第一句英译中的averages为股票用语,指的是"(若干种股票的)平均价格";第二句英译中的average则为保险用语,意为"海损费用"。相比之下,汉语则分别用了两个不同的词语。

③ 在开立新账户时,敝公司有一例行公事,即向客户要求提供商业证明人。

英译:When opening new accounts, it is our practice to ask customers for trade references.

对比分析:references在普通英语中的意思是"参考",而在商务情景中意义得到了引申,即具有专业词义——"证明人"。

④ 必须与协议第一款相符。

英译:It must be in conformity with the first article of the agreement.

对比分析:article的普通词义是"文章",而在商务合同中则表示"条款"。

⑤ 你有权向学校索取差旅补贴。

英译:You are entitled to claim a traveling allowance from the school.

⑥ 我们向轮船公司就有关损失提出索赔。

英译:We claimed on that shipping company for the loss involved.

对比分析:在普通英语中claim最常用的词义是"要求,认领",在商务英语中它则意为"索赔"(demand or request for a thing considered one's due)。相比之下,汉语则需要分别用不同的词语来表达两个不同但关系密切的概念。

⑦ 经销商同意在出示时予以承兑,凭所附提单以即期汇票的方式支付。

英译:The distributor agrees to accept, on presentation, and to pay with exchange, sight draft against B/L attached.

⑧ 保险以 CIF 发票总金额的110%投保仓至仓水渍险、偷窃提货不着险、战争险。如果保费总额超过规定限度，额外的保费由买方支付，并应在有关信用证内注明。

英译：Insurance to be effected covers only marine WPA, TPND, warehouse to warehouse and WR at 110% of the total CIF invoice value. Should coverage on risks and the amount exceeding these limits be required, the additional insurance premium is for the Buyers' account, and shall be embodied in the relevant L/C accordingly.

对比分析：商务英语的一个重要词汇特征就是大量使用缩略形式的专业术语，所以汉英翻译应突出这一特征，使译文更专业、更地道。

2.2 对商务汉英词汇翻译的启示与警示

2.2.1 启示：实现从"普通词义"向"专业词义"的翻译转换

词汇有一般含义（用于文学和社会生活方面的含义）与特殊含义（用于专业方面的含义）之分。商务英语中的许多词汇都具有这一特点。这类词汇可以一词多用，出现在不同专业领域中表达的概念也会截然不同。以 policy 为例，该词在一般意义上作"方针""政策"解，如 a business policy of the company（该公司的经营方针）。但是，该词用在保险业中却作"保单"解，这就是该词的特殊含义。因此，在进行翻译选词时，我们要注意区别词语的一般含义和特殊含义，做到用词准确、翻译恰当。

请对比分析以下商务汉英翻译实例：

⑨ 抵押行会雇用一些能讲西班牙语的这类中介人来调查贫困地区中谁的信贷风险最小。

英译：Mortgage banks will hire people like Spanish-speaking entrepreneurs to find out who is a good credit risk in the poorer communities.（叶玉龙、王文翰、段云礼，1998）

对比分析：entrepreneur 一词在一般意义上作"企业家"解，但用于特殊的专业领域时，其专业引申意义是"中介人"。

⑩ 这是支付给他向保险公司索赔的偿金。

英译：Here is the payment to satisfy for his claim against the insurance company.

对比分析：satisfy 的含义相当于 pay，属于正规用法，常见于商业文件中。

⑪ 只要愿意参加在中国举办的贸易交易会，只要愿意制作汉语宣传说明资料，那些以前曾有出口经验，特别是有出口到亚洲其他地区经验的公司将有更大的成功机会。

英译:Companies with previous experience of exporting (particularly to other parts of Asia) who are willing to participate in trade fairs in China and who are prepared to produce trade literature in Chinese will have the greatest chance of success.

对比分析:英译中 literature 作 printed matter for publicity(宣传说明资料)解,而非一般意义上的"文学"。

2.2.2 警示:避免翻译不专业、不地道

因为不熟悉专业知识或不懂行,商务汉英词汇翻译经常出现不专业、不地道的情况。请对比分析以下商务汉英翻译实例:

⑫ 土纸

误译:soil paper

改译:handmade paper

⑬ 花茶

误译:flower tea

改译:scented tea

⑭ 山野菜

误译:mountain wild vegetables

改译:wild vegetables

对比分析:在上例中,误译都是一字一字地死译(word-for-word translation),改译采用了与行业相统一的专业地道的译名。

⑮ 王婆卖瓜,自卖自夸。

误译:You are praising the melons you sell yourself.

改译1:You are making sales pitches about your goods.

改译2:A dealer in rubbish sounds the praise of rubbish.

对比分析:在上例中,误译属于凭空想象的自译、误译,改译1属于意译,改译2就属于灵活对等翻译。

区别词的一般含义和专业含义需要掌握一定的专业知识。因为处理这类多义词的关键在于理解词义。熟悉专业有助于辨别、理解多义词在特定专业中的含义,可以更好地避免与其一般含义相混淆。如果对所涉及的专业不熟悉或对这类词的特殊含义比较陌生,翻译就容易出错。因此,译者需要格外小心,勤查字典,而不能望"词"生义。多义词的专业含义在较为完备的词典,尤其在专业词典中一般都有专条列出。只有尽可能多地接触并掌握商务英语词语的特殊意义或用法,我们才能在进行商务汉英翻译时做到准确、得当。

第三节　商务汉英褒贬词义对比分析与翻译

◈ 3.1　商务汉英褒贬词义差异对比分析

在汉英两种语言中,词语都会带有它们的感情色彩,因为语言的使用者对所描绘的事物都有喜欢与厌恶之分,这就决定了词语的褒贬修辞色彩。在概念意义层次上,词的修辞意义可分为褒义(commendatory)、贬义(derogatory)和中性(neutral)。比如,同样是形容一个人爱说话,"辩才无碍"就是褒义词,与英语的 eloquent 相对应,而"喋喋不休"就是贬义词,与英语的 garrulous 相当。再如,propaganda, problem, politician, self-indulgence, malpractice, serious 等英语词语含有贬义,而与之对应的英语中性或褒义词语是 publicity(或 exposure to the media)、issue(或 question)、statesman、enjoyment、practice、outstanding 等。

请对比分析以下汉英翻译实例:

① 货物的质量和价格已经影响到我们对欧美的出口。

英译:The quality and price of the goods have affected our export to Europe and America.

② 一些员工正在拼命适应一些新技术。

英译:Some members of staff are struggling to cope with some of the new technology.

对比分析:例①中,从汉语字面上看,"影响"并无褒贬之分;而英语 influence 一词为中性词,读者从中看不出事情的好坏,辨不出是积极还是消极之义。但是,从语境来看,产生影响的是不好的东西(质量不好而价格偏高的货物),因此选用含有贬义的 affect 一词来翻译,似乎更恰当。从例②来看,"拼命"一般属于中性词,但是语境表明,它用的并非不好不坏的中性词义,而是消极词义,所以选用同样含有消极词义的 struggling 可以传译出汉语原义——因素质不高,适应新技术有很大的困难,员工因此干得费劲。

3.2 对商务汉英词汇翻译的启示与警示

3.2.1 启示：褒贬有别，准确翻译

在同义词组或同义词群中，词的感情色彩极为精妙、细致，我们要充分注意其褒贬或积极/消极（positive/negative）意义。例如，表达"影响"这一词义的英语词语有influence，impact 和 affect（或名词形式 affectation），它们之间就有或褒或贬或中性的色彩之分。affect 往往带有贬义色彩，而 influence 和 impact 一般有着中性词义色彩。此外，词义的褒贬大多数是由上下文决定的。所以，商务汉英翻译就应力求表达准确，确保读者能够根据语境准确无误地理解和把握词语的褒贬修辞义。

请对比分析以下汉英翻译实例：

③ 最近，他有件急活，所以，他干得太过劳累了。

英译：He's been overtaxing himself a bit lately for he is doing a rush job.

对比分析：例③英译中的 overtaxing 所含贬义正好与汉语词语"太过劳累"的感情色彩相一致，就比中性词语 working hard 更恰当。

④ 核保人认识到这一点，当然不会给他的代理同事出难题，但是他又有工作要做，其中部分工作是确保那些预期快要"死"而想方设法去买保骗保的企图不能得逞。

英译：The underwriter realizes this and certainly does not set out to make life difficult for his agency colleagues. However, he has a job to do. Part of that job is to ensure that people who attempt to buy policies because they expect to "die" soon do not succeed in fooling him and his company.

对比分析：succeed 一词本身并无褒义、贬义之分，属于中性词。但是在语境中，它被用来表示"买保骗保"这个不怀好意的企图，因此它就染上了贬义的修辞色彩。

3.2.2 警示：不可褒贬不分

有些英语词语的褒贬修辞意义并非表层词义，而是深层词义，所以很难一眼被识别。我们在辨别商务汉英褒贬词义时要准确把握，否则就会误译、错译。

请对比分析以下汉英翻译实例：

⑤ 价廉物美

误译：cheap and good

改译：economical and good/ inexpensive and good

对比分析：cheap 一词有"便宜无好货"的消极修辞义，使人联想到假冒伪劣商

品。通过分析比较，我们发现，应选择 economical 或 inexpensive 这两个词比较恰当准确。

⑥ 时间很紧，所以我们认为准时备妥货物交货很成问题。

误译：Time is pressing, so we've found it a big <u>question</u> to get ready for the shipment on time.

改译：Time is pressing, so we've found it a big <u>problem</u> to get ready for the shipment on time.

对比分析：question 和 issue 为中性词。上例谈论的是时间紧迫而交货有问题的麻烦事，根据语境，我们应选用含有消极意义的 problem 一词来表示交货的困难。

另外值得注意的一点是，有些英语词汇，特别是一些短语介词，其后要接含有褒义或中性的词，如 in consideration of, due to, because of。而另一些词语，如 owing to, beset by, troubled by 等，谈论的大多是贬义的事情或不好的消息。

请对比分析以下汉英翻译实例：

⑦ 由于贵公司的信誉一直良好，我方可以同意 D/P 付款。

误译：<u>Owing to your consistently good credibility</u>, we can accept payment by D/P.

改译：<u>In consideration of your consistently good credibility</u>, we can accept payment by D/P.

对比分析：owing to 与 in consideration of 都可表示"由于"，但是例句中的原因为积极的褒义——your consistently good credibility，所以我们应选用 in consideration of 这个短语介词。in consideration of 既可表示"考虑到……""作为……的报酬"，又可引申表示"由于"，但后面接的词语应是褒义的。

第四节　商务汉英正式与非正式语体词义对比分析与翻译

◆ 4.1　商务汉英正式与非正式语体的词义差异对比分析

在同义词组或同义词群中，词的语体修辞色彩也极为精妙、细致，我们也应充分注意辨别其不同的语体修辞意义的细微差异。请对比分析表 4.1（简·沃特森，2004）中的同义词的不同语体修辞意义。

表 5.1　同义词的不同语体修辞意义

语体正式词	语体中性词
await	wait for
anticipate	expect
ascertain	determine, find out
alleviate	lessen / ease
advise	tell
aggregate	total
application	use
utilize	use
expedite	speed up
initiate	start / begin
subsequent	after
demonstrate	show
necessitate	require
obligation	duty
substantial	large
objective	aim / goal
subsequently	later / since
notwithstanding	but, despite / regardless of
variation	change
eventuality	result, outcome
forward	send
signify	mean

对比分析："语体正式词"一栏中的词偏长，大多来自古拉丁文、古希腊文或从法语借用而来，其语体较正式，一般只用在像商务合同、契约之类的语体极正式的文体翻译中。相比之下，"语体中性词"一栏中的词较短，它们一般都是来自古英语，其语体较随便，属于中性词，既可以用在日常口语交际中，也可以用于像商务备忘录、商务信函那样的语体不那么正式的文体翻译。

汉英两种语言的同义词或短语很多，它们的语体等级不同，表达的语体修辞色彩不一样。不同语体有着不同的修辞规范，并选用语体等级不同的词语表达修辞立意。译者在进行商务汉英翻译时应树立语体修辞意识，也就是说，时刻对原文语篇的语体属性保持高度的敏感和觉悟。在建构译文语篇时，我们应先考虑语篇服务的活动领域、社会用途，以及由此而来的语体属性，从而确保选择恰当而正确的语体。商务翻译确立并运用语体修辞意识的指导作用,对准确而得体的修辞意义表达是很重要的。修辞意义又名"修辞色彩"(王德春,1987)。修辞色彩包括"感情评价色彩"和"语体语域色彩"(张会森,2003)。词汇、语法形式、句子结构可以具有修辞色彩,同样由它们构成的语篇也是具有修辞色彩的。修辞色彩的浓淡在很大程度上是修辞立意的表现和修辞优化的结果。修辞优化就是炼词炼句,追求"语随境、文适体",提高语篇的可读性(readability)。

请对比分析"请"字在英译中的不同表达方式及其语体修辞效果:

① 请看一下上一次的会议记录。

英译:Please take a look at the minutes of our previous meeting.

② 请告知我方订货何时运出。

英译:Kindly advise us when our order will be shipped.

③ 请报100吨黄豆实盘。

英译:We shall appreciate it if you will make us a firm offer for 100 metric tons of soybeans.

对比分析:在以上三例中,please 最常用,既可用于口语语体,也可用于书面语体;而 kindly 所表示的语体色彩较浓,多用于书面语体;"We shall appreciate it if you will ..."这种用法最正式,往往只用于正式的书面语体中。

◆4.2 对商务汉英词汇翻译的启示与警示

4.2.1 启示:语随境,文适体

4.2.1.1 因人而异,选用不同语体

读者对象不同,选用的语体就不同。比如,公司对公司的商务信函就会有较重的"公事公办的持重感",词句十分正式;而关系亲密的贸易伙伴之间的业务信函所用语体就不会那么正式,词句比较通俗自然。

请对比分析以下汉英翻译实例:

④ 我们非常抱歉,你们11月15日订购函上所说的那种货,没有现货可供。

英译:We are sorry to tell you that we do not have in stock any of the articles you said in your order of November 15.

⑤ 兹复贵公司11月15日的订购函。贵公司所述货物现无货可供,甚为遗憾。

英译:In reply to your order of November 15, we regret to advise that we do not have in stock any such articles as you described.

对比分析:例⑤用词用语多为书面或学术语汇,语体正式。如果这封回函是给初次订货的客户的话,这种正式语体的风格较为可取且得体。相比之下,例④措辞

通俗易懂,使人感到亲切自然。很显然,这种中性语体(neutral style)的风格属于直白的当代商务英语风格。

⑥ 特此订购以下产品:……

英译:We are pleased to place an order for the products specified below:…

⑦ 我们想订以下产品:……

英译:We would like to place an order for the following products:…

对比分析:如果关系较亲密的生意伙伴之间的"一般性往来"电邮用例⑥的说法,就会使人感到别扭做作,给人一种虚伪的感觉;若改用例⑦的说法,读起来就自然多了,也顺畅多了。但是,例⑥的说法出现在一封新客户写来的订购函里,也是自然得体的。

4.2.1.2　因时而变,选用不同语体

文风不是静止不变的,而是不断变化的。这就是一个时代风格的问题。"时代风格是因时代因素而产生的语言运用特点的综合。随着时代变迁,语言形式也在变化,可以分成今用语、过时语、陈旧语、古语、废语等。此外,不同时代有不同的风貌和时尚,在语言运用上呈现不同的格调,即时代风格。"(方梦之,2004:65)例如,20世纪五六十年代,商务英语信函写作还倾向于使用烦琐、冷僻难懂的行话,而在今天,"随着现代语言的发展演变,书信语体日趋崇尚自然、朴素、率直和简洁的风格。某些曾属于信函套语的咬文嚼字的措辞现在已经非常罕见。例如,开头用的'We beg to acknowledge …',结尾用的'Awaiting your reply, I am …'或'I remain …',凡属此类在过去十分流行的极其正式的用法现已不合时宜,而在现代商务英语信函写作中,已经渐渐显得古板陈旧或过于烦琐"(连先,2002:112)。翻译即写作,所以商务汉英翻译应因时而变,选用不同的语体风格。

请对比分析以下汉英翻译实例:

⑧ 贵函敬悉,不胜感激。

英译:We have for acknowledgment with thanks the receipt of your letter.

⑨ 你的来函已经收到。

英译:We have received your letter.

⑩ 兹奉告,贵方32234号发票已收悉。

英译:Please be advised that we have received your invoice No. 32234.

⑪ 你方32234号发票已收到。

英译:Your invoice No. 32234 has been received.

对比分析:例⑧⑩属于过时的套语,行文拖沓,语义晦涩难懂,不合时宜。相比之下,例⑨⑪用词简洁明快,通俗易懂。

4.2.2 警示:不要文不得体

我国现在使用的许多商务英语写译教材充斥着传统文体风格的样信。这些教材对我国学生和商贸工作者产生了极大的负面影响,很多人仍在大量使用那些早该被扔进垃圾堆里去的陈词滥调(hackneyed and stereotyped expressions)却浑然不知。

因此,随着国际商务信息传递方式和语言的现代化,商务英语写译与时俱进,摈弃了传统信函使用的那些过时的(obsolete)、晦涩的(obscure)商业行话(commercialese/jargon)或过于程式化的公文文体(stereotyped officialese),转而崇尚简洁直白(direct)和自然朴素(plain)的文体风格。如果对现代商务英语与传统商务英语的文体风格把握不当,英译就会发生偏差。

请对比分析以下汉英翻译实例:

⑫ 十分感谢你方就这几点提供有关这家公司的真实情况。

误译:We shall appreciate it if you will give us your frank opinion on these points regarding the company.

改译:Thank you very much if you will give us your frank opinion on these points about the company.

⑬ 这三项工程的总价为593 000美元。

误译:The aggregate cost of the three projects amounts to US $593,000.

改译:The total cost of the three projects is US $593,000.

对比分析:例⑫⑬的第一句英译多为传统风格的商务英语语句,其中所用标有下划线部分的大词表明,传统商务英语的语体极为正式。对于此类语体程度较高的大词或高深学术语汇,在当代商务英语写译中我们应尽量避免使用。相比之下,第二句英译所用词语的语体程度没有那么高;此类小词多为通俗词语,既可用于口语,也可用于书面语。在此,提请注意的是,使用小词或通俗语汇是当代商务英语修辞的大势所趋。

此外,当代商务英语写译已不再像传统商务英语那样倾向于使用一些晦涩的、过时的套语或浮夸之辞,而是崇尚自然而精练的言辞表达,使商务英语具有了较浓的当代气息。

请对比分析以下汉英翻译实例:

⑭ 务必在4月8日前上交调查问卷的回馈。

误译:Your response to this questionnaire should be submitted by April 8.

改译:Could you please respond to this questionnaire by April 8?

对比分析:误译的用语属于过时的套语,行文拖沓,用词陈腐晦涩;所用名词化短语显得冗长乏味,过于拘泥。相比之下,改译用词简洁明快。

⑮ 随函附寄邮资已付的邮票,敬请本月月底前回复。

误译:Will you be kind enough to send us a reply before the end of the month for which a stamped envelope is enclosed?

改译:Will you please send us a reply in the enclosed envelope before the end of the month?

对比分析：误译的用语属于老套的商业行话,晦涩造作。相比之下,改译直截了当,通俗自然。

第五节 商务汉英正反义对比分析与翻译

5.1 商务汉英正反义的差异对比分析

汉英两种语言都有从正面(肯定)或反面(否定)进行表达的方式,但两种语言使用正反、反正的表达方式存在差异。这种正反不同的表达方式在商用汉英中也有体现。汉语的反面表达方式多于英语。相比之下,英语的肯定表达多于汉语。这种差异特别是在一些标识语、商用习语中比较常见。

请对比分析以下汉英翻译实例：

① 暂时不要发这份文件。

英译:Please withhold the document for the time being.

② 他无权签署这份合同。

英译:He was beyond his power to sign the contract.

③ 1954 年,《米勒杀虫剂修正案》详细规定了制定未加工农产品杀虫剂残留标准的程序。

英译:In 1954, Miller Pesticide Amendment spells out procedures for setting safety limits for pesticide residues on raw agricultural commodities.

④ 因特网的股价呈自由降落之势,许多股票还算幸运,没有跌破每股一美元——使数十亿美元的投资灰飞烟灭。

英译:Internet stocks are in free fall, many of them lucky to top a buck a share—sending billions of dollars of investment up in smoke.

对比分析:上例汉语原文均是反面表达方式,带有诸如"无""未""没有"等表示否定意义的词,而对应的英语译文则是肯定表达。

5.2 对商务汉英词汇翻译的启示与警示

5.2.1 启示:进行正反式转换

汉语中有些从正面表达的句子被翻译成英语时更适合使用反面的表达方式。反之,汉语中有些从反面表达的句子对应的英译则习惯用正面表达方式。这种翻译方法就是正反式转换法(mutual transformation of affirmative and negative expressions),亦称"反译法"。但是,在有些情况下,汉英两种语言的思维表达方式一样,那么正正或反反对应转换的译法也就顺理成章了。

请对比分析以下汉英翻译实例:

⑤ 虽然目前石油供过于求,但任何一位认真的观察家都认为,石油是一种很快就要枯竭的资源。

英译:Despite the current oil glut, no serious observer believes that this is anything but a rapidly diminishing resource.

⑥ 凭票退还押金。

英译:No deposit is to be refunded unless the ticket is presented. (谢金领,2007)

对比分析:例⑤⑥的汉语原文表达的是肯定意义,而英译表达的却是否定意义。汉英翻译采用的转换法是正反转换法。

⑦ 酒好不怕巷子深。

英译:Good wine praises or sells itself. / Good wine needs no bush or crier.

⑧ 好货不愁销。

英译:Good ware makes quick markets. (周锡卿,1987)

⑨ 每次电脑急修,该公司收费60美元,最初半小时的维修不另收费,此后每小时收费30美元。

英译:The company charges US $60 to attend a PC emergency, including the first half-hour, and US $30 for every half-hour after that.

对比分析:例⑦⑧⑨的汉语原文都是采用否定表达的形式,而英译的表达方式恰恰相反。

5.2.2 警示:不要因正反形式完全对应而使英译不地道

不同民族在思维方式及语言表达上存在差异,一种语言从反面表达的内容,另一种语言为求语用、修辞相当,或出于语言习惯可能会以肯定的说法来翻译原文否定的形式,或以否定的说法来翻译原文肯定的形式。(方梦之,2003)由此可见,汉英翻译不应拘泥于外在形式,而应按照汉英语用、修辞习惯进行地道的翻译转换。

请对比分析以下汉英翻译实例:

⑩ 游客止步!

误译:Tourists, Please Stop!

改译:Staff Only. / Employee Only. (谢金领,2007)

对比分析:汉语原文采用了否定意义的表达方式。误译强调一字一句地死译,也是乱译;改译按照英语标识语的习惯表达,转换成了肯定的表达方式。

⑪ 请勿将头伸出窗外!

误译:Please do not put your head out of the window!

改译:Keep Head Inside Vehicle! (谢金领,2007)

对比分析:汉语原文的表达方式是否定式。误译属于不符合英语表达习惯的汉语式英译;改译就套用了英语的肯定表达方式。

⑫ 童叟无欺,市无二价。

误译:No cheating to old and young people and do not sell at different prices.

改译:Be honest with all customers and sell at a fair price. / Neither old nor young are cheated. (安亚中、张健,2008)

⑬ 货有高低三等价,客无远近一般看。

误译:Our tariffs may be low or dear, but we won't treat you differently, no matter whether you come from far or near.

改译:Our tariffs may be low, our tariffs may be dear, but we'll treat you all the same, who come from far or near. (尹帮彦,2006)

⑭ 售出概不退货。

误译:All goods are not to be returned when sold.

改译:All sales are final.

对比分析:英译以正面表达来转换汉语原文的反面表达。反正式转换表达对于汉英两种语言来说都是地道且恰当的。

思考与练习

1. 思考题

（1）商务汉英词义在哪些方面表现出不同之处？

（2）如何跨越词义之间的差异进行翻译转换？

2. 句子翻译

（1）大多数小店已被并入大公司。

（2）技术落后的国家可以低价引进最新技术，而无须负担研究、发明和开发的费用。

（3）有人发现会计做假账。

（4）我认为,这套住房至少可以卖到每平方 5 600 美元。

（5）我们正在做钢铁多头生意。

（6）收到卖方的交货通知,买方应在交货期15—20天前,开具一个以卖方为受益人的、可转让的、可分期的、不可撤销的信用证,金额与发货总额等值。

（7）我们是美国重要的大量经营纺织品的商号。

（8）此项投资可由我方来筹集贷款。

（9）我们对该货投保全险。

（10）我们能够向你方报相当优惠的价格。

（11）通道禁止摆摊。

（12）有规则就有例外。

（13）你们过去是,现在是,将来仍然是我们的客户。

3. 语篇翻译

- 语篇1

大力实施本土化战略

实施本土化对跨国公司来讲是一项十分重要并且是一箭双雕的战略决策。它不但能有效降低向东道国派遣高级管理人员的成本,与此同时,还能充分利用东道国相对低廉的人力资源。从长远来看,把当地优秀的经理人员提拔到决策者的位子上来是十分明智的选择,因为他们比较熟悉本国的法律法规,了解本国的市场行情,绝无文化方面的障碍,并能有效地与当地各部门进行沟通。简而言之,他们更熟悉本国政府制定的游戏规则。但要吸引并留住这些优秀人才,跨国公司必须做一件实实在在的事情,即给他们提供自身发展和事业进步的机遇。以中国这个新兴市场国家为例,跨国公司对其投资与日俱增,如今已吸引的外商投资总量仅次于当今的头号发达国家——美国,因而跨国公司对中国本土优秀人才的竞争便十分激烈。他们明白一个简单的道理:市场竞争归根结底是人才的竞争,谁掌握了人才谁就占尽了先机,再配以雄厚的资本、先进的技术以及行之有效的管理方法和运作手段,他们也就掌握了搏击市场风浪、克敌制胜的法宝。

● 语篇 2

中国经济在世界经济中的作用

进入 21 世纪,特别是在中国打破重重阻挠加入世贸组织之后,中国经济在世界经济中的作用已受到世人瞩目。由于世界生产链的重新分工和转移,中国成为世界上的制造大国,进而带动了许多发展中国家经济的发展,它们向中国出口资源、农产品和制造业半成品,中国也向全世界提供价廉物美的工业品。

英国《经济学家》2005 年 7 月 30 日这一期分析了中国经济在世界经济中的地位和作用,认为"中国几乎推动着世界经济正在发生的一切","全球通胀率、利率、国债收益率、房地产价格、工资、利润和商品价格现在越来越受中国政策的驱动,这可能成为至少半个世纪以来世界上最深刻的经济变化"。

中国实行改革开放政策 28 年来,中国经济保持了 9.4% 的增长速度,并且在诸多领域取得了骄人的成绩。中国的社会主义制度得到了加强,因为它把社会主义的基本社会制度和市场经济体制恰当地结合了起来;生产力得到了空前发展,人民生活水平得到了显著提高;综合国力显著增长,经济结构有了调整。因而中国经济在世界经济中的地位有了提升,成为世界经济向前发展的一种推动力。

● 语篇 3

尊敬的先生:

你公司第 TY678 号报价收到了,很遗憾,报价和当前市场趋势不一致。

目前在欧洲,亚洲销售商增多了,同时东欧货也增多了。主要卖主唯恐市场份额下降,又再降低价格。因此,FH 集团愿接受去年的价格水平一定有充足的理由。

根据我公司掌握的情报,FH 集团的策略是出较好的价格,尽量多购中国材料,然后同他们自己的材料一起,按较低的欧洲市价出售。由于从中国购进的材料仅占全部销量的一小部分,这样做所付出的费用为他们自身材料的利润空间所弥补。这意味着,当其他竞争者退出后,中国供货商就会发现较难出售,不得不向 FH 集团统治市场的压力低头。

希望贵公司重新考虑这一问题并能提出新的报价。

此致

敬礼

2020 年 6 月 6 日

第六章

商务汉英词类用法对比分析与翻译

Identify the problems in the following translations

① 按贵方要求,我方已经给贵方寄去最新产品目录一份和样品一套,供贵方参考。

英译:As you require, we have sent you a copy of our latest catalogue and a set of samples for you to examine.

② 成功地实现单一市场的前提就是有的公司必有所得,有的公司必有所失。

英译:A precondition for the success of the single market is that some companies must lose some market shares and others must win some market shares.

③ 根据来函条款,我方决定试订下列货物。

英译:We have decided to order the following as a trial on the terms stated in the letter. (余富林等,2003)

汉语与英语相比,形态特征没有那么明显。在词类划分上,形态在英语中发挥着重要作用,而汉语基本上是按照词在搭配及上下文中的功能来确定其词类的,因为汉语词的形态特征的普遍性远不及英语。由此可见,作为两大不同语系,汉英在词的形态特征和词类用法上存在差异,特别是在汉语的动词与英语的名词、介词等词类用法上有着显著的差异。

有着发达的派生构词法的英语可以灵活地把动词派生成名词。因此,相比汉语而言,英语有着 Simeon Potter 在他的《英语的变化》(*Changing English*,1969)一书中指出的名词优势于动词的倾向(preponderance of nouns over verbs)。英语这种倾向于多用名词或名词短语来表示动作、行为概念和品质特征的语言现象就是所谓的名词化(nominalization or noun phrases)现象。汉语则不然。由于汉语具有连动结构和兼语结构的语言修辞特征,且缺乏形态变化,动词在汉语中用得较多,形容词可以直接用作动词。这就是汉语的动词优势。

此外,英语的名词优势也造成了其介词优势(连淑能,1993)。英语介词不仅数目和种类多,而且使用非常频繁,搭配能力很强,含义也很丰富。英语介词包括单个介词(如:in,at,on,with)、合成介词(如:inside,onto,without,throughout)和短语介词(如:in front of,on behalf of,according to,with reference to)。据乔治·欧·寇姆(George O. Curme)的统计,英语各类介词大约共有286个。介词在英语中十分活跃,是连接词、短语或句子的常用手段。英语介词的这种特点和用法可能是汉语所没有的。汉语的介词大多是从动词演变而来的,没有形态变化,与动词之间很难区别,两者经常被互换使用。

在有着"客观、真实、准确、简洁"(谢建平,2008)的用词特点的商务英语信函、报告、合同、计划书等应用文体写译中,英语具有名词和介词优势的言语修辞特征与效果就更加得到彰显。

第一节　商务汉英动词与名词用法差异对比分析与翻译

1.1　商务汉英动词与名词用法的差异对比分析

比较起来,汉英两种语言在用词上有明显不同:在汉语中,由于具有连动结构和兼语结构,动词在句中可以频繁出现;而英语倾向于多用名词(词组)来表示动作、行为和其他概念。这种名词化现象在英语书面语体中是十分常见的。认识两种语言的这一差异对于英译有着重要的修辞指导作用。

在商务汉英文体中,上述差异就表现得更加明显。据统计,商务英语中,200个小句含有同等数量甚至更多数量的名词化短语。这就表明,名词化现象在商务英语中更加普遍。但相比之下,汉语中名词化现象就不太常见,商务汉语也是如此。这就是汉英两种语言在选词用词上的显著区别之一。

请对比分析商务汉语中的动词与商务英语中的名词(特别是商务汉语中的连动结构、兼语结构与商务英语中的名词化短语)之间的差异:

① 未经我们经理许可,我们不能向你方提供数量折扣。

英译: We can not allow you any quantity discount without our manager's permission. / We can not allow you any quantity discount if our manager does not permit it.

对比分析:汉语原句所用的动词"许可"在英语译文中被转换成了名词permission。这就表明汉英两种语言分别有着使用动词和名词的民族语言情结或习惯。

② 鉴于货运量很小,我们同意破例接受付款交单。

英译:Considering the small amount of goods shipped, we agree to make an exception by accepting the payment by D/P.

对比分析:汉语原文采用了连动式结构"破例接受",而英译则发挥名词优势,采用名词 exception 和名词化短语 accepting the payment by D/P。

③ 一个具有宏伟发展计划的发展中国家,为了有效地实施其发展计划,可能需要进口大量资本货物、技术、原材料和其他输入资源及消费品。

英译:A developing economy with an impressive development plan requires large imports of capital goods, technology, raw materials and other inputs and consumer goods to carry out the plan effectively.

对比分析:汉语原文使用了一个连动式结构"需要进口",而英译则将"进口"这个动词译成了名词 imports。

④ 在过去的几年里,AT&T 裁掉了数千名经理和雇员,而他们中的许多人已经在该公司忠心耿耿地工作了二十年甚至更长的时间。

英译:In the past years AT&T dismissed thousands of managers and employees through downsizing, though many of these people have twenty or more years of loyal employment with the firm.

对比分析:汉语原文所用的动词在英译中被分别转换成了由动词派生而来的名词 downsizing 和 employment。

⑤ ……或者可以这样安排,派遣我们的代理把样品送到你们办公室供你们检验,费用由我们负担。

英译:… or alternatively it can be arranged by sending our representative to your office with samples for your inspection at our expense.

对比分析:汉语原文使用了连动结构或兼语结构"派遣我们的代理把样品送到你们办公室供你们检验",英译则使用了动名词 sending、派生名词 inspection 等进行了灵活的对等转换。

由此可见,这就是汉语动词优势与英语名词优势的修辞差异。汉英分属两大不同语系,因此它们在构词、用词习惯、表达方式上有极大的差异。汉语多使用连动结构和兼语结构,动词可在句中频繁出现。但是,汉语缺乏像英语那样强大的派生和词类转换能力。汉语缺乏形态变化,形式相同的词可以是名词,也可以是动词,还可以是形容词或其他词。为数不多的汉语名词化短语有相当大的比例是西方语言对汉语影响的结果,如许多带"化""性""度"等词尾的名词化词语或短语。相比之下,英语语法要求一个分句只能有一个限定性动词作谓语动词,限定性动词有时态、语态、人称、数等变化;如果分句还要使用动词,就得使用诸如动词不定式、动名词、分词等非限定性动词形式。但是,英语的派生(derivation)和词类转换(conversion)能力极强,它可以通过添加名词性后缀、动词等词类的方式直接转化生成大量的名词化词语或抽象名词,如:the <u>conclusion</u> of difficult negotiations, the <u>formulation</u> of export sales contract, the <u>participation</u> in GATT, the <u>involvement</u> in international economy and trade activities, a <u>decline</u> in industrial production and a marked <u>upturn</u> in inflation, the <u>fall</u> in the growth rate of the world economy。

因此,需要注意的是,文体正式程度很高的商务英语要求选用名词化词语,这是因为商务英语用词简约、语篇简短。同时,这也是商界"时间就是金钱"理念在商务英语写译中的体现。由此可见,名词化词语的选用反映了商务英语语篇用词正式、语言经济的言语修辞特征。

◆ 1.2 对商务汉英词类翻译的启示与警示

1.2.1 启示:"化动为静"

如上所述,汉英两种语言在词类使用方面有一定的差异:汉语句子中动词占优势,英语句子中名词占优势。商务英语写译有着较多使用名词或名词化短语的倾向,所以在汉英翻译转换中,我们必须遵照汉英两种不同语言的修辞习惯,"化动为静"。

请对比分析以下汉英翻译中的动词和名词之间的词类转换:

⑥ 在发展中国家中,中国<u>吸收</u>的国外投资额最大。在20世纪末的几年里,中国<u>平均</u>每年吸收的外资额高达400亿美元左右。中国<u>入</u>世后更是引来了更多的投资。

英译:Among developing nations, China has been the largest <u>recipient</u> of foreign investment, <u>averaging</u> about US \$40 billion per year during the late 1990s. <u>Membership</u> in the WTO has further resulted in even higher levels.

对比分析:汉语句子所用动词"吸收"和"入"在英译中被转换成了名词。此外,汉语副词"平均"也被转换成了英语动名词 averaging。

⑦ 正如您可从我方1月份所寄产品目录中了解到的那样,我们的毯子<u>暖和</u>、<u>柔软</u>,并易于保管。它<u>集中</u>了所有上述优点。

英译:As you realized from the catalogue we have sent in January, our blanket is a perfect <u>combination</u> of warmth, softness, and easy care.

对比分析:汉语原句连用了三个动词和动词短语,而英译则发挥英语的名词优势,并列使用了三个名词和名词短语。而且,英译将汉语动词"集中"转换成了名词 combination。

⑧ 根据来函条款,我方决定试订下列货物。

英译:We have decided to place a trial order for the following on the terms stated in the letter. (余富林等,2003)

对比分析:汉语原句所用动词"试订"与英译中的名词短语 trial order 实现了词类转换。

1.2.2 警示:发挥英语的名词优势,防止出现英译"多动症"

汉语偏爱动词的修辞倾向可能会对商务英语翻译产生负面影响。因此,商务汉英翻译须警惕汉语偏爱动词的行文风格,避免译出动词用得过多的汉式英语。

请对比分析以下商务汉英翻译实例:

⑨ 成功地实现单一市场的前提就是有的公司必有所得,有的公司必有所失。

误译:A precondition for the success of the single market is that some companies must lose some market shares and others must win some market shares.

改译:A precondition for the success of the single market is that there must be losers as well as winners. (叶玉龙、王文翰、段云礼,1998)

对比分析:此例误译就是受到了汉语偏爱动词的修辞倾向的负面影响。英译把汉语原文所用动词照译过去,结果就成了汉式英语。改译发挥了英语的名词优势,把汉语动词转换成英语名词,这样译文不仅地道而且简练。

⑩ 我们也认识到越来越需要使某些经济部门实行工业化。

误译:We also realize that it is more and more necessary to industrialize some sectors of the economy.

改译:We also realize the growing need and necessity to industrialize some sectors of the economy. (张新红等,2003)

对比分析:正是受到汉语多动词的修辞习惯的影响,误译没有对汉语原文的动词进行名词转换,结果出现了汉式英译现象;改译成功地进行了汉语动词与英语名词之间的转换,译文地道且经济。

第二节　商务汉英动词与介词用法差异对比分析与翻译

◆ 2.1　商务汉英动词与介词用法的差异对比分析

汉语的介词功能相对简单，而且汉语介词多由动词演变而来，无形态变化，两者之间往往难以区分。相比之下，英语介词不仅使用频率高、搭配能力强，含义也十分丰富。英语介词既可以用来表示具体含义，如时间、地点、方位、距离等，也可以引申表示抽象概念，即用于表示动作。英语介词的这种功能是英语的一大优势。英语造句几乎离不开介词，而汉语常不用或省略介词。

在商务英语中，介词或介词短语使用相当频繁，搭配能力很强，并且用法灵活、含义多变。汉语原本是没有介词的。即使有，也为数不多。

请注意观察以下商务汉英信函中的粗体画线部分并进行对比分析：

①

尊敬的哈里森先生：

感谢**接到**您 2004 年 5 月 18 日的来电。

非常抱歉没有及时**给**您寄送衬衫样品。延误寄送样品是因为我们的生产部经理戴维·莫瑞病了三周。衬衫样品现已**在**路上，您应该能在三日内收到。

我为延迟给您带来的不便再次表示歉意。希望我们的样品能令您满意。

此致

敬礼

英译：

Dear Mr. Harrison,

Thank you **for** your telephone call **of** May 18, 2004.

I am extremely sorry **for** the delay **in** sending the sample shirt **to** you. It was late because David Murray, our Production Manager, has been sick **for** three weeks. The sample is now **on** its way and you should get the sample **within** three days.

I apologize again **for** the delay and I hope the sample will meet **with** your satisfaction.

Yours sincerely

对比分析：汉语信函所用三个动词短语"接到……来电""给您""在路上"分别

由英语介词短语 for your telephone call, to you, on its way 加以转换。再者,短短一封信函就用了 10 个介词。由此可见,商务英语信函中有很多灵活的介词用法。

英语的名词化可以使文字简练、表达简洁。英语介词也可以起到同样的修辞功能。介词的使用体现了简洁、经济与客观的商务英语信函的文体修辞特点。

请对比分析以下商务汉英翻译实例:

② 这是一艘<u>开往</u>美国旧金山的货船。

英译:This is a freight ship <u>for</u> San Francisco.

对比分析:用于转换汉语原句的动词"开往"的介词 for 可以起到定语从句"that sails for San Francisco"的作用。

③ 中国<u>有着</u>世界五分之一的人口,并且<u>还是</u>世界上经济发展速度最快的国家之一,因此它就成了全球商贸投资的主要目标。

英译:China, <u>with</u> one fifth of the world's population and one of the fastest rates of economic growth, is a major target <u>for</u> global business.

对比分析:汉语原句连用了两个动词"有着"和"还是";而英语则发挥介词优势将汉语的前一个分句转换成一个介词短语 with one fifth of the world's population and one of the fastest rates of economic growth。

◆ 2.2 对商务汉英词类翻译的启示与警示

2.2.1 启示:进行动词与介词互译转换

在商务汉英翻译中,我们可以在汉语动词与英语介词之间进行互译转换。

请对比分析以下商务汉英翻译实例:

④ 2004 北京国际旅游博览会<u>汇集</u>了来自世界 25 个国家的 210 个参展商,具有宏大的包容性,不仅包括众多出入境旅游项目、全新旅游线路推介,更涵盖多种旅游产业衍生品,展览的品类异常丰富。

英译:<u>With</u> 210 exhibitors <u>from</u> some 25 countries <u>under</u> one roof, Beijing International Tourism Expo (BITE) 2004 showcases a great variety of destinations and diversified products, including hotels, attractions, meetings and specialized services.

⑤ 违反合同的一方<u>有责任</u>采取一切必要措施减轻已经发生的损失。

英译:The party who sets up a breach of the contract shall be <u>under a duty</u> to take all necessary measures to mitigate the loss which has occurred. (叶玉龙、王文翰、段云礼,1998)

⑥ 本杂志每年四期,全年年订阅 49 美元,<u>外加</u> 16 美元的邮寄费用。

英译：Annual subscription for four issues of this journal is US $49.00 plus postage and handling (US $16.00).

对比分析：以上三例都是把汉语原句的动词转换成英语的介词。

⑦ 贵公司代表对我方产品有兴趣，并要求给他们寄送更详细的资料，供他们做进一步考虑。

英译：Your company's representatives expressed interest in our products and asked that additional details be sent to them for further consideration.

⑧ 这是表示赞成在处理国际问题时应由一个机构进行商讨的论据，而不是表示反对这种做法的。

英译：This is an argument for, not against, an institutional approach to international problems.

对比分析：汉语原句的动词短语与英语的介词短语在英译中进行了恰当而得体的转换，以此发挥了英语的介词优势。

2.2.2 警示：发挥英语的介词优势，避免汉语动词负迁移

汉语偏爱使用连动结构和兼语结构，而英语偏爱使用介词。鉴于汉英在动词与介词使用上的较大差异，英语初学者在商务汉英翻译中可能不时会犯该用介词而用动词的修辞失误。因此，商务汉英翻译应避免受汉语偏爱动词的修辞习惯的负面影响，尽量减少汉语修辞习惯对商务英语的负迁移。

请对比分析以下商务汉英翻译实例：

⑨ 6月份的价格是根据原来的合同定的，并削减了我方的利润。

误译：The June price was according to the original contract and cut down our own profit.

改译：The June price was based on the original contract at a sacrifice of our own profit.

⑩ 作为回复，我方特此确认向贵方出售500打运动衫。

误译：To make a reply to your letter, we confirm our sales to you of 500 dozens of sweaters.

改译：In reply, we confirm our sales to you of 500 dozens of sweaters.

⑪ 按贵方要求，我方已经给贵方寄去最新产品目录一份和样品一套，供贵方参考。

误译：As you require, we have sent you a copy of our latest catalogue and a set of samples for you to examine.

改译：At your request, we have sent you a copy of our latest catalogue and a set of samples **for your examination**.

对比分析：误译中，汉语原句所用动词均一字一句地被转换翻译成了英语的动词，这是汉语动词用法对英译的负面影响。

由此可见，我们该用介词而用动词的修辞失误在商务英语写译中时有发生。
请对比分析以下商务汉英信函翻译实例：

⑫

尊敬的约翰逊：

非常感谢贵方 2004 年 5 月 3 日的来函。

我方为延误很长时间回复贵方信函，表示真诚的歉意。我方最近把公司总部迁到位于本市南部的新址，结果延误了大量询价函的回复。搬迁现已结束。我方可以向贵方保证延误之事今后再也不会发生。

随信附寄贵方所要产品目录。望贵方能继续把我方作为贵方的主要供货商。

此致

敬礼

有待修改的英译：

Dear Mr. Johnson,

Thank you very much for your letter of 3 May 2004.

We wish to offer our sincere apologies for **that we delayed to reply to your letter for a long time**. We have recently moved our headquarters to a new location in the south of the city and this has **led to the result that we delay to reply to inquiries for a considerable amount of time**. The move has now been completed and I can assure you that there will be no more delays in the future.

The catalogs you require are enclosed and I hope that you will continue to use us **to be your main supplier**.

Yours sincerely

修改的英译：

Dear Mr. Johnson,

Thank you very much for your letter of 3 May 2004.

We wish to offer our sincere apologies **for the long delay in replying to your letter**. We have recently moved our headquarters to a new location in the south of the city and this has resulted **in some considerable delay in replying to inquiries**. The move has now been completed and I can assure you that there will be no more delays in the future.

The catalogs you require are enclosed and I hope that you will continue to use us **as your main supplier**.

Yours sincerely

对比分析：通过对比分析以上英译，我们发现，在第一个译文中，译者因缺乏英语介词优势的修辞意识，在该用介词的地方用了动词，这就使得译文不够明快简练。相比之下，第二个译文因恰当而得体地使用短小简洁的介词短语而使译文更显"英语味儿"，更符合英语修辞习惯与规范。

思考与练习

1. 思考题

（1）汉英两种语言在词类用法上有什么显著差异？特别是在商务汉英信函中词类用法的差异是什么？

（2）鉴于商务汉英在词类用法上表现出来的差异，可以采用的翻译策略和方法有哪些？

2. 句子翻译

（1）该公司由于管理不善而破产。

（2）这些贸易自由化措施旨在促进更有效地利用本国资源。

（3）备忘录中已经写明，我们愿意向贵方用户提供技术服务。

（4）为了促进双边贸易，中国化工进出口总公司和美国一家大公司达成如下协议。

（5）总公司根本不知道这项促销活动，因而没有装运该产品的计划。

（6）另外，这也是选择股票的主要手段。

（7）在汽车工业中使用塑料，已经大大地增加了塑料的消费量。

（8）采用本公司的全套新设备可大大降低废品率。

（9）请及时付款。

（10）经济学家们深信，这种趋势是不可避免的。

（11）他详尽地问起我们产品的情况。

（12）他们之间的关系有一个特点，就是以礼相待。

（13）我们必须确保，这样汇付佣金不违反当地的规定。

（14）轻纺工业产品的花色品种增多，质量继续有所提高。

（15）中国的富强与发展不会对任何国家构成威胁。

3. 语篇翻译

● 语篇1

从你方9月20日来信获悉,在我们装运你方订单43号的货物中,有一箱到达时损坏情况十分严重。经查,这批货物系用牢固的新木箱包装,适合长途海运,我们只得断定,你们没有留心把这箱货物储存好。

在收到你们来信后,我们立即请了你地的一位公证人会同你方职员前往现场检查那箱损坏的货物。10月3日,该公证人发来了一份检查报告说,就所见的情况而论,正在谈及的那箱货要么是放在外面给大雨淋过,要么就曾掉进水里,你们那位职员公正、友好,他看了以后承认情况属实。

我们接着又叫运输部门进一步研究此事,经与船公司联系,船公司说,整批货物到达情况良好,他们可以肯定损坏是在货物到了你们手中以后这段时间里发生的。在此情况下,我们不得不遗憾地说,对这一损坏我们歉难承担责任。

我们知道这只箱子里装有我们针织机的某些重要部件,机器没有这些部件就不会运转。因此,你若认为需要的话,我们将乐于按发票价格着手再供一批同样的部件,并尽最大努力在两星期内交货。

等候你们答复。

● 语篇2

上月29日来函收到。感谢贵方给我们一个机会担任贵方在本地的代理。

正如你们所知,我公司经营化工产品有很长的历史。我们坚信,我们能用我们的信誉和广泛的业务联系为你们提供良好的服务。拥有这些优势,我们认为在推销贵方产品和开拓贵方产品市场方面不会有任何困难。我们对贵公司提出的建议很感兴趣。如果你方代理协议条款可以接受,我们会十分高兴。敬请贵方在最方便的时刻将代理条款航寄我们。

至盼早复。

● 语篇3

如果日本各公司断然采取西方国家裁员的做法以增加利润,日本一度令人美慕的失业率将极可能飙升至两位数。虽然日本的终生雇佣制明显地在走向解体,但是鉴于大幅度裁员刺激经济的动机与要求保留工作岗位的社会压力和政治压力相冲突,许多经济学家仍无法断定日本是否会出现失业率急剧上升的局面。以一个较为仁慈和温和的做法——调整经济,可以缓解社会的动荡不安,因为许多人担心早已创纪录的失业率若再增长一倍就会导致社会不安定。

评论家们认为,高失业率还会限制利润的增长和抑制经济活力,特别是如果不采取大胆步骤为增长型产业敞开大门的话。一些经济学家认为,用不同的方法计算,按美国标准,日本的失业率早已接近7%,与1992年美国7.8%的最高失业率相去不远,而当时美国已经走出两年的经济衰退期。

第七章

商务汉英句法对比分析与翻译

Identify the problems in the following translations

① 产品没有市场、长期亏损、扭亏无望和资源枯竭的企业,以及浪费资源、技术落后、质量低劣、污染严重的小煤矿、小炼油、小水泥、小玻璃、小火电等,要实行破产、关闭。

英译:Enterprises that cannot find any market for their products, entail long-term losses but are not expected to turn round, and suffer from the drying up of resources and small coal mines, refineries, cement works and glass factories and small thermal power plants that have been wasting resources, or are technologically backward, or are manufacturing poor quality products, or have caused severe pollution should also be forced to declare bankrupt or close down.

② 他们对订购的裙装式样已经达成了一致,这是一件好事。

英译:They have reached an agreement on the style of the dresses ordered. It is a good thing.

③ 对于世界经济暂时的不景气,中国民航业有着充分的信心去克服。(李长栓,2004)

英译:As regards the present slowdown in the world economy, the Chinese civil aviation is fully confident in overcoming it.

作为特殊用途的语言变体,商务汉英(广告除外)有其独特的句法修辞特征。一般来说,商务汉英句法各有规律可循,但总体上结构严谨、简练准确、句意完整、逻辑严密。值得注意的有以下几点:

- 一般来说,长句用得较多,文体就较庄严(dignified)、高雅(lofty);短句用得较多,文体就较通俗(conversational)、轻松(light)。在商务英语文体中,长短句交错使用,以避免单调(monotonousness),而短句更适合商务信函文体的写作(Gartside, 1989)。但为保证语言的准确性和逻辑性,合同与协议的句子比较长,每句话都表达一个完整的意思(谢建平,2008)。

- 商务汉英文体很少使用任何形式的疑问句和感叹句,而较多使用陈述句、祈使句。
- 商务汉语较多使用圆周句。相比之下,商务英语较多使用松散句。
- 英语常用被动式,采用物称表达法;汉语常用主动式,采用人称、泛称或隐称表达法(连淑能,1993)。物称较多地用于商务文体,特别是用在商务英语文体,其目的是使文字更加客观。
- 英语被动语态在应用文体、科技文体中用得极为普遍。被动语态普遍使用除了语言结构上的原因之外,还有"语义价值"(semantic value)上的原因:被动语态常用来表示说话者对所提出的话题(或人或事或物)持有某种客观态度,因而比较婉转。

上述这些句法特征均与商务汉英是一种特殊用途的语言变体(广告除外)有关。因为追求利润和效益,所以商务活动的信条就是"时间就是金钱""效益就是生命"。因此,商务汉英的句法简洁高效,具体表现就是采用信息含量极高的简单句、并列句、复合句、并列复合句等。

第一节 商务汉英意合与形合之间的句法差异对比分析与翻译

1.1 商务汉英意合与形合之间的句法差异对比分析

从句法结构来分,句子分为简单句(simple sentence)、并列句(compound sentence)、复合句(complex sentence)和并列复合句(compound-complex sentence)。商务文体对句法的一大要求就是保持完整性、严密性和逻辑性。因此,商务汉英文体较多地使用诸如"因为""因此""以便""鉴于""关于"和 therefore, that, because, so that, regarding 之类的过渡与衔接词语(transitional and cohesive words/phrases)。正是由于对关联词语的大量使用,商务汉英的语句偏长,特别是在商贸合同、商务报告、商务计划书等商务汉英正式文体中,长句比比皆是。但相比之下,商务汉语因其意合型语言行文特征而短句居多;商务英语因其形合型语言行文特征而长句居多。

由于汉英分属意合型语言与形合型语言,汉英句法结构与语序完全对应或基本对应的情况很少。汉语是意合型语言,其句法结构比较松散,各部分的衔接靠的是语义和逻辑。只要在上下文中意思能被理解,汉语就较少使用衔接词、介词等形合手段。因此,汉语句子具有结构短小、排比连动、运用灵活、富有弹性的特点。例如：

① 本厂是专业生产航空、宾馆、酒店、铁路、游轮等场所用中、高档拖鞋的厂家，产品有"可洗型""环保型""一次型"等几大类，畅销中国，远销日本、新加坡、欧美国家，款式达数百种，可供客户选择，也可应客户要求设计定样，欢迎国内外客户洽谈合作。

分析：这篇企业产品简介就只使用了一个句号，中间均用逗号隔开。句式简短，大多都是动宾搭配的无主句，前后排比连动，较少使用衔接词。

相比之下，英语属于形合型语言。为了前后连贯，英语比汉语使用更多的衔接词、介词等形合手段。所以，英语的句法结构比较严谨，各部分通过使用衔接词紧密地衔接成一个整体。

请对比以上所给汉语产品简介的英译：

② We are a professional manufacturer of all kinds of slippers which are widely used in airplanes, hotels, trains and travel ships. Our products include "washable slippers", "environmentally-friendly slippers", "disposable slippers", etc. They are well sold in the domestic market and exported to Japan, Singapore, Europe and America. There are hundreds of styles for customers to choose from. Moreover, the styles can also be customized according to customers' specific needs. Customers from both home and abroad are welcome to our company for business negotiation.

分析：英译将汉语原文的一句话译成了主谓成分齐全的六句话。英译根据前后的逻辑关系进行整合，并添加必要的关系代词和连词，使得前后衔接紧密。

汉英两种语言在行文修辞上的差异就自然而然地导致了这样一个结果：汉语短句多，英语长句多。

请对比分析以下商务汉英信函翻译实例：

③
敬启者：

你方1999年12月2日来函已经收悉。获知贵公司想在罐装食品行业与我方建立贸易关系，我方十分高兴。

按照你方要求，我方航空邮寄产品目录一份，并附一套小册子，以供你方参考。

如果产品目录所列任何商品符合你方要求，请具体询价，我方将马上寄去报价单。

同时，在第一笔生意做成之前，请将你方银行行名告知我方。

谨启

英译：

Dear Sirs,

With reference to your letter of December 2, 1999, we are glad to learn that you wish to enter into trade relations with this corporation in the line of canned goods.

In compliance with your request, we are sending you by air a catalogue together with a range of pamphlets for your reference.

If any of the items listed in the catalogue meets your interest, please let us have your specific inquiry, and our quotation will be forwarded without delay.

In the meantime, you are requested to furnish us with the name of your bank prior to the conclusion of the first transaction between us.

Sincerely yours

对比分析： 汉语信函有五句，而只用了一个复合句，因为汉语这种意合型语言没有英语那么多的关联词可供使用。相比之下，英译只有四句，而复合句就有两句。并且，英译信函所用介词随处可见，如 with reference to，in the line of canned goods，in compliance with your request，by air，together with a range of pamphlets，for your reference，in the catalogue，without delay，in the meantime，prior to the conclusion of the first transaction between us 等。英译信函不长，但全文共用介词20多个。

◆ 1.2 对商务汉英句法翻译的启示与警示

1.2.1 启示：该合则合，该分则分

汉语句子结构比较松散，而英语句子结构比较严谨。为了取得较好的英译效果，译者在句型结构上应当进行转换：把汉语原句拆开，采用英语丰富的形合手段，搭建英译的"主—谓"句法框架，充分发挥英语"主—谓"提携机制，对汉语原文的信息重新加以组合。所以，进行商务汉英翻译时，我们该合则合、该分则分。

1.2.1.1 合译

汉语没有动词的非谓语形式，没有关系代词，较少使用介词、连词，所以从表面上看，汉语句子结构以并列句较多。相比之下，英语更加形式化，分句之间的连接往往用连词、关系代词或关系副词直接表示出来，形成层次分明的复合句。在商务汉英翻译中，我们经常要对原句结构做较大的调整或改变，即根据英语形合型语言特点，对按照汉语意合型语言特点组合起来的竹节形的不间断语句或流水句进行剖析，继而做合译处理。也就是，把汉语中用逗号甚至用句号相连的短句根据一定的逻辑关系重新组合成讲究层次的

英语长句。

请对比分析以下商务汉英翻译实例:

④ 合资企业使其参与者能够募集起资金去修建广场,同时还给予他们一种力量。在遭受几次突如其来的、有可能阻止广场竣工的困难和工程延期之后,这种力量使他们依然幸存下来。

英译:The joint venture enabled the participants to raise the money to build the square and also give them the strength to survive several unanticipated challenges and delays that might have prevented the square's completion.

⑤ 在危机过去很久以后,失望的股东们仍对那些有争议的决定感到愤怒,这些决定使他们与红利无缘。两名研究人员被指派去研究董事会的绩效。

英译:Long after the crisis, disappointed stockholders were still angry with the disputed decisions that denied their dividends. Two researchers were appointed to study the performance of board of directors.

⑥ 我们已将寄来的目录和图纸转交几家大厂。现已接到上海一家工厂愿意承办的答复。

英译:We have forwarded the catalogs and drawings you sent us to some large manufacturers and now have an affirmative answer from a factory in Shanghai.

⑦ 这些早期的企业家几乎白手起家却创造了宏大的产业,在千百万美国人看来,他们恰如早期拓荒时代的英雄,走进美国一望无际的荒野,将森林变成了农场、村庄和小城镇。

英译:The fact that these early entrepreneurs built great industries out of very little made them seem to millions of Americans like the heroes of the early frontier days who went into the vast wilderness of the United States and turned the forests into farms, villages and small cities.

对比分析:以上汉英翻译均采用了合句法。例④将汉语的两个独立语句合并成英译中的复合句;例⑤也是把汉语的两个简单句合译成一个英语复合句;例⑥将汉语的两个独立语句合译成一个英语句子;例⑦也是把汉语的两个语句合并成英译中的复合句。

1.2.1.2 分译

汉语的一句话有时比较长,句子界限并不明显;而英语语句受形式逻辑的支配,句法严谨。所以,我们进行汉英翻译时经常需要断句。根据上下文,我们可以运用分割、融合、颠倒、插入、重复等技巧,将汉语长句分成若干个短语、分句、单句、独立成分。分译可以把一个汉语长句拆分成两句甚至三句。

请对比分析以下商务汉英翻译实例：

⑧ 从贵公司9月5日函获悉,贵方拟购会计部使用的电脑软件。

英译:We received your letter of September 5, 2004. In your letter, you asked about purchasing software for use in your accounting department.

⑨ "革新技术、壮大员工、创新管理、顾客至上"是贝赛德(传动装置集团)的企业精神,它推动着贝赛德的迅速壮大和发展,使我们始终处于传动装置行业的领先地位。

英译:It's all part of what we call the Bayside Way. It involves technical innovation, continuous employee development, creative management and a strong customer focus. It's what drives Bayside's exponential growth and continues to make us the leader in motion control.

对比分析:以上汉英翻译均采用了分句法。例⑧的英译将汉语的一个句子拆分成英译中两个独立的语句;例⑨的英译则是把汉语原句拆分成三句话。

1.2.2　警示:不要受汉语"意合"的负面影响

1.2.2.1　警惕英译不连贯

汉语没有英语那么多的起连接作用的连词、关系代词/副词、介词等,句子与句子之间的连接比较松散,较少使用连接词,其逻辑关系通过意合来显示。相比之下,英语则使用较多的连接词来连接词与词、短语与短语、小句与小句、主句与从句,使语义前后连贯,富有逻辑严密性。如果不清楚汉英两种语言的这种差异,商务汉英翻译就可能出现逻辑不严谨或前后不连贯的句法修辞失误。

请对比分析以下商务汉英翻译实例：

⑩ (因为)目前没有舱位,我方不能安排9月装运发货,请见谅。

误译:There is no space available, we are sorry that we can't arrange for September shipment.

改译:We are sorry that we can't arrange for September shipment <u>because</u> there is no space available.

⑪ 这是高峰时间,饭店里闹哄哄挤满了人。

误译:It was the peak hour. The restaurant was seething with people.

改译:It was the peak hour <u>and</u> the restaurant was seething with people.

对比分析:以上误译受汉语意合型语言习惯的负面影响而不连贯,缺乏逻辑严密性。改译充分发挥英语的形合手段优势,把汉语原文的两个或三个小句融合成英语并列句。

1.2.2.2 警惕英译出现不间断句

因受汉语思维表达习惯的影响,许多学生在商务汉英翻译中该用连接词而没用,译出来的句子前后缺乏连贯,显得松散,很像汉语的竹竿句或流水句(serial clauses)。在商务汉英翻译中出现不间断句(run-on sentences)的修辞失误现象比较普遍。因此,我们务必要提防此类情况的出现,努力迎合英语形合型语言特点,在该用连接词的地方用连接词,把汉语几个短句合成英语的一个长句。

请对比分析以下商务汉英翻译实例:

⑫ 如果有问题,可以询问我方代理,他可以给您提供帮助。

误译:If you have problems, you can ask our representative, he may give you help.

改译:If you have problems, you can ask our representative, who may give you help.

⑬ 随函附寄我方试订单一份,请供现货。

误译:Enclosed is our trial order list, please supply us with your current goods.

改译:Enclosed is our trial order, and please supply us with goods from stock.

对比分析:以上误译因没用衔接句子的关系代词或连词而出现句法修辞问题——出现不间断句;改译所用关系代词和连词使英译句法严密、逻辑性强。

⑭ 他们对订购的裙装式样已经达成了一致,这是一件好事。

误译:They have reached an agreement on the style of the dresses ordered. It is a good thing.

改译:It is a good thing that they have reached an agreement on the style of the dresses ordered. (潘红,2004)

对比分析:上例误译纯属汉英之间一字一句地对译、硬译,而改译就采用了英语名词性从句和形式主语 it 的句式,使得译文更有形合型语言的句法特征。

1.2.2.3 警惕英译"该分不分,该合不合"

汉英句式存在较大差异,我们在进行英译时千万要警惕"该分不分,该合不合"的不合逻辑、前后不太连贯的情况发生。

请对比分析以下商务汉英翻译实例:

⑮ 海峡两岸经贸关系经过20年的发展,逐步形成了互补互利、日益紧密的经贸合作格局。两岸贸易额从1979年的0.77亿美元,增长到1999年的257亿美元。20年间两岸贸易总额超过1 600亿美元。到1999年年底,台湾在大陆投资项目近4.4万个,合同金额达446.7亿美元,实际投资为240亿美元,占大陆引进外商投资总额的7.8%。

误译:The economic and trade relation between the Mainland and Taiwan Province has greatly improved in last 20 years and has formed the structure of close cooperation and mutual supplement. The total trade volume between the two sides has increased from 77 million in 1979 to 25.7 billion in 1999 in US dollars. The total trade volume for the last 20 years is as high as 160 billion. By the end of 1999, total investment projects from Taiwan Province reached 44 thousand, the contracts' amount is 44.67 billion and the actual investment amounts to 24 billion. The number accounts for 7.8 percent of the total foreign investment in China.

改译:The economic and trade relations between the Mainland and Taiwan Province have greatly improved in the past 20 years, and a structure of close cooperation and mutual benefit has formed. Annual trade volume between the two sides increased from US $77 million in 1979 to US $25.7 billion in 1999, and the past 20 years totaled as much as US $160 billion. By the end of 1999, the number of investment projects from Taiwan Province reached 44,000, with contracts worth US $44.67 billion, and the actual use of US $24 billion. This number accounts for 7.8 percent of the total foreign investments in China.

对比分析:上例误译则是"该分不分,该合不合"导致的结果。因此,英译就显得有些汉式英语,缺乏英语意合型语言的特征。而改译充分发挥英语句法优势,将原文第二句和第三句合并,这样更合乎英语句法要求。

第二节 商务汉英尾重与头重之间的信息结构差异对比分析与翻译

◆ 2.1 商务汉英尾重与头重之间的信息结构差异对比分析

从信息结构来看,在汉英书面语体中形成了以信息重心为着眼点的三种句式:松散句(loose sentence)、圆周句(periodic sentence)和平衡句(balanced sentence)。圆周句又叫"掉尾句"或"尾重句",它是末端中心(end-focus)或句尾中心原则在语言交际中的应用。圆周句的特点是主要信息或实质部分迟迟不出现,直至句尾,以此造成一种悬念,吸引读者的注意力。圆周句结构较严谨,多用于正式语体。松散句又称"松弛句"。它与圆周句恰恰相反,它把主要信息或实质部分首先提出来,随后附加修饰语或补充细节。从属分句在主句之后的复合句就是松散句。松散句不像圆周句那样严谨有力,多用于日常谈话及非正式的书面语体中。另外,还有一种具有排比修辞功能的平衡句,这种句式可以达到信息均衡、结构工整的修辞效果。在商务汉英中,为了达到不同的修辞效果,松散句、圆周句和平衡句可以被交错使用。相比之下,商务汉语较多使用圆周句,而商务英语较多使用松散句。这一点是汉英两种不同语言在思维表达模式上的不同之处。

请对比分析以下商务汉英翻译实例:

① 即使是那些没有被告知情况严重的投资者都很清楚可能产生的后果,<u>这一事实给我们留下了极其深刻的印象</u>。(圆周句)

英译:<u>We were most impressed by the fact</u> that even those investors who were not told of the serious situation were quite aware of its potential outcome.(松散句)

② 我们已经开始了经营代销英国货物的业务,<u>特此通告</u>。(圆周句)

英译:<u>I have the honor to notify you that</u> we have commenced a business as commission agents for British goods.(松散句)

对比分析:例①②清楚地表明,汉语偏爱使用圆周句,而英语偏爱使用松散句。

究其原因,汉语句子一般注重尾重,状语、定语等修饰语往往在谓语动词或名词中心词之前。这就像演戏一样,把压轴戏放在后面。英语则相反,常常首先考虑信息的主题,然后按照"主—谓"语法框架常规一一排列。定语,特别是短语式定语和定语从句,通常在中心词之后;状语的位置比较灵活,可在句首,可在句尾,也可被插入句中。

请对比分析以下商务汉英翻译实例:

③ 该公司在美国纽约百老汇大街34号<u>设有办事处</u>。

英译:<u>The company operates a branch office</u> at 34 Broadway, New York, USA.(常玉田,2002)

④ 该货轮于2003年12月22日上午8时离开加拿大魁北克,将于2004年3月<u>2日抵达英国伦敦</u>。

英译:<u>The ship left Quebec, Canada</u>, at eight o'clock a.m. on the morning of December 22, 2003 and <u>is due to arrive in London, England</u>, on March 2, 2004.(常玉田,2002)

对比分析:汉语原文中,句子的信息重心都在末尾,而英译则将主要信息提至句首。

◆ 2.2 对商务汉英句法翻译的启示与警示

2.2.1 启示:实现信息重心的转移

汉英语句在信息结构的安排上有所不同,商务汉英翻译应根据汉语尾重而英语头重的差异进行恰当而地道的转换。

请对比分析以下商务汉英翻译实例：

⑤ 人们在家里利用网络进行远程通信的时代已经到来。

英译：<u>The time has come</u> when people telecommute by using the Web from home.

⑥ 请在规定的装船期前30天开出信用证。

英译：<u>Please establish the L/C</u> 30 days before the prescribed time of shipment.

对比分析：上例汉语原句均把主要信息"时代已经到来"和"开出信用证"放在尾部；而在英译中，信息重心被转移至句子的开头。

2.2.2 警示：英译"变"序，避免"尾重"

在商务汉英翻译中，我们必须了解汉英在逻辑顺序上的差异，照顾到"汉语重尾重、英语重头重"的语言表达顺序的差别，否则就极有可能译出一些不符合英语表达习惯的句子。

请对比分析以下商务汉英翻译实例：

⑦ 收到你方信用证30天内发货。

误译：Within 30 days after receipt of your L/C, <u>goods will be shipped</u>.

改译：<u>Goods will be shipped</u> within 30 days after receipt of your L/C.

⑧ 在4月至6月，分三批均装。

误译：During April to June in three equal lots, <u>shipment is to be made</u>.

改译：<u>Shipment is to be made</u> during April to June in three equal lots.

⑨ 在国际奥运会评估委员会4天的考察中，北京市并没有特意采取措施控制市区交通。

误译：During the ongoing four-day inspection tour by an International Olympic Committee evaluation commission for the city's bid to host the 2008 Olympic Games, <u>Beijing took no specific measures to control its traffic flow</u>.

改译：<u>Beijing took no specific measures to control its traffic flow</u> during the ongoing four-day inspection tour by an International Olympic Committee evaluation commission for the city's bid to host the 2008 Olympic Games.

对比分析：以上误译都是没有进行汉英信息重心从句尾向句首的转换。

⑩ 产品没有市场、长期亏损、扭亏无望和资源枯竭的企业，以及浪费资源、技术落后、质量低劣、污染严重的小煤矿、小炼油、小水泥、小玻璃、小火电等，<u>要实行破产、关闭</u>。

误译：Enterprises that cannot find any market for their products, entail long-term losses but are not expected to turn round, and suffer from the drying up of resources and small coal mines, refineries, cement works and glass factories and small thermal power plants that have been wasting resources, or are technologically backward, or are manufacturing poor quality products, or have caused severe pollution should also <u>be forced to declare bankrupt or close down.</u>

改译：<u>Bankruptcy and closing are the only options</u> for enterprises that cannot find any market for their products, entail long-term losses but are not expected to turn round, and suffer from the drying up of resources. Small coal mines, refineries, cement works and glass factories and small thermal power plants that have been wasting resources, or are technologically backward, or are manufacturing poor quality products, or have caused severe pollution should also be forced to declare bankrupt or close down. (常玉田, 2002)

对比分析：汉语原文属于典型的意合型语句，主语罗列了高污染、高耗能、低效益的小企业，然后才表达中心意思。像误译那样不断句重组、不变序改译，只会译出汉语式英语语句。

⑪ 此项贷款若属抵押贷款，<u>本协议应有借方书面声明，证明贷款银行有权将上述抵押品作为贷款抵押</u>。

误译：<u>The agreement shall be supported by the borrower's written declaration that the named securities acceptable to the bank are in pledge for repayment</u> if the loan is under collateral security. (松散句)

改译：If the loan is under collateral security, <u>the agreement shall be supported by the borrower's written declaration that the named securities acceptable to the bank are in pledge for repayment</u> of the loan. (圆周句)

对比分析：汉语原文属于典型的圆周句。原译将汉语圆周句译为英语松散句，则显得随意，先于结果发生的条件却置后，只起到补充作用。相比之下，改译所用圆周句按事物内在规律性表达，贴切、自然、一丝不苟（杨一秋, 2003）。

第三节　汉语突出话题与英语突出主语的句法结构差异对比分析与翻译

3.1　汉语突出话题与英语突出主语的句法结构差异对比分析

汉语是话题（topic）突出的语言。比如，"这部车他只花了400美元，跟白捡的一样"就是一句典型的突出话题——"这部车"的汉语语句。汉语注重话题而不是主语，在句法关系上作为施事者的主语往往可以被省略。只要句子意思表达清楚，逻辑主语有没有就不是主要的。正如语言大师王力所说，主语并非中国语法所需求，所以在凡主语显然可知的时候，以不用为常。例如：

① 待剩下的问题都解决之后就应立即开始安装。

英译：The installation should be commenced as soon as all the remaining problems have been cleared up.

② 香港与世界上其他大多数地区的不同之处在于其变化的速度。

英译：The pace of the change distinguishes Hong Kong from most of the other parts of the world.

相比之下，英语是主语突出的语言。英语主语是谓语讨论或描述的对象。所以，用英语斟词造句就必须有主语。例如：

③（期）盼早日订货。

英译：We are looking forward to receiving your order asap.

④ 须立即交货。

英译：Immediate delivery would be required.

由于英语每个句子都得有主语，因此对于某些汉语句子不用主语的空缺，英译就需要用物主代词 it 来填充。例如：

⑤（该职位）有时需要在业务时间加班，但公司提供丰厚的一揽子福利条件。

英译：You will sometimes be required to work unsocial hours but an excellent benefits package is offered.（潘红，2004）

⑥ 承你方订货，实感荣幸，祝你们推销货物圆满成功。

英译：It is certainly a pleasure to have this order from you and we wish you the best of success in your sales promotion of the goods.

3.2 对商务汉英句法翻译的启示与警示

3.2.1 启示：英译须补出主语

我们在商务汉英翻译中,应时时牢记英语"主语"的概念,或补出主语,或改选主语,或用 it 来填补汉语无主句的主语空缺,或将汉语无主句译为形式主语。

请对比分析以下商务汉英翻译实例：

⑦ 首先要积极调整出口商品结构,进一步扩大机电产品出口,加快纺织品、服装、轻工业产品等传统出口商品的升级换代,提高高新技术产品的出口比重,增加农产品的出口。

英译：First of all, it is imperative to adjust the export product mix: we must expand exports of electric and mechanical products, speed up the upgrading of such traditional commodities as textiles, garments and other light industrial products, increase the proportion of the exports of high and new technology products, and boost exports of farm produce.

⑧ 据发现,987号商品所含的那种化学成分没有达到合同规定要求。

英译：<u>It</u> was found that the chemical content of Item 987 is not up to the contract stipulation.

⑨ 有的设计师在面料、服装设计上创造了许多动物或其变异图案纹样,这些是不是他们心目中的图腾？抑或是他们的审美观顺应了相当一部分人的需要？都有可能。

英译：We often see animal patterns or their variations on material or a finished garment. Could they be the totems of the designers? Or are they merely designed to go with many people's sense of beauty? <u>Both</u> are likely.

对比分析：上例的汉语原句均为无主句。例⑦的英译将汉语原句中的状语改写成了英语的主语；例⑧的英译是把 it 用作形式主语；例⑨的英译补出了隐含的主语 both。

3.2.2 警示：英译不要缺少主语

汉语偏重话题说明而隐称主语,英语偏重"主语—谓语"结构而必须有主语,鉴于汉英之间的这种句法修辞差异,商务汉英翻译中就可能出现缺少主语的句法修辞失误。

请对比分析以下商务汉英翻译实例：

⑩ 希望我们建立平等互利的贸易关系。

误译：Hope that we can enter into equal trade relations to our mutual benefit.

改译：It is hoped that we can enter into equal trade relations to our mutual benefit.

⑪ 盼早日收到贵方订单。

误译：Look forward to your order at an early date.

改译：We are looking forward to your order at an early date.

对比分析：上例误译都是将汉语无主句死译成无主语的英语句子。改译或补出了形式主语it，或加上了汉语隐含的主语we。

第四节　商务汉英人称与物称之间的句法修辞差异对比分析与翻译

4.1　商务汉英人称与物称之间的句法修辞差异对比分析

汉语多用有生命的词语作句子的主语，它还比较多地使用拟人化的说法，行为主体或句子主语常常由人或以人为本的机构来担当。这就是汉语突出人称（personal）的句法修辞倾向。

英语的句法修辞特点之一就是其物称（impersonal）主语的倾向，即英语有着以抽象名词和物质名词作主语的句法修辞特点。在文体正式的书面英语中，这种句法修辞倾向就更明显。利奇（Leech）和斯瓦特维克（Svartvik）在《英语交际语法》（1974：25）一书中指出"Formal written language often goes with an impersonal style; i.e. one in which the speaker does not refer directly to himself or his readers, but avoids the pronouns I, you, we. Some of the common features of impersonal language are passives, sentences beginning with it, and abstract nouns."。钱歌川在《英语疑难详解》（1978：178）中指出："我们说英文时，惯常都要用人或生物作主语，而英文则爱用无生物作主语。"比如，英语习惯使用"It is my hope that …"这种非人称主语，而不常用"I hope that …"。物称较多地用于商务英语文体，其目的是使表述更加客观。

请对比分析以下商务汉英翻译实例：

① 我们可以肯定，如您能将我们的产品和其他供应者的类似品种进行公正的比较，您定会相信我们的价格是合理的，并乐于接受我方2008年3月15日函中的报价。

英译：It is our firm belief that a fair comparison of quality between our products and similar articles from other sources will convince you of the reasonableness of our prices and as a result, you will be ready to accept what we quoted in our letter of March 15, 2008. (孟广君,2009)

② 如果不能把名字和脸对上,你可能会失去赚大钱的生意机会。

英译:Failure to connect a name and a face can cost you a lucrative business opportunity.

③ 如果您稍稍浏览英国伯明翰新展览中心举行的食品饮料展的宣传册,您就会随即感到:亲临会展,一定不虚此行！因为该会展吸引了英国食品饮料行业的专家达40 000多名,展会内容和活动新颖独特,曾被许多参展商们誉为"2004年度英国规模最大的食品饮料展"。

英译:A glimpse of the brochure will make you feel that it is worth the efforts for the visit to Food & Drink Expo at the NEC, Birmingham, UK, which attracted well over 40,000 industry professionals from across the entire food and drink industry in Britain, with a variety of creative programs or activities and is embraced by many exhibitors as the UK's biggest events for the whole food and drink industry in 2004. (孟广君,2009)

对比分析: 例①②③的汉语原句均以"人"为句子主语,其英译也无一例外地把句子的主语转换成了"物"。这种"人""物"之间的汉英转换符合英语的语言表达习惯。

中国哲学主张"天人合一""物我交融",强调主体意识,强调人对客观事物或人本身的作用或影响。因而汉语句子习惯以人或拟人化的事物为出发点来叙述世界万物。相比之下,西方哲学重视理性,强调客观。思维的目标往往指向外界,探求客观世界对人的影响。因而英语句子常常用物或抽象概念作主语,倾向于让事物以客观事实的形式表现出来。英语语言的这种客观性特征在商务英语实用文体中更加突出。

请对比分析以下商务汉英翻译实例:

④ 该公司二季度共出口各种重型设备49台(套),赚取外汇总计880万美元。

英译:The export of 49 heavy-duty equipment pieces in the second quarter this year has earned the company a total of US $8.8 million in foreign exchange. (常玉田,2002)

⑤ 这几年,中国的经济快速而健康地发展。

英译:The recent years have witnessed a quick and healthy development in China's economy.

对比分析: 例④的汉语原句采用了一个类似于人的名词作话题,而英语翻译是将汉语原句中的"出口"这一事实用作句子主语;例⑤在英译时把汉语原句的状语"这几年"转换成了句子主语。这种转换使英语语言表达更加客观。

4.2 对商务汉英句法翻译的启示与警示

4.2.1 启示:实现从人称到物称的转换

"英语常用被动式,采用物称表达法;汉语常用主动式,采用人称、泛称或隐称表达法。"(连淑能,1993:83)中国人习惯于主体思维,常以具体的人来陈述客观事物和事实,因此汉语中以人为话题的句子很多。西方人习惯于客体思维,常以客观事实作为说话的对象,以物为主语。商务汉语中以人为话题的句子在英译时常常需要被转译为以客观事物为主语的句子。因此,在商务汉英翻译中,我们应根据汉英两种语言之间的区别,实现从汉语人称到英语物称的转换。

请对比分析以下商务汉英翻译实例:

⑥ 我们被展销会上展出的那辆轿车给迷住了。

英译:The beautiful car exhibited at the exhibition really caught our eyes.

⑦ 我们发展企业集团,要遵循客观经济规律,以企业为主体,以资本为纽带,通过市场来形成,不能靠行政手段勉强撮合,不能盲目求大、求全。要在突出主业、增强竞争优势上下功夫。

英译:The development of enterprise groups should abide by the law governing the economy, and enterprises should be regarded as the main body and capital as the link. Enterprise groups must be formed by the market and should not be produced by administrative means. There should not be a blind chase to make them as large and all inclusive as possible. Efforts should be made to emphasize their main business and increase their superiority in competition. (常玉田,2002)

对比分析:例⑥的汉语原句的主语是人,而英译则是将用作宾语的"那辆轿车"转换成了英语的主语;例⑦的汉语原句的主语是"我们",而英译中的主语变成了表示行为的名词化短语 the development of enterprise groups。

4.2.2 警示:不要"人""物"不变

在英语里,人和物都可作句子的主语,而汉语在这个位置上一般只放指代人的词(潘文国,1997)。鉴于汉英两种语言间的这种差异,我们在商务汉英翻译中必须注意英语"物称"的修辞倾向,否则就会发生误译。

请对比分析以下商务汉英翻译实例:

⑧ 他借了另一笔助学款,进了大学。

误译:He got another grant and entered the university.

改译：Another grant took him to the university.

对比分析：上例原译的错误就在于受到了汉语偏爱人称的句法修辞习惯的负面影响，而没有进行从汉语人称到英语物称的转换。

⑨ 特别是在销售部，人们感到，经理对员工所付出的努力并不赏识。

误译：Particularly in the Sales Department, the staff feel that managers are unappreciative of their efforts.

改译：The perception that managers are unappreciative of staff efforts is particularly noticeable in the Sales Department.（Wood, 2002）

对比分析：上例原译只是字对字式的死译，它在英译中没有进行汉语人称与英语物称的转换。做了物称转换的改译顺应了商务英语报告客观性文体修辞的要求。

第五节　商务汉英主动语态与被动语态之间的句法修辞差异对比分析与翻译

5.1　商务汉英主动语态与被动语态之间的句法修辞差异对比分析

在英语中，被动语态是人们比较喜欢使用的一种表达形式。而被动语态在商务、法律等领域的英语应用文体中的使用情况如何呢？

英语被动语态在应用文体、科技文体中用得极为普遍。被动语态强调受事者，有将它置于话题主位（thematic position）的语用功能；被动语态常用来表示说话者对所提出的话题（或人或事或物）持有某种客观态度，因而比较婉转。例如：

① 与敝公司有着多年生意往来的查尔斯先生向阁下推荐了贵公司。

英译：Your firm has been recommended to me by Mr. Charles, with whom we have done business for many years.

② 如蒙早复，不胜感激。

英译：Your early reply will be highly appreciated.

③ 来宾请出示入场券。

英译：Visitors are requested to show their tickets.

④ 买卖双方同意按下列条款买卖下述商品，并签订本合同。

英译：This Contract is made by and between the Buyer and the Seller, whereby the Buyer agrees to buy and the Seller agrees to sell the under-mentioned commodity according to the terms and conditions stipulated below.

相比之下,汉语较少使用被动句,这在商务汉语中也是如此。在许多情况下,汉语通过许多非被动形式来表达被动意义。现代汉语中没有"被"字的被动句源自古代汉语,比有"被"字的被动句的历史更悠久(王力,1957)。这一点体现了汉语被动语态的复杂性。尽管汉语被动语态需要用"被"来表示,但是汉语只在不得已的情况下才用"被"字句,因为"被"字句一般被认为是很书面化的语言,而且让人感到别扭。汉语的被动语义可以通过"给""让""受""由""遭""加以""得以"等词语来表达。有时,当受事主语与动词搭配而语义不会造成误解时,干脆就不用句中表示被动的词语,如"书已经卖完了"。由此可见,汉语不太用含有"被"字的被动句。例如:

⑤ 所有易货合同项下供货的支付都得通过清算账户结算。

英译:All payments for the supply of goods under the barter contract shall be settled through the clearing account.(叶玉龙、王文翰、段云礼,1998)

⑥ 该笔生意系由贵方贸易部经理格兰特先生与我方销售部经理李小姐口头确认的,每吨单价为40美元。

英译:The business is confirmed verbally by your Business Manager Mr. Grant to our Sales Manager Miss Li at a price of US $40 per ton.

◆ 5.2 对商务汉英句法翻译的启示与警示

5.2.1 启示:进行变"态"处理

汉语多用主动语态,而英语多用被动语态。因此,在商务汉英翻译中,我们需要在以下三种情况下做变"态"处理。

5.2.1.1 基于汉英差异,译成英语被动句

由于汉英两种语言在被动句使用上的差异,有些汉语主动句要被译成英语被动句。具体来讲,汉语非人称主语主动句、无主句、不定人称句等常被译成英语被动句。

请对比分析以下商务汉英翻译实例:

⑦ 任何企业都可以以合伙的方式经营。

英译:Any business may be operated as a partnership.

⑧ 软件出口享受优惠利率的信贷支持。

英译:The export of software is backed by credit with concessionary interest rates.

⑨ 必须强调,买方应于收到本合同之日起三日内签字并返还合同的副本,如买方不这样做,卖方保留取消合同的权利。

英译:It must be essentially stressed that the Buyers are requested to sign and return the duplicate of this Contract within three days from the date of receipt. In the event of failure to do this, the Sellers reserve the right to cancel the Contract.

⑩ 人们都认为那些单证早已寄出。

英译：Those documents <u>are supposed</u> to have been sent out.

对比分析：例⑦⑧的汉语原句的主语是非人称主语"任何信息情报"和"软件出口"，所以英译都进行了变"态"处理；例⑨的汉语原句是无主句，英译进行了语态转换；例⑩的汉语原句的主语的不定人称代词"人们"隐含在英译的被动语态之中，所以更显简洁。

5.2.1.2 出于修辞目的，译成英语被动句

为了行文方便或流畅，出于修辞目的，我们常把一些汉语主动句译成英语被动句，使句子主语保持稳定。

请对比分析以下商务汉英翻译实例：

⑪ 美国贸易代表团是10点到的，我们热情接待了他们。

英译：The American trade delegation arrived at 10:00 o'clock and <u>was given</u> a hearty reception.（余富林等,2003）

⑫ 我们确认已经收到贵方9月25日的订单，并保证按时交货。

英译：We acknowledge receipt of your order of 25 September, <u>which will be shipped</u> to you on time.

对比分析：例⑪⑫的汉语原句中的第二个动词出于修辞目的都被转换成英译中的被动语态。

5.2.2 警示：警惕汉语无"被"字句对英语的负面影响

由于受汉语无主句、不用"被"字表示被动意义的影响，中国学生的"被动意识"不强。所以，商务汉英翻译中该用被动语态却没用的句法修辞失误比较常见。

请对比分析以下商务汉英翻译实例：

⑬ 过几年，这里将建一个全新的工业园。

误译：In a few years, here will build a brand-new industrial park.

改译：<u>A brand-new industrial park</u> will be built here in a few years.

⑭ 必须强调产品的更新换代。

误译：We must emphasize the upgrading of product.

改译：<u>Emphasis</u> must be laid on the upgrading of product.

⑮ 对文物出口的年代是有限制的。

误译：The export of relics that date back beyond a defined dividing year has restriction.

改译:Restriction is imposed on the export of relics that date back beyond a defined dividing year.

⑯ 这项工程搬迁了许多工厂和学校。

误译:This project has moved many factories and schools.

改译:Many factories and schools had to be relocated for the implementation of this project.

⑰ 办公室不准抽烟。

误译:The office allows nobody to smoke.

改译:Smoking is forbidden in the office.

对比分析:例⑬⑭的汉语原句都是无主句,误译"照葫芦画瓢",也译成了无主句,改译都是把宾语提前用作英译主语,所以语态就发生了转换。例⑮的汉语原句虽没有用"被"字,但是它暗含被动的语义,所以误译所用主动语态显然不对,改译灵活地将原文加以变"态",这更加有利于英译语句的平衡。例⑯⑰的汉语原句虽有主语,但主语不是动作执行者,误译只是从表层结构出发,不假思索地把汉语原句进行了逐字硬译,错误地译成了英语主动句。只要稍加分析,我们就会发现汉语原句的主语不是真正的主语,英译须进行变"态"处理,译出真正的主语。

思考与练习

1. 思考题

(1) 在句法层面上,商务汉英之间的主要差异有哪些?

(2) 如何跨越商务汉英之间的主要差异,实现有效的汉英翻译转换?

2. 句子翻译

(1) 当时的经济繁荣是几个因素共同作用的结果。

(2) 您会注意到我们的每一个产品都是用百分之百的天然原料制成的。

(3) 人们赚钱后很快花掉,随着汽车销量与流量的增加,汽车业从经济繁荣中获利颇丰。这意味着给汽车制造、公路修筑、路边餐馆建造以及广告业这些方面创造了更多的就业机会。

(4) 在本进口许可证被批准后,我们将开立以贵方为受益人的不可撤销的信用证。

(5) 我们为这次耽误给您和其他老客户造成的不便深表歉意。

(6) 我们就此事已经与法律顾问联系过。他们告知我们:如果你方对我方提出索赔的指控,我方将不负法律责任。

(7) 你们的人参酒质量很好，但包装较差、瓶子易碎、纸盒太薄，对于我们今后的订货，请每瓶套一只泡沫塑料套，并装在较厚的纸盒内，否则我们只能放弃这项业务。

(8) 出口商必须很好地考虑运往国外货物的包装，并尽量按买方的要求包装货物。

(9) 出口包装的结构必须考虑到经济与实效。出口商应记住，货物应该采用一种能保证安全到达目的地和便于在转运中搬运的方式进行包装。

(10) 我们的印花棉布系用木箱包装，内衬牛皮纸和防潮纸。每箱30匹，一花五色，平均搭配。

(11) 每年的两届交易会把几乎所有的外贸公司和出口商品集中起来，统一到广州展出、成交，减少了我们到国外推销的支出，外商也可只派少数人到会选购，不必花大量的人力到我各口岸寻找生意，节省了买卖双方的费用，深受国外经营各种商品的中小客商的欢迎。

(12) 为适应国际市场的变化和国内客户的需求，适时加大了开拓业务的力度。

(13) 本机床厂创建于1935年，自1949年新中国成立后，经过大规模的改建和扩建，成为中国最大的车床生产专业厂，技术实力雄厚，工艺手段先进，具有现代化的设备条件和管理水平，计量与试验测试装置齐全，因此生产的产品性能稳定、质量优异。

(14) 更为重要的是，法国人没有能够在诸如机床、照相机、计算机等需求量最大的、他们称之为拳头产品的市场上占据重要的一席之地。

(15) 浙江真丝印花绸采用精细手工印制，花样新颖别致，色彩鲜艳夺目，实是各式名贵服装和礼服的理想的高级用料。

3. 语篇翻译

- 语篇1

由于我厂进行了生产效率检查，促使厂内普遍采取了更迅速有效的操作方法，现在我厂的生产效率已经提高了50%以上，经理部拟在办公室职工中开展同样的检查制度以降低成本。为了适应外部环境的激烈竞争，我们的意图是寻求减少不必要的工作环节的方法。经理部鼓励职工提出改进办公室工作常规的建议，并将给予提出最切实可行的建议者一个月额外工资的嘉奖。请于下个月月底前将建议提交总经理办公室。

- 语篇2

观念创新是西门子公司的一个悠久传统。原来的西门子霍尔斯克公司已发展成为今天在世界电气和电子市场上富有高度革新精神的领导者。由西门子有限公司和一大批海内外子公司组成的当代西门子公司继续在前进的道路上建起一座座里程碑。

西门子公司在35个国家拥有生产设施并且构建了一个全球性的销售网络。它拥有30多万雇员，是世界电气、电子工业中最大的公司之一。其1986—1987年财政年度销售额为540亿德国马克。远见卓识和坚实可靠的管理与朝气蓬勃的活力和改革创新的热情相结合，这就是西门子公司的特点所在。

- 语篇3

尊敬的先生：

  谢谢你公司5月6日提出关于600台"牡丹"牌电视机的订货，但是由于你公司坚持以在圣诞节前交货为条件，我公司深感遗憾，不能像过去多次供货那样供应这批货物。

  目前生产厂商无法满足对这一型号电视机的需求。我公司曾于一个月以前提出24台的订货，但被告知，所有订单均将严格按次序排队，我方订单在2月初以前无法得到处理。

  从今晨收到你公司电传中获悉，你方买主不愿意考虑其他牌号，建议你公司试同北京的中国轻工业品进出口公司联系，他们或许能帮助你公司解决。

谨启
2020年5月10日

- 语篇4

哈尔滨冰雕节

  可能没有其他地方会比1月份的哈尔滨更寒冷彻骨，但这并不意味着人们会因此只待在家里不出门。相反，届时会有许多来自世界各地的人们相聚在冰天雪地的哈尔滨，庆祝一年一度的冰雕节。冰雕节于每年的1月5日至2月25日举行，来自世界各地的参赛选手参加角逐，竞争"最佳冰雪艺术奖"。入夜，当千万盏闪烁的彩灯照亮冰雕时，五彩缤纷的冰雕显得更加迷人。

第八章

商务汉英语段语篇对比分析与翻译

Identify the problems in the following translations

① 该厂能生产大衣、西装、时装、衬衣、毛衣等不同类型服装的上千个花色品种纽扣,产品规格齐全、品种繁多、造型新颖。

英译:The factory can produce various new types of buttons in thousands of different designs for coats, suits, fashions, shirts and sweaters. They come in different colors and specifications.

② 本奶粉含有维生素 A、B_1、B_2、B_6、B_{12}、C、D、E、K、PP、胡萝卜素、蛋白质和乳脂,以及强化维生素 A 和 D,其营养价值与新鲜牛奶相同。(翁凤翔,2007)

英译:This milk powder contains vitamins A, B_1, B_2, B_6, B_{12}, C, D, E, K, PP, carotene, protein, and milk fat, plus enrichment with vitamins A and D and it gives you the same nutritional value as fresh milk.

③ 目前,居民储蓄存款增加较快,银行资金比较充裕,利率水平较低,市场价格稳定,国债余额占国内生产总值的比重仍在安全线以内,发行长期建设国债还有一定的空间,不会有大的风险。

英译:At present, people's savings deposits have increased considerably. Banks have sufficient funds. Interest rates are low. Market prices are stable. The ratio of national debts to GDP is still within safe limits. There is still room for issuing more long-term treasury bonds for construction without incurring great risks.(李长栓,2004)

在商务汉英语篇中,无论是商务信函、商务合同,还是商业广告、企业简介,大多都有分段的问题。分段的目的是使文章条理清楚、意思明确。商务汉英的语段倾向于短小。以商务信函为例,短小语段不仅使信函外表美观,而且能使读者更快地抓住写信者表达的要点(Gartside,1989)。

组句成段,布局谋篇。"篇"就是以某种方式构合在一起、以达到某种整体修辞意图而采用的一系列相互关联的交际功能。旨在"有事说事"不加评述的商务汉英应用文的语篇大多不长,如商业通知、商业备忘录、商业信函等,其中有些语篇短到只有一句话,甚至一个词、一个短语,如商务标识语、商业广告、商标品名等。但在此,我们主要关注至少有几个句子的语篇。

经过仔细分析商务汉英的不同语段语篇,我们发现,在语段语篇的组织结构、思想内容安排、谋篇布局上,汉英两种语言都有明显不同。由于翻译极少在段篇这个层次上操作(Newmark,1988),所以下面将简略地对商务汉英语段语篇层面上的差异进行对比分析,继而浅探商务汉英语段语篇层面上的翻译转换问题。

第一节　商务汉英语段差异对比分析与翻译

1.1　商务汉英语段差异对比分析

1.1.1　商务汉英语段结构组织的差异对比分析

汉语的说明描叙特点是按时间顺序、动作次第展开,思维和话语的推进顺势而下。汉语的断句不太严格,但这无碍汉语表达。古汉语的文章一般不断句,更不要说分段了。一般来说,汉语语段没有明确的主题句,而英语语段十分强调主题句。一个好的语段必须有一个完整意思,而这个完整意思往往是通过主题句来组织的。主题句揭示语段的中心思想,其他语句都是围绕它来展开论证或说明的。

请对比分析以下商务汉英语段实例:

①　当前,经济全球化、保险金融混业经营的趋势增强,科技革命迅猛发展,全球保险产业结构调整的步伐加快,国际保险资本进行了史无前例的大规模兼并、重组,跨国保险公司在全球保险市场上的竞争实力和地位重新形成。面对国际保险业发展的新潮流,我国保险业既面临引进更多资金、技术和管理经验,促进产业结构优化升级的发展机遇;也面临着保险市场主体增多,国际化竞争日趋激烈的严峻挑战。在这样的历史条件下,中国保险行业协会的成立对我国保险业站在时代高度、以更加积极的姿态迎接保险市场开放的挑战、抓住机遇加快发展、提高国际化竞争能力、实现整体的产业开放具有重要意义。(常玉田,2002)

② These cultural challenges exist side by side with the problems of doing business in a foreign language. Language, of course, is full of difficulties—disaster may be only a syllable way. But the more you know of the culture of the country that you are dealing with, the less likely you are to get into difficulties. It is worth the effort. It might be rather hard to explain that the reason why you lost the contract was not the product or the price, but the fact that you offended your hosts in a light-hearted comment over an aperitif. Good manners are admired: they can also make or break the deal.（琼斯、亚历山大，2000）

对比分析：通过对汉语语段与英语语段进行对比分析，我们发现，汉语语段没有一个总览全段的中心句。而英语语段则不同，它的第一句就是一个概括全段中心思想的主题句。另外，我们还发现，汉语语段内部句子中的逗号使用频繁，表明汉语断句的随意性较大；英语语段内部句子之间使用了大量的连词、介词、关系代词、关系副词和其他关联词，语句之间衔接紧密。

以上涉及的是商贸报刊文章中的语段情况。虽然上述情况可以说明汉英语段结构组织之间的一般差异，但是商务汉英语篇不同于一般性文章，它们大多是应用性实用文体，并且"体中有体，类中有类"。因此，商务汉英文体在语段结构组织上有其特别要求：一事一段（One point, one paragraph.）。正如 Gartside（1989）所说，"In business writing we tend to divide our material into small topics and to use shorter paragraphs than is customary for literary work"。既然是一事一段，那么商务汉英语篇（商务信函、通知、广告、合同、说明书、报告）大多篇幅不长，语段大多较短，独句段所占比例不小。在商务汉英短小语段中，一般是找不到主题句的。客观地说，按照"一事一段"的原则来布局组段，主题句是根本不需要的。这是商务汉英语篇对语段的客观反映与真实要求。

此外，像商务报告、报价函、说明书、合同、信用证之类的商贸汉英语篇，大多采用分项列表法来组织语篇，其中的语段很短，大多只是一个短语。但有一点，无论是汉语语篇，还是英语语篇，分项列表中的项目前往往有一个提纲挈领式的关键词。

请对比分析以下商务汉英语段：

③ 汉语说明书：

"长城"牌方便面

品种：鸡蛋面、番茄面、茄汁面、麻辣面、虾黄面、肉松面。
特点：快速方便，营养丰富，味美价廉，老幼皆宜。
方法：沸水冲泡 5 分钟即可食用；若煮沸 2～3 分钟味道更佳。
方便面将为您的就餐提供省时、省力等种种方便。

××食品总厂方便食品车间生产

④ 汉语商品调研报告

外商对我国抽纱质量的反映

去年外商对我国抽纱出口提出 80 起索赔或退货要求,个别口岸高达 20～30 起。索赔数量之大,在我国抽纱出口史上前所未有,给国家造成很大的经济损失,严重地影响了我国抽纱在国际市场上的声誉,挫伤了经营者的信心,也影响了我国抽纱的出口。

对方提出索赔的原因有以下几种:

a. 质量不符合要求

这几年由于经营抽纱的口岸增多,产区盲目生产,很多绣花女工没有经过严格培训就接受了抽纱加工任务,结果出现了绣工粗糙、漏工缺线、针脚不齐、芭花不平、尺寸做小、接拼露针眼、锁扣露毛边等不符合质量要求的现象。据统计,绣工质量差的约占整个索赔的半数以上。

b. 工作差错

有些业务员由于外语水平不高,没有完全理解外商的要求,或者在谈判时没有做详细记录,结果把外商对原料的选择、花型的修改、颜色的搭配、包装要求等搞错了。如有一个德国商人下订单时,再三说明要独幅绣花台布,而我方却做成了拼幅绣花台布,外商要求索赔30%。

c. 包装问题

以往各口岸对抽纱进行包装时,一般都以棉纱绳捆扎,现在多用塑料绳。由于塑料绳是化纤材料制成的,有的会透过牛皮纸和塑料袋将其本身颜色沾染在抽纱品上。对此,外商要求索赔。

此外,还有些口岸没有按照外商的要求进行包装,造成外商在国外返工,增加了外商的费用。

d. 货物发错

仓库人员由于工作粗心,将抽纱的颜色、规格、型号等发错。

e. 原料用错

抽纱原料不符合要求,布匹经纬纱横竖不齐,疵点较多,绣花线颜色褪色,等等。

f. 检验不严格

有些抽纱出现污点、水渍、黄斑、油迹、受潮、熨烫不平等现象。

g. 其他方面的原因

如超配发放、品种归类搞错、发放不及时等造成索赔。

抽纱是我国出口达数亿美元的"拳头"商品,在国际市场上享有一定的声誉。但是最近几年以来,特别是从去年起,抽纱质量急剧下降,外商意见很大。

为了开创抽纱出口的新局面,建议做到:

a. 各级领导要把抽纱质量提高到重要的议事日程上来抓，完善各项规章制度，建立岗位责任制。

b. 停止盲目发展绣花队伍，对绣工要进行严格考核，不符合条件的不准从事绣花业。

c. 抽纱工针有数百种之多，各地区都有传统特点。各分公司应根据本地区的绣花能力接订单，严禁抢客户、争订单，不顾本地区的加工能力搞成交。

d. 加强对业务员的培训。业务员要懂外语、熟悉商品、熟悉业务的各个环节。

e. 在推销库存货时，对存放时间较长的抽纱品，在出运时要打开包装检查，防止受潮、褪色的商品出口。

⑤ 英语产品说明书

Kenwood Dynamic Microphone MC-550 Instruction Manual

Main Features

- The magnet is made from neodymium so that high level and high quality sound is produced.

- The unit employs a double dome diaphragm in order to achieve a well-balanced sound quality from the lower range to the upper range.

- A light duty CCAW (aluminum wire) is employed for the voice coil in order to achieve a crystal clear sound quality.

- A reliable Canon brand connector is employed.

Operating Instructions

- Insert the microphone plug into the microphone terminal.

- Flip the microphone switch to the "ON" position and adjust the volume with the volume control knob on the amplifier.

- When handing the microphone to somebody else or when finish using, flip the microphone switch to the "OFF" position.

Handling Precautions

- If the microphone head is covered by hand or the microphone is approached to the speaker, a howling sound may be generated. This phenomenon of howling is caused by the microphone picking up the sound output from the speaker. To prevent this, first decrease the volume, then place the microphone so that it is not pointed to the speaker and that there is a sufficient distance between the microphone and the speaker.

- The microphone is sensitive equipment. Do not drop, hit it or apply strong shock to it.

- Do not store the microphone in a place with high temperature or humidity.

Pointer for Proper Use of Microphone

The optimum distance between the microphone and the mouth is from 5 to 10 centimeters. If the microphone is too close to the mouth, the sound may be unclear with too much enhanced base (proximity effect) or may be uncomfortable to ears with pop noise generated every time when the singer breathes in and out.

Specifications

Type	Dynamic microphone
Directivity	Undirectional
Impedance	600 ohms
Frequency response	60 to 17,000 Hz
Sensitivity	−52 dB
Cords	6 mm dia., 5 m. With 6.3 mm dia. Standard phone plug
Dimensions	Max diameter 54 mm; Max length 170 mm
Weight	215 g, without cord

⑥ 商务英语报告

Report on Ramsden Breweries and Bute Chemicals: Investment Potential

Introduction

This report aims to assess which company, either Ramsden Breweries or Bute Chemicals, we should invest in.

Ramsden

The company had mixed results last year; although turnover increased by approximately 25%, net profit rose by less than 4%. However, restructuring may be able to eliminate these inefficiencies and expected growth in the drinks industry suggests opportunities for increased profits.

Bute

Results were disappointing, with turnover and profit both falling slightly. Nevertheless, the company managed to increase its dividend to shareholders. The rumored merger seems likely to push up the share price considerably.

Conclusion

Despite the merger rumors, any investment in Bute Chemicals would involve a risk. Ramsden, on the other hand, despite its present inefficiency, is still profitable and has definite potential for further growth.

Recommendation

We would recommend investment in Ramsden Breweries.

对比分析: 以上商务汉英语篇的语段短小,少则几个名词短语并列在一起组成一个语段,多则两三个句子。这就是"一事一段"的商务文体对语段布局要求的体现。

1.1.2 商务汉英语段内句与句之间的关联词对比分析

一个语段内,句子的组织安排要符合逻辑顺序(logical order),做到句子之间上下衔接、前后连贯,以利于中心思想的明确表达。使用关联词(linking words)可以增强语段的连贯性。这些关联词是指示读者的路标,使读者期待下面发生的事,提高读者的理解速度。另外,关联词还可以起到许多不同的作用:强调思想;表示时间顺序或过程;表示因果关系、比较、对比;等等。

请对比分析商务汉英翻译中可以使用的不同类别的关联词:

(1) 表示进一步说明的关联词有:此外/additionally、又/again、也/also、同样地/likewise、此外/moreover、此外/furthermore、和/and 等;

(2) 表示因果关系的关联词有:因此/accordingly、因此/as a result、所以/consequently、因此/for this reason、所以/so、因此/therefore、因此/thus、既然如此/under the circumstances、因为/because 等;

(3) 表示事件顺序或过程的关联词有:然后/after、以前/before、最后/finally、第一/first(ly)、第二/second(ly)、同时/meanwhile、其次/next、当……时候/when、直到/until 等;

(4) 表示澄清、举例的关联词有:例如/for example、比如/for instance、我的意思是说/I mean、即/that is、换言之/to put it another way、换言之/in other words、也就是说/that means、即/namely 等;

(5) 表示矛盾或转折关系的关联词有:实际上/actually、但是/but、然而/however、事实上/in fact、却/instead、虽然/though 等;

(6) 表示比较的关联词有:像/like、同样地/similarly、与……一样/the same as 等;

(7) 表示对比的关联词有:与……相对/as opposed to、相比之下/by contrast、相反/conversely、相反地/on the contrary、另一方面/on the other hand 等;

(8) 表示总结的关联词有:总之/in conclusion、总的来说/to sum up、下结论说/to conclude、简而言之/in short、简言之/in brief 等;

(9) 表示强调的关联词有:特别/in particular、特别/especially、尤其/particularly 等;

(10) 表示让步的关联词有:无论如何/anyway、无论如何/at any rate 等;

(11) 表示一般性的关联词有:一般来说/generally speaking、一般地/in general、通常地/normally、一般来说/as a rule、通常/usually 等。

除了上述种种外显衔接之外,汉英两种语言都使用词语重复或同义词来实现语段内的语句衔接。"重复"是汉语的一大衔接手段:同一词语或词组可以在文中重复出现,以求表达准确有力。这与汉语的意合型语言特征有关。因缺少连词、代词、介词在语篇衔接中的帮助,汉语依靠词语的简单重复来增加句子的凝聚力便是很自然的了。但是,英语也常使用"重复"来达到语段内语句之间的衔接。例如:

⑦ 由于不同行业正逐步开始依赖一些共同的技术,新技术使公司开展多元化经营变得更加容易。例如,微软公司正忙于扩大经营范围,从事有线电视、移动通信和网络视频业务。这家美国软件巨头拥有美国电信电话公司50亿美元的股权……

英译:New technology is making it easier for companies to diversify as different industries come to rely on common technologies. Microsoft, for instance, is busily diversifying into cable and mobile telecommunications as well as WebTV. The US software giant has a $5bn equity stake in AT&T, which recently bought Media One for $57bn. Under the deal, Microsoft will succeed in … (Wood, 2002)

◆ 1.2 对商务汉英语段翻译的启示与警示

1.2.1 对商务汉英语段翻译的启示

1.2.1.1 以段为单位来翻译

与单句相比,段落更有利于翻译时的综合考虑,可供译者调整语序、选择句型的余地较大。与句子相比,语段不是一连串句子的简单组合,而是一个语义的整体。语段内各句之间有连接、替代、省略、照应等关系。因此,进行汉英翻译时,我们要对汉语原语段进行必要的调整,以保证英译段落的完整性和连贯性,使译文重点突出、传神流畅。

请对比分析以下商务汉英翻译实例:

⑧ 我们要进一步加强税贸协作,加快退税进度,减轻外贸企业的负担,改变接受单证时间,由原10—20日提前至5—15日,力争受理后30天内退税完毕,进一步落实自营进出口生产企业"免、抵、退"税收政策,为企业用好用活外贸资金创造条件。

英译:The taxation authorities will reschedule the receiving dates of documents from the 10th -20th every month ahead to the 5th -15th, and try to pay the rebates within 30 days after receipts of applications. Moreover, the tax offices will continue to implement the policies of "exempting, offsetting and rebating" taxes and duties to enterprises permitted to export on their own, and by doing these to create conditions for them to make the most of their fluid assets. (常玉田,2002)

1.2.1.2 "拆段"翻译法

汉英两种语言在段落组织上有差别。汉语可将所讲述的几个不同的内容囊括在一个段落之中,而英语通常按叙述的细节分段。对于具有同样内容或长度的文章,英语往往段落数量多一些,这在报刊文章中十分显著。汉译英中的"拆段"是指将原文中比较长的段落化整为零,按内容细节分段译出。

请对比分析以下商务汉英翻译实例:

⑨

重庆南部新城开发建设征集策划运作单位

重庆主城区南部新城,面积33平方公里,重庆李家沱和马家溪两座长江大桥横跨其间,是商家置业的黄金口岸。为实现国家西部大开发战略,我们计划进行全面开发建设。诚征"新城"策划(规划)运作单位,有意者请与重庆市巴南区西部办联系。

英译:

Request for Proposals for Development Plans
The "New Town" Project of Chongqing

The office of the Development of the Western Regions in Banan District, Chongqing City, invites qualified urban planners to submit proposals to design and plan the full-scale development of the New Town in the southern section of the city proper.

The site of the project, with a total area of 33 square kilometers, is a spectacular setting strategically located, embracing the two Yangtze River bridges at Lijiatuo and Majiaxi. It is a port promising unrivaled opportunities for commercial and real estate investments.

The project is part of the effort to implement the national program for the development of the west regions of the country. A decision has thereof been made to carry out a full-scale development of the "New Town" project, which calls for competitive proposals of development plans. Interested parties are advised to apply to the Office of Bana District for the Development of the Western Region.

1.2.2 对商务汉英语段翻译的警示

1.2.2.1 不受汉语语序约束,英译变"序"

商务汉英语篇的许多语段是独句段。语段中的唯一句子往往较长,结构较为复杂。翻译成英语时,我们要对汉语原语段中独句的语序进行重新调整和安排,否则就会有悖于英语的句法修辞习惯;有时,还要将其拆分成几句,以避免汉语"流水句"式的汉式英译。

请对比分析以下商务汉英翻译实例:

⑩
速溶全脂奶粉

本速溶全脂奶粉选用优质 A 级牛奶精制而成,加水即可调成营养丰富的天然牛奶。

本奶粉含有维生素 A、B_1、B_2、B_6、B_{12}、C、D、E、K、PP、胡萝卜素、蛋白质和乳脂,以及强化维生素 A 和 D,<u>其营养价值与新鲜牛奶相同</u>。

有待改进的译文:

Instant Full Cream Powder

This instant full cream powder is made from the Premium Grade A milk. To prepare it you simply mix the powder with water and instantly you have nutritious, natural full cream milk.

This milk powder contains vitamins A, B_1, B_2, B_6, B_{12}, C, D, E, K, PP, carotene, protein, and milk fat, plus enrichment with vitamins A and D and <u>it gives you the same nutritional value as fresh milk.</u>

改译:

Instant Full Cream Powder

This instant full cream powder is made from the Premium Grade A milk. To prepare it you simply mix the powder with water and instantly you have nutritious, natural full cream milk.

<u>This milk powder gives you the same nutritional value as fresh milk</u> because it contains vitamins A, B_1, B_2, B_6, B_{12}, C, D, E, K, PP, carotene, protein, and milk fat, plus enrichment with vitamins A and D.

对比分析: 汉语语篇的第二段只有一个长句。原译文从表面上看并无大碍,语义信息在英译中并无流失。但是,我们仔细分析一下会发现,汉语原文属于圆周句,这完全符合典型的汉语"尾重"的信息结构特征,但是按照汉语圆周句的修辞结构所做的直译就有些不符合英语的修辞表达习惯。英语偏爱松散句,一般把信息重心置于句首。由此可见,改译顺应了英语的修辞表达习惯,不失为得体而地道的英译。

1.2.2.2 不受汉语原文束缚,进行增、删、补、改

汉语喜欢连用四字结构或三字结构,有时"一发而不可收拾",就会产生浮夸渲染的负面修辞效果;相比之下,英语注重客观而精确的表达。所以,英译就需要增、删、补、改。

请对比分析以下商务汉英翻译实例:

⑪迪庆藏族自治州位于云南省西北部滇、川、藏三省市交界处,这里有冰山雪

川、江河峡谷、湖泊草甸,美丽而宁静。川内以藏族居民为主,还居住着傈僳族、纳西族等 20 多个民族。长期以来,这里各民族和谐相处,创造了独特而灿烂的文化——山川秀美、民风淳朴、历史悠久,<u>与詹姆斯·希尔顿笔下的香格里拉极其相似</u>。

误译:Diqing Tibetan Autonomous Prefecture, located at the junction of Yunnan and Sichuan Province and the Tibet Autonomous Region, is filled with glaciers, deep canyons, meadows, and lakes, so it is beautiful and tranquil. Residents here are mainly Tibetans who coexist peacefully with over 20 other ethnic groups, including Lili and Naxi groups, thus creating a unique and splendid culture that is reflected in beautiful scenery, simple, honest and unspoiled people and a long history. It remarkably resembles that of the Shangri-la described in Hilton's novel.

英译:Located at the junction of Yunnan and Sichuan Province and the Tibet Autonomous Region, the scenery in picturesque Diqing, filled with glaciers, deep canyons, meadows, and lakes, <u>remarkably resembles that of the Shangri-la described in Hilton's novel</u>. Residents here are mainly Tibetans who coexist peacefully with over 20 other ethnic groups, including Lili and Naxi groups, thus creating a rich and unique culture.

对比分析:原汉语语段为旅游宣传介绍材料。整个语段符合汉语尾重的修辞结构特征,但是英译时不能一字一句地对译、死译(如上示误译),而应该按照英语的信息结构特征和形式逻辑要求进行重组,把段尾句子"与詹姆斯·希尔顿笔下的香格里拉极其相似"提前,并将破折号后的汉语惯用的(并无多大实际意义的、浮夸的)评述性话语"山川秀美、民风淳朴、历史悠久、文化丰富"省去不译,这样译文结构更加紧凑、信息更加突出。(贾文波,2004)

1.2.2.3 不受汉语语段限制,英译"拆段"

汉语语段偏长,而商务英语语段编排的一个重要原则是"一事一段",所以英译应拆段,避免英译语段过长。

请对比分析以下商务汉英翻译实例:

⑫ 改革开放和创办经济特区以来,珠海市外经工作取得了长足的进展,珠海经济特区的经济与国际经济日益相连,整体素质不断提高。当前,经济发展和改革开放都进入了新的历史阶段,为了适应新形势,营造功能型的环境优势,拓宽投资领域和融资渠道,推动珠海市外经工作向更广的领域、更深的层次发展,必须采取一切切实可行的措施。

误译:Since the adoption of reform and opening up policies and the establishment of special economic zones, Zhuhai of Guangdong Province has made tremendous progress in its foreign trade and international cooperation. Increasingly linked to the global economy, the Zhuhai Special Economic Zone has been improving itself in every aspect of the growth endeavor. Now that both the economic development and the opening up have entered a new phase, the following measures are to be made and adopted in an effort to build up a friendly environment in which different functions can be undertaken smoothly, to broaden both the areas for foreign investment and appropriate financing channels, and to push Zhuhai's foreign trade and cooperation on to yet another new stage.

改译：Since the adoption of reform and opening up policies and the establishment of special economic zones, Zhuhai of Guangdong Province has made tremendous progress in its foreign trade and international cooperation. Increasingly linked to the global economy, the Zhuhai Special Economic Zone has been improving itself in every aspect of the growth endeavor.

Now that both the economic development and the opening have entered a new phase, the following measures are to be made and adopted in an effort to build up a friendly environment in which different functions can be undertaken smoothly, to broaden both the areas for foreign investment and appropriate financing channels, and to push Zhuhai's foreign trade and cooperation on to yet another new stage.（常玉田，2002）

对比分析：原汉语语段仅有一段，这种情况在汉语语篇建构中司空见惯。相比之下，英语语段较短，一事一段，简明扼要，层次分明。

第二节　商务汉英语篇差异对比分析与翻译

2.1　商务汉英语篇差异对比分析

商务汉英的应用范围十分广泛，在长期使用过程中，根据事务的性质和应用的场合逐渐形成了固定的篇章结构形式和言语程式。作为商务应用文文体，商务汉英的语篇主要包括商务信函、商务报告、商务合同、商务计划书、产品说明书、企业宣传资料、商业广告、旅游宣传资料、商用标识语等。一方面，不同语篇有着不同的篇章格式和言语程式；另一方面，同一语篇的篇章格式和言语程式还表现出汉英两种语言的不同思维表达上的差异。倾向于螺旋式（spiral pattern）思维表达的中国人喜欢使用较间接（indirect）的语言表达方式,而偏爱线性思维表达方式(linear pattern)的西方人则倾向于较直接(direct)的语言表达方式。请观察分析以下信函：

①

Dear Jeremy,

I won't bore you with the details but the bottom line is someone in inventory control (who was terminated as a result) wasn't doing his job and we've run out of stock on several important items unexpectedly. Needless to say we're in "crisis mode" and we depend on you to <u>fill the attached order at once</u>. Please call if there's a problem with this.

Sincerely yours,

Dustin Bodack

②

Dear Jeremy,

<u>Please rush the attached order as fast as you can</u>. We have run out of stock unexpectedly. Will you help us out?

To be sure you got this order and to check on its status—as well as to thank you personally for whatever you can do to speed up the shipment—I'll call you Thursday morning.

Sincerely yours,

Dustin Bodack

（霍莉·罗迪克,2005）

对比分析：例①的订货函有些像是中国人所写或所译,信函的写法可能受到汉语思维表达习惯的影响而不够开门见山。信函一开头就是一通解释,说明紧急订货的缘由——"someone in inventory control (who was terminated as a result) wasn't doing his job and we've run out of stock on several important items unexpectedly"。如果读者不耐烦的话,就很可能随手将其扔进了废纸篓。商人大多很忙,没有时间也没有耐心读这种婆婆妈妈的信函。按照国际商务英语信函的语篇建构模式,如果所写的不是坏消息,信函就应有事说事、直截了当。信函一开头最好就直奔主题,如例②的信函开头——"Please rush the attached order as fast as you can."。由此可见,不同民族的思维、不同语言的篇章修辞模式是不同的。

2.2 对商务汉英语篇翻译的启示与警示

2.2.1 启示：调整改写，归化转换

既然汉英两种语言在篇章模式与言语程式上存在差异，商务汉英语篇翻译就应根据不同的语篇类型，按照汉英相应的篇章模式和言语程式进行调整改写，做归化转换处理。请对比分析以下商务汉英翻译实例：

③ 从晋代开始，峨眉山一直为佛教普贤道场，是中国四大佛教名山之一，距今已有一千多年的文化史。峨眉山高出五岳、秀甲天下，山势雄伟，景色秀丽，气象万千，素有"一山有四季，十里不同天"之妙喻。清代诗人谭钟岳将峨眉山佳景概为十景："金顶祥光""象池夜月""九老仙府""洪椿晓雨""白水秋风""双桥清音""大坪霁雪""灵岩叠翠""罗峰晴云""圣积晚钟"。现在人们又不断发现和创造了许多新景观。进入山中，重峦叠嶂，古木参天，峰回路转，云断桥连；涧深谷幽，天光一线；灵猴嬉戏，琴蛙奏弹，奇花铺径，别有洞天。春季万物萌动，郁郁葱葱；夏季百花争艳，姹紫嫣红；秋季红叶满山，五彩缤纷；冬季银装素裹，白雪皑皑。

峨眉山以优美的自然风光、悠久的佛教文化、丰富的动植物资源、独特的地质地貌而著称于世，素有"峨眉天下秀"的美誉。唐代诗人李白诗曰："蜀国多仙山，峨眉邈难匹。"明代诗人周洪谟赞道："三峨之秀甲天下，何须涉海寻蓬莱。"当代文豪郭沫若题书峨眉山为"天下名山"。古往今来，峨眉山就是人们礼佛朝拜、游览观光、科学考察和休闲疗养的胜地。

英译：<u>Known for</u> a thousand years as one of the four Buddhist sacred mountains in China, Mt. Emei is <u>hence featured by</u> its Buddhist cultural heritages together with its diverse geographical land-forms and beautiful scenery. Now many new sights have been found and developed in the mountain areas besides its ten old ones such as Elephant Bath Pond, Cave of Nine Old Men, the Hongchunping Mountain Glen, etc. <u>Filled with</u> weird peaks, tranquil valleys, winding roads, abrupt waterfalls, luxuriant vegetation, aged trees as well as wild animals (especially the playing monkey groups), the mountainous scenery abounds in changes with seasons, <u>which</u> earns Mt. Emei the reputation of "The Most Elegant Mountain" in China and has been of all ages a resort for sightseeing, pilgrimage, the health recuperation and even scientific researches. (贾文波，2004)

对比分析：通观汉语全文，上下段内容多处重复，并且不少语言表达并不具体，纯粹出于汉语行文需要，以渲染诗情画意来感染读者或潜在游客。若我们将原文全

盘译出,势必造成译文行文堆砌、语义重复。其实,从原文下划线部分即可看出这两段文字的实际含义:前一段为细节描述,后一段为评述性总结。在对原文的信息进行抽象概括之后,英译重新行文布局,对原汉语语篇予以整合,将原文两段合并成译文的一段。增减补改后的译文表明,对原文信息的选择一定要根据翻译目的和译语读者的需要,不可全盘皆取。

2.2.2 警示:增删补改,避免死板硬套

在对诸如商业广告、企业简介、旅游宣传资料之类的商务汉英"呼唤型"功能语篇或文本进行翻译转换时,切忌死译、硬译。正确的对策是不受汉语原语篇的篇章布局的束缚,根据译入语的篇章模式和言语程式,按照译文读者的语言文化习惯,进行增删补改,不拘一格。

请对比分析以下商务汉英翻译实例:

④ 改革资金缴拨方式,将以多重账户为基础的分散收付制度,改为以国库单一账户体系为基础、资金缴拨以国库集中收付为主要形式的现代国库管理制度。

误译:Chinese government will reform its capital payment and allocation style, and change the decentralized revenues and expenditures system on the basis of multiple accountings into the modern treasury management system with the treasury unitary accounting system as its basis and treasury concentrated revenues and expenditures as its main style of capital payment and allocation.

改译: The Chinese government will set up a modern treasury management system by replacing the current multiple accounts with a single account, thus centralizing collection and allocation of funds.

对比分析:照原文一字不漏地译出来,译文就很啰唆冗余,比如,capital payment and allocation style, revenues and expenditures, accounting 重复出现两次。所以,在不改变汉语原义的基础上,改译对原文进行了简化处理。

思考与练习

1. 思考题

(1) 商务汉英在语段结构上有什么差异？可以采用的有效翻译转换策略有哪些？

(2) 商务汉英在篇章结构上有什么差异？可以采用的有效翻译转换策略有哪些？

2. 句子翻译

(1) A：他们在附近超市买饮料吗？

　　B：不，不过我们在这里买。

(2) 联邦、州和地方各级政府力求增强公众的安全感，确保公平竞争，并提供一系列普遍认为更适于公有企业而非私有企业来管理的服务。

(3) 如有管辖法院认为此项贷款协议中的某一部分无效或无法执行，此项贷款协议的其余部分将仍然有效并可在法律允许的最大范围内付诸实施。

(4) 如果可能的话，请她一块吃午餐以加深了解。把这当作一次招聘面试，因为事实就是如此。

(5) 此后，曾去函佩龙先生不下四次，说明若亲自前往领取项链，须行程200英里，十分不便，故请代为邮寄，但均无回音。可否请您与佩龙先生联系，请其尽快将项链寄来？

(6) 成年之前就患有的听力失聪会逐步严重并伴随人的一生。虽然听力失聪是世界第一健康问题，但几乎90%的患者都任其发展而不去治疗。对成千上万的患者来说，常规治疗听力失聪的办法有经常去医院，进行昂贵的检查、校正以改善你的听力。现在由于有了晶体助听器，解决听力问题变得非常方便。几乎90%的轻度失聪的人及上百万听力衰退的人都能得到晶体助听器的神奇帮助。而且，它的优良设计是节能型的，电池可以连续使用几个月。现在，有了晶体助听器，医生可以通过一个小型的扩音器有效地帮助人们治疗听力问题。

3. 语段语篇翻译

● 语篇1

到一定的时候，你无疑需要引进新的机器、物品以及工作程序，而这些都有可能引发新的隐患。如有重大变化，你必须把它考虑进去。不管怎么说，对风险随时做出新的评估是件好事。虽说不要因为每一细小的变化或每项新的工作内容就对风险评估重做修改，但是如果一项新的工作本身就带有新的重大隐患，你就有必要对此做出相应的考虑，采取一切必要措施以减少风险。

- 语篇 2

公司非凡的研发能力使洛克希德公司在航天、导弹、太空及军事电子工业方面独具优势。它使我们成为更有实力的竞争者，使我们更有能力主持国家的优先项目，也更有能力开发出质量可靠、价格适宜的技术。所有这些优势正是人们期望一流航天公司所具有的，也正是您能从洛克希德公司得到的。

- 语篇 3

可口可乐的新招是全球首创的立体电视广告，可口可乐将通过杂货店和连锁快餐店，向全国观众分发 4 000 万副特制的立体电视观赏眼镜。这点子虽然聪明，但这种标新立异的做法却遭到有些评论家的公开谴责。政治专栏作家乔治·威尔抱怨说："如今的广告宣传实在做得太过分了。"那么，立体广告是要，还是不要？对登广告者来说，这真是一个问题。

- 语篇 4

狩猎和植物采集经济统治达几十万年才让位于农业经济。农业经济延续了 10 000 年左右。随后是工业经济。工业经济最早于 18 世纪 60 年代始于英国，最先于 20 世纪 50 年代初结束于美国。现在，信息经济已经行程过半，从开始到结束将持续 75—80 年，于 21 世纪 20 年代后期结束。然后人们准备迎接下一种经济形式：生物经济。

- 语篇 5

重要的不是经营什么而是办公地点

随着大千世界似乎逐渐趋同，顾客们感到难以区别无数种相似的产品和服务，因此人们认识到公司形象在赢得顾客和留住顾客方面起着越来越重要的作用。

然而，对于"公司形象"的内涵为何，人们意见不一。有些公司认为，"公司形象"仅仅局限于一个易认的标识和一句好记的口号。而另一些公司则认为，"公司形象"有着更广泛的内涵：它涉及从选择明星做产品的广告代言人，到选择接待室的壁纸颜色，再到选择实际的办公地点。实际办公地点的选择乍一看没什么，实际上更能体现公司的特点及其理念。花点时间考虑一下各种选择以及每一种选择对潜在的顾客意味着什么吧！

你是否想把公司的地点选在市中心的古式建筑，摆出公司富有传统、历史悠久，但也许是十分因循守旧的企业形象？还是会迁入远离市中心的专门设计的商业新区，与成功的跨国公司（或者可能是你的竞争者）为邻，以强调乐观、自信和现代感？甚至在破旧的工业园区边缘安一间不起眼的办公室与厂房毗邻，也可以显示贵公司的职业道德和对必需品投资的重视，而不是浪费金钱在会议室布置些小摆设，如米罗或莫奈的画。

III. 分论 (2)

> *Translating consists in reproducing in the receptor language the closest natural equivalence of the source language message, first in terms of meaning and secondly in terms of style.*
>
> ——Eugene A. Nida
>
> 即使书写或翻译一份公告、通知都需要作者驾驭言简意明的表达手段,做到适体,即最简单的艺术性。
>
> ——刘宓庆

第九章

商务汉英文体对比分析与翻译

Identify the problems in the following translations

① 打开门,恭候您的就是您梦寐以求的家。无论您企盼的是一座乡间宅第,抑或是一间摩天大楼的顶屋,翻开下面几页就可以看到世界上最高雅的住宅供您选择。(商务广告)

英译:The home of your dreams is waiting for you now. What do you want, a country house or a penthouse in the sky? Just open the booklet, you'll find the world's most elegant houses.

② 新公司应建立经营管理机构负责企业的日常经营管理工作。

英译:The new company shall establish a management office which shall be responsible for its daily management.

③ 对于贵方的合作,我方深表感激之情。

英译:Thanks for your cooperation.

文本创作者在创作时所传达的语言信息对形式的选择绝不是随意的(random),也不是无目的的,而是必然有一定的修辞立意(rhetorical preconception)。作为一种社会交际手段的翻译,必须关注源语的具有修辞功能的形式立意,因为形式立意是意义转换的组成成分,缺了它,源语的全部意义就不能尽可能忠实地被传达出来。针对商务语篇无修辞审美的问题,刘宓庆(2001:100)批评指出,"语言表达无时无刻不伴随着审美(包括审美意识活动、审美判断和审美功效),即使书写或翻译一份公告、通知都需要作者驾驭言简意明的表达手段,做到适体,即最简单的艺术性"。2003 年,他进一步明确指出,只要原文承载意义、具有语言交际功能、有翻译价值、有交流传播目的,在翻译中就必然存在一个遣词酌句的审美问题……有人认为翻译文艺小说要审美,翻译科技论文、法律条文、合同契约等非文艺文体不要审美就是因为他们没有看到翻译中不分文本一律要求遣词酌句等文字优化工作本身就是审美活动。刘宓庆在此特别强调的是,非文艺文体肯定有修辞审美问题，译者也必须有修辞审美意识（rhetorical and aesthetic awareness），通过文字优化工作来进行准确而得体的翻译活动，以确保审美功效。例如，在对"付现交货"（动宾+动宾：结构对称工整）这个短语进行翻译时，译者只有在对其进行修辞审美分析之后，才能对其修辞进行优化处理，以保证功能对等翻译，如 cash on order（名词+介词+名词：结构对称工整）。

以上所说的文体其实就是语篇所用的语域，就是按照文本所用语域划分而来的语篇类型。商务汉英的主要文体或语篇类型有商务信函、商务报告、商务合同、商务计划书、产品说明书、企业宣传资料、商业广告、旅游宣传资料等。"当我们观察各种语境中发生的语言活动时，我们发现，针对不同情境选用的适用语言类型是各不相同的。"（Halliday, 1964）。

第一节　商务汉英文体特征对比分析与翻译

商务英语是在商务环境中应用的英语（Jones & Alexander, 1989），所以它必定就有着受商务语境制约的不同于普通英语的文体特征。商务汉语也是如此。

总的来说，商务文体"用词简练规范，内容具体，专业性强；句式结构严谨，表达准确，句意完整；语篇独具特色，语体正式，措辞礼貌"（谢建平，2008：179）。所以，在商务汉英文体翻译中，我们应时刻对语篇文本的文体属性保持高度的敏感和觉悟。翻译时，我们应先考虑语篇文本服务的活动领域，以及由此而来的文体属性，从而确保选择恰当的文体语言进行英译转换。"语贵适境，文贵适体"在具有语言服务于社会功能这个特点的商务文体翻译中表现得非常显著。

请对比分析以下商务汉英翻译实例：

① 本协议的任何一方都不得在本协议有效期间，采用出售、抵押、赠送或其他与履行本协议规定的义务不相一致的方式，处理其拥有的合营公司的任何股份。

英译：Neither of the parties hereto shall at any time during the continuance hereof deal with any of the shares of the Joint Company owned by it whether by sale, pledge, gift or otherwise in any manner inconsistent with the carrying out of its obligations thereunder.

对比分析：此例属于契约合同文体，句式较长，用词正式。汉语原文使用了诸如"不得""本""其"这样的语体正式的字词或古文言词。相应地，英译则使用了一些古体词，如 hereto, hereof, thereunder 等。这些都是合同或协议所具有的重要的文体语言特征。

② 此报盘以我方最后确认为准。

英译：This offer is subject to our final confirmation.

对比分析：汉语语句为外贸报盘套语，具有法律语言的文体特征，英译再现了原文的文体信息。

③ 人们普遍感到，公司竞争对手提供的工资水平较高。

英译：It is generally felt that the company's competitors offer higher levels of remuneration.

对比分析：汉语语句为商务报告调查结果的常用句型。与汉语原文相比，英译采用被动语态来陈述调查结果，这就反映了"语言朴实、客观公正"的报告文体特征。

④ 九铁动力 拓新领域（九铁广告）

英译：The Way Ahead

对比分析：此例属于广告文体，句式简短，用词抽象，带有文学语言色彩。汉语原文选用汉语惯用的四字结构，前后对称；英译用词更加简练，诱发人们的想象力。由此可见，汉英广告翻译已经基本脱离了翻译框架，属于重新创造的一类。（张新红等，2003）

除了上述有别于普通汉英的商务文体的文体语言特征以外，诸如商务信函、商务报告、商务合同、产品说明书等商务文体的子文体自有其本身的文体语言特征。

◆ 1.1 商务信函的文体特征及其翻译

商务信函"重纪实，少文饰"，有着"公事公办的持重感"，所以文体正式，语言简练，行文规范，表达准确，语篇具有较强的语域特征和目的性。商务汉英信函翻译应该把握上述商务信函的文体特征，尽量达到商务信函翻译的标准——"事实准确、礼貌得体"（马会娟，2005）。

请对比分析以下商务汉英翻译实例：

⑤ 所有电传报盘五日内有效，发电传的那一日包括在内。

误译：All offers by telex are open for five days.

改译：All offers by telex are open for five days inclusive of the date of dispatch.

对比分析：误译漏译了原文的信息内容，所说时间不够详尽精确。

⑥ 在我们这样大的公司，订货少于 2 000 件，我们很少接受。

误译：In a company as large as ours, we seldom take an order of less than 2,000 pcs.

改译：Please note that it is not our common practice to take an order of less than 2,000 pcs.

对比分析：第二句英译与第一句英译相比更委婉间接,因此也就更礼貌得体。

◆ 1.2 商务合同的文体特征及其翻译

商务合同属于契约体,具有法律语言的特征。合同语言庄重,行文规范,措辞严谨,正式程度较高。为了确保商务汉英合同翻译规范得体,我们需要参照执行"准确完整、通顺得体"的翻译标准(马会娟,2005)。

请对比分析以下商务汉英翻译实例:

⑦ 保险责任:从被保险人踏入本保险单上指定的航班班机(或等效班机)的舱门开始到飞抵目的港走出舱门为止,被保险人因遭受意外伤害,自伤害发生之日起180日内身故或残疾,保险公司按所附给付比例表进行一次性给付。

英译：Coverage: This policy covers the Insured from his/her embarkation onto the aircraft as per the flight number designated in this Policy (or a replacement flight) to his/her disembarkation out of the aircraft at the designated destination. In case the death or disablement befall on the Insured within 180 days since the accident occurred during the aforesaid flight, the Company will pay the Insured or his/her appointed beneficiary for a recoverable claim in a lump sum as per the Indemnity Scale attached hereto.

对比分析：此汉英合同的保险条款用词庄重得体,如"自伤害发生之日起180日内""as per the Indemnity Scale attached hereto"等;措辞严谨,如"从被保险人踏入本保险单上的指定的航班班机(或等效班机)的舱门开始到飞抵目的港走出舱门为止""from his/her embarkation onto the aircraft as per the flight number designated in this Policy (or a replacement flight) to his/her disembarkation out of the aircraft at the designated destination"。此外,英译还补加了 during the aforesaid flight 这个介词短语,是为了避免人们误解成离开机舱后半年之内由于别的原因而出现意外也有索赔的权利。(常玉田,2002)

⑧ 异议索赔:如果卖方不能在合同规定期限内把整批或一部分的货物装上船,除非人力不可抗拒原因或者取得买方同意而修改合同规定外,买方有权在合同装船期满二十天后撤销未履行部分的合同。如果货到目的口岸而买方对品质有异议时,买方可以凭卖方同意的公证机构出具的检验报告,在货到目的口岸三十天内向卖方提出索赔,卖方须根据实际情况考虑理赔或不理赔,一切损失凡由于自然原因或属于船方或保险公司责任范围内者,卖方概不负赔偿责任。如果买方不能在合同规定期限内将信用证开到或者开来的信用证不符合合同规定,卖方可以撤销合同或延期

交货,并有权提出索赔要求。

英译:Discrepancy and Claim: In case the Sellers fail to ship the whole lot or part of the goods within the time stipulated in this Contract, the Buyers <u>shall</u> have the right to cancel the part of the Contract which has not been performed <u>20 days following the expiry of the stipulated time of shipment</u>, unless there exists a Force Majeure cause or the Contract stipulation has been modified with the Buyers' consent. In case discrepancy on the quality of the goods is found by the Buyers after arrival of the goods at the port of destination, the Buyers may, <u>within 30 days after arrival of the goods at the port of destination</u>, lodge with the Sellers a claim which should be supported by an Inspection Certificate issued by a public surveyor approved by the Sellers. The Sellers <u>shall</u>, on the merits of the claim, either make good the loss sustained by the Buyers or reject their claim. It is agreed that the Sellers shall not be held responsible for any loss or losses due to natural causes of the Insurance Co. ; <u>in case the Letter of Credit does not correspond to the Contract terms and the Buyers fail to amend thereafter its terms in time</u>, after receipt of Credit opened by Buyers does not reach the Sellers within the time stipulated in the Contract, the Sellers shall have the right to cancel the Contract or to delay the delivery of the goods and shall have also the right to claim for compensation of losses against the Buyers.

对比分析:汉英合同的异议索赔条款的措辞同样庄重严谨,如"除非人力不可抗拒原因或者取得买方同意而修改合同规定外"(unless there exists a Force Majeure cause or the Contract stipulation)、"如果买方不能在合同规定期限内将信用证开到或者开来的信用证不符合合同规定"(in case the Letter of Credit does not correspond to the Contract terms and the Buyers fail to amend thereafter its terms in time)等。特别值得一提的是,英语译文所用表达权利与义务的 shall 和古体词 thereafter 更为合同的神圣与庄严增添了不少色彩。

◆ 1.3 商业说明书的文体特征及其翻译

商业说明书包括产品说明书和企业宣传说明书。企业宣传说明书旨在对企业和其他商业组织进行介绍、说明,以使其在大众心目中树立良好的社会形象。产品说明书旨在对产品的性能、特征、用途、用法等进行介绍、说明,以便消费者购物时做出正确的选择。说明书必须"通俗易懂,对企业或产品进行客观描述,有一说一、有二说二,不能用任何夸大的语言来欺骗大众或消费者"(翁凤翔,2002:253)。根据商业说明书的文体特征,我们在进行汉英商业说明书翻译时应该遵循以下翻译标准:简明客观,地道规范,特别是对产品说明书进行翻译时应注意广告美学功能(李明,2007),保持其技术和知识的传播性(谢金领,2007)。

请对比分析以下商务汉英翻译实例:

⑨ 注意事项
- 请将瓶竖直放置于儿童触及不到且阴凉之处。
- 不可饮用。若不慎误服,应立即饮下大量牛奶或开水,并请医生治疗。
- 勿与眼接触。若不慎入眼,请用清水冲洗15分钟以上,并请医生治疗。
- 使用时请戴上乳胶手套。

英译:

CAUTIONS
- Keep out of reach of children and keep bottle upright in the cool place.
- Do not drink. If swallowed, take plenty of milk or water and consult a physician.
- Avoid contact with eyes. If it gets into the eyes, flush with water for at least 15 minutes and consult a physician.
- Wear rubber gloves during use.

对比分析:汉英产品说明书中的注意事项或须知条款言简意赅,如汉语"勿""且"等,又如英语 if swallowed, during use。因为属于须知条款,所以所用句式均为祈使句。

⑩ "老城隍庙五香豆"流传至今,颇受东南亚华侨宠爱,生意兴隆,口碑载道,尝者百吃不厌,齿颊留香。

英译:

"Old Town God's Temple Five-Flavored Beans" have long been a favorite snack among many overseas Chinese in Southeast Asia. They have been selling well with a good reputation. You will never be fed up with this snack. Once you have some of them, their good flavor will linger long in your mouth. (刘法公,2004)

对比分析:产品说明书具有与商业广告类似的文体特征:语言极具渲染力,具有煽情功能。

1.4 商业广告的文体特征及其翻译

作为极具"商业价值的实用文体"(秦秀白,1986:197),商业广告总是具有很强的说服力,其作用就是"引人注目、唤起兴趣、刺激欲望、令人信服、敦促行动"(秦秀白,2002:298);其主要文体特征是简洁明快、通俗易懂,富于描述、表现力强、诙谐幽默、富于美感

(谢建平,2008)。遵循"劝购功能相似"的原则,商业广告汉英翻译并不要求字字对等的"忠实"翻译,而是要实现一种极为灵活的对等,即译文的受众是否像原广告的受众一样乐于掏钱购买商家所宣传的产品(马会娟,2004)。

请对比分析以下商务汉英翻译实例:

⑪ 衣食住行,有龙则灵。(中国建设银行龙卡广告)

英译:

Your everyday life is very busy,

Our *Long*Card can make it easy.

对比分析:汉英广告都实现了广告文体的"呼唤功能"和"劝诱功能",特别是英译把 Long(龙)写成了斜体,以便与英语单词 Long 区别开来。(顾维勇,2005)

⑫ "贵州茅台酒 38% V/V"系贵州茅台酒的系列产品,是用贵州茅台酒经先进的科学方法精制而成的白酒。它既保持了酱香浓郁、典雅细致、协调丰满、回味悠长等贵州茅台酒的独特风格,又具有加水、加冰后不混浊和风格不变等特点,<u>深受国内外各界人士的欢迎</u>。(李明,2007)

英译:

Maotai Liquor 38%, Your New Expression of Life

<u>Want to break away from convention?</u> Get ready for a new life? Then <u>try our new Guizhou Maotai Liquor 38%</u>. An unconventional blend of tradition and innovation. It unleashes your passion for life. Rich. Aromatic. Extra fine. Crystal-clear. Life has never been expressed better. Maotai Liquor 38% (V/V), the new born star that draws cheers worldwide.

Maotai Liquor 38%, <u>your new expression of life</u>. <u>Anything you ask for</u> ... the answers are all in it.

Express yourself better. With Maotai Liquor. <u>As always</u>. (李明,2007)

对比分析:汉语广告始终突出的是产品本身,所用句式均为陈述句;而英译则采用了大量的以用户为中心的祈使句,如"Then try our new Guizhou Maotai Liquor 38%.""Express yourself better."等,还采用了两个省略 You 的"Want to break away from convention? Get ready for a new life?"的疑问句。此外,英译广告词甚至没有翻译汉语原文略显自夸而无多大实际意义的评述性话语——"深受国内外各界人士的欢迎"。

第二节 对商务汉英文体翻译的启示与警示

2.1 启示：分析与优化文体修辞，英译分"体"别类

文体修辞的基础是语域（register），译者通常是通过它来掌握源语的文体特色。词汇、语法形式、句子结构、篇章模式等都有修辞色彩，并可用来实现特定的文体修辞意图或目的。在修辞优化过程中，译者主要通过炼词炼句，提高源语与译语语篇的可读性，以及确定文体风格及其对应体式等方式。

商务领域涉及的文体类型较多，有公文体（如：商业信函）、广告体（如：商务广告）、契约体（如：商务合同、协议）、应用体（如：请柬、说明书）、论说体（如：商贸评论）等。对于如此繁杂的文体类型，若无敏感的文体修辞意识，译者在进行汉英翻译时就有可能"跑调串体"，出现文体修辞失误。

请对比分析以下商务汉英翻译实例：

① 贵方须更换受损的轴承。

误译：You have to replace the damaged bearings.

改译：We will appreciate it if you replace the damaged bearings.

对比分析：此例是一句商务信函用语。误译语气生硬，没有传译出源语正式的文体风格信息。改译语气委婉，文体正式，实现了译语与源语文体风格信息的对等转换。

2.2 警示：切合原文文体，不能"跑调串体"

语篇由于受其使用范围的制约而有各种不同的类型，不同的语篇类型有着不同的语篇构建模式。语篇信息的发送者和接收者对语篇使用场合的适切性都很敏感，语篇范围的错位要么导致出现异常的修辞效果，要么就会使交际失败。不同的语篇类型总是有自己使用频率较高的词汇、句式和语篇结构。因此，商务英语言语交际者要对不同语篇类型的特点做到心中有数，并不断提升自己的文字修养（李运兴，2000）。也就是说，在商务汉英文体翻译中，我们应"文贵适体"：时刻对语篇的文体属性保持高度的敏感和觉察。在充分把握语篇的社会用途和文体属性的基础上，我们应该选择恰当的文体，以达到刘重德（1979）在《试论翻译的原则》一文中所说的"切"（切合原文文体风格），从而避

免出现"跑调串体"等文体修辞失误。

比如,下面是一位新手草拟的一份"跑调串体"的商品推销函:

② 我公司的女装,品种繁多,有美如柳丝的长裙和睡衣,有艳比玫瑰的旗袍和裙衫,有花团锦簇、五彩缤纷的绣衣、大衣和短衫,有富丽如牡丹、淡雅如幽兰的胸罩和衬衣。艳而不凡,美丽不俗。无论是选料、设计款式还是一针一线,均经过精心加工制作。

分析:经理读后认为该信函用词华丽,过于文饰,显然不符合商务文体写作修辞的规范与要求。商界人士时间宝贵,各种商务文书应当在涵盖需要传达的信息的基础上,做到言简意赅、文字质朴。为此,经理把那些华丽的修饰语全部划掉,然后再做英译。

英译: Our company has a good assortment of women's clothing, such as dresses, pajamas, mandarin gowns, embroidered clothes, overcoats, short gowns, brassieres and shirts. Both the materials and designs are well chosen, and they are all meticulously processed.

由此可见,在商务语篇建构中,文体的定位有着十分重要的作用。我们在翻译时应把文体修辞属性准确地反映出来。

思考与练习

1. 思考题

(1) 商务汉英在文体类别上表现出什么差异?

(2) 商务汉英如何分门别类地进行不同文体的翻译转换?

2. 句子翻译

(1) 本公司已宣告解散。原址房屋已经出租,为清理旧收支账款,现于 T 街 10 号设立办事处,特请知照。

(2) 贵方的样品与报价实在令人难以接受;若告知易于接受的最优惠价格,我将电告订购与否。

(3) 我们未收到贵公司所寄的提单及发票,贵公司来函中未见该文件的任何附本,请原谅。

(4) 800 美元每台的价格我方可以接受,但条件是你方应将订货数量增至 3 000 台。

(5) 货物装船后,您方可按发票金额开立汇票向我方提款。

（6）纸板箱作为一种包装容器已在国际贸易中广泛使用。因此,对它们的适航性,你们不必担心。

（7）据我们所知,保险公司接受投保纸板箱装的货物的偷窃、提货不着险。万一发生偷窃,你们可以放心,保险公司将给予赔偿。

（8）纸板箱的货物被窃的痕迹比装木箱的易于察觉,这将有助于你们从保险公司那里得到赔偿。

（9）我们男衬衫的包装为每件套一个塑料袋,五打装一个纸箱。内衬防潮纸,外打铁箍两道。

（10）运到我们口岸的货物必须在汉堡转船,因此你们的包装必须具有适航性,并能经得起运输途中的粗暴搬运。

3. 语篇翻译

● 语篇1

公司简介

瑞安地产有限公司[Shui On Properties Limited（SOP）]原为瑞安集团旗下的主要房地产发展公司,1985年起已在中国内地发展业务,在内地市场拥有近二十年的经验。自集团于2004年把内地的主要地产发展项目注入新成立的瑞安房地产有限公司后,瑞安地产现时主要从事地产投资,在中国香港、中国内地及纽约均有投资项目。

瑞安地产的主要地产投资项目包括:

*上海瑞安广场及城市酒店

*香港瑞安中心

*纽约曼哈顿区"Riverside South"地产发展项目(占20%权益)

● 语篇2

服务公司的员工忠诚度

那些雇用成千上万个收入低下、工作单调的员工的旅馆、商店和餐饮连锁店的老板们发现一个事实:不加区别地对待这些"廉价劳动力"导致员工的流动率居高不下,而且会使他们付出高昂代价。

总部设在美国俄亥俄州的克利夫兰市,在全国拥有"儿童世界""温馨记忆"等专卖店的科尔公司发动了一场"人力资源战争",努力招募并留住较好的员工。

员工们必须回答下列问题:你为什么喜欢在这里工作?在过去的一年里,你想过辞职吗?如果想过,那是为什么?我们的公司该如何改善、不断创造更好的工作环境?员工们回答说他们想得到更好的培训机会,与上司更好地交流,而最重要的是,他们想要老板"让我感受到我并非可有可无"。经过努力,人员流动量减少了一半多;那些全职销售人员的流动量则减少了大约1/3。

万豪公司,一个酒店旅馆集团公司,也已决定在留住员工方面花费更多的资金,希望这样可以节省招聘和训练新员工的开销。因为该公司曾在一年内不得不招募至少27 000人次员工来填满8 800个按小时计费的职位。

为了减缓人员的流动速度，万豪公司必须让各个管理层接受一个简单信息：对公司忠诚、工作积极的员工让顾客满意，从而创造更丰厚的利润，提高股东的满意度。加强对中层管理人员的训练减缓了人员流动速度，改变奖金分配办法也减缓了人员的流动速度。

同时，万豪公司对其员工的要求更加苛刻。公司筛除了以金钱为主要动机的求职者，即那些被公司贬称为"工资至上者"的求职者。这些人虽然很少，却显然构成了服务业劳动大军中极具破坏性的部分。万豪公司在员工工作态度调查表中发现：罗伊·罗杰斯连锁酒店大约只有20%的员工认为薪酬是他们工作的首要原因，在万豪连锁酒店，也大约只有30%的员工这么认为。

许多服务业的中层管理人员认为比起处理要得到更多承认和更多交流的要求来说，对付加薪的要求更加简单易行。这些管理人员需要改变他们处理问题的方式。调查表明：全美国零售店的13 000名员工在被问及如何为18种工作理由排序时，他们把"高薪"放在第三位。排在第一位的是"工作受到肯定"，第二位是"人格受到尊重"。

● 语篇3

备忘录

发件人：董事长　　　　　要求：　　　　　阅后：
收件人：人事部经理　　　　办理　　　　　张贴
发件日期：2020年3月18日　评论　　　　　存档
　　　　　　　　　　　　　信息讨论　　　退回
　　　　　　　　　　　　　　　　　　　　转递：_____

事由：安装咖啡机
董事会正考虑在各部门办公室安装自动咖啡机。实施之前欲知如下情况：
　（1）自动咖啡机的利用率将有多高；
　（2）需要购进多少台；
　（3）是否会节省目前所用煮咖啡的时间。
请提供对下列问题的看法：
　（1）员工们将对此有何反应；
　（2）可以如何与工会讨论此事。
如有可能，请在4月1日董事会前呈报。

第十章

汉英商标对比分析与翻译

Identify the problems in the following translations
① "孔雀"牌电视机
英译:"Peacock" colour TV
② "白翎"牌钢笔
英译:"White Feather" pen
③ "轻身"减肥片
英译:Obesity-Reducing tablets

　　商标(trademark)是一种商品表面或包装上的标志、记号(图画、图案、图形、文字等),使这种商品和同类的其他商品有所区别。随着市场经济的发展,我国对商标的命名越来越看重。汉语商标有着丰富的文化内涵。有些商标文雅尊贵、情深意浓,如"黑妹"牌牙膏、"满庭芳"牌肥皂、"丽人"牌雨伞。有的商标取名于名山、名城、名人、名舍,使人一见商标便联想到其产地,如"天一阁"牌椅子(宁波)、"泰山"牌拖拉机(山东)、"黄鹤楼"牌电吹风(武汉)等。还有的商标来自神话传说和历史文化典故,如"杜康"牌白酒。汉语商标中的这些文化内涵要通过翻译完整地反映于英译之中十分困难,因为汉英两种语言的读者的文化背景差异很大,必然会导致文化因素的传递障碍。然而,汉英两种语言所涉及的文化差异并不能阻止我们采用灵活的翻译手段做适当的调整,将汉语的文化寓意通过种种变通手段反映到英译之中(顾维勇,2005)。

第一节 汉英商标的语言文化差异对比分析

汉语中原来并无"商标"一词,它是一个由英语 trademark 意译而来的外来词。trademark 传统上被译成"牌""商牌""品牌""货牌"等,而现在大多被翻译成"商标"。商标虽小,但是蕴含的文化信息十分丰富。语言是文化的重要部分,商标能够反映出一个民族的悠久历史和文化。(翁凤翔,2002)

"当今的时代是文化制胜的时代,文化是明天的经济,商业竞争既是商品品质的竞争,又是文化品位的竞争。因为消费者购买商品,除了对其物值效用的认同外,更注重商品的文化内涵和文化品位,注重商品所展示的民族文化传统和现代的文化风尚、文化个性。如果商品名字不符合消费者的文化传统心理,消费者就不会认同,更不会喜爱。"(黎运汉,2005:282-283)

无论是汉语商标用词,还是英语商标名称,它们都倾向于选用蕴含高品位的文化词语、有褒美意义的词语、吉利的口彩语和具有美好象征意义的动植物名称。但是,我们在进行商品命名时应该注意不同文化的禁忌。比如,意大利人偏爱玫瑰而讨厌菊花,日本忌用菊花作为商标,原因是菊花在日本常用于葬礼,表示哀悼。

相比之下,汉语以动植物命名的商标居多,以褒美词义外显之词命名的商标多于英语商标。

◆ 1.1 以动植物命名的汉英商标文化现象

选用在各自文化中有着美好象征意义的动植物命名的商标在汉英两种语言中都有,比如我国的"熊猫"牌电视机和"小天鹅"牌洗衣机、美国的"苹果"(Apple)牌电脑、日本的"蓝鸟"(Bluebird)牌汽车等。但是,汉语商标或我国出口的商品以动植物命名的商标居多,如"双鹿"(Pair Deer)、"小熊猫"(Little Panda)、"凤凰"(Phoenix)、"海燕"(Petrel)、"喜鹊"(Magpie)、"牡丹"(Peony)、"红山茶"(Scarlet Camellia)、"五羊"(Five Rams)、"小白兔"(Little Rabbit)、"蝙蝠"(Bat)、"骆驼"(Camel)、"雄狮牌"(Lion)、"马牌"(Horse)等。其中,牡丹自古就被誉为"花后""国色天香",是我国的国花,象征着荣华富贵;羊、猫、兔象征着温顺和平;喜鹊象征着吉祥喜庆;蝙蝠象征着幸福美好;雄狮象征着"雄壮有力、具有男子汉威力";等等。

同时,译者在进行出口商标汉英翻译时也需要注意避讳具有不同文化联想意义的动植物名称。例如:

Narcissus(水仙花):那耳喀索斯是希腊神话中爱上自己影子的美貌少年。相传,那耳喀索斯是河神刻斐索斯与水泽女神利里俄珀之子。他是一位长相十分清秀的美少年,却对任何姑娘都不动心,只对自己的水中倒影爱慕不已,最终在顾影自怜中抑郁死去。他死去的地方长出一种花,人们就根据他的名字给其取名叫 narcissus(水仙花)。后来,Narcissus 就成了"孤芳自赏者"和"自我陶醉者"的代名词。由此可见,以 narcissus 作为商标的出口商品可能不太会受西方顾客的喜欢。

Lily(百合花):百合花在汉文化中被看作吉祥之花,白色的百合花是纯洁和美丽的象征。但是,在英国和印度,白色百合花用于丧礼,忌用此花贺喜、赠人。所以,在使用"百合花"作为出口产品商标时需要谨慎。

Lotus(荷花):又称"莲花",汉语中有"出淤泥而不染,濯青涟而不妖"的诗句赞美荷花。在上海,有"碧莲"牌糖果;在湖南,有"莲蓬"牌热水瓶。在西方国家,"荷花"也是常用商标;而在日本,荷花则被视作不吉利之花,因为荷花在日本被用作祭奠供品。所以,"荷花"牌商品销往日本时需要改名。

Jasmine(茉莉花):中国人偏爱茉莉花,喜欢茉莉花茶(Jasmine tea),但茉莉花茶在东南亚滞销,原因是"茉莉"与"没利"同音,为当地人所忌讳。

Petrel(海燕):它那种不畏暴风雨、勇于冲出乌云和风浪的勇敢精神令深受高尔基的《海燕》这首散文诗影响的我们钦佩。但是,西方人对其并无好感,他们认为暴风雨中的海燕预示着灾难、纠纷,可能带来厄运、黑暗,所以"Petrel"牌的商品很难赢得西方人的青睐。

Dragon(龙):中国人称自己是"龙的传人",把龙看作民族的图腾,对其倍加崇拜。因此,许多商品以龙的形象和名称作为品牌,如"金龙牌""龙泉牌""双龙牌"等。这些品牌一旦被译成 dragon,便会令西方人望而生畏。原因是,在英语里 dragon 是一种凶恶的、嘴里吐火的、能给人带来厄运的怪物,是魔鬼撒旦的化身,是邪恶的象征,这也是"亚洲四小龙"被翻译成 Four Asian Tigers 的缘故。

Bat(蝙蝠):我们认为蝙蝠是一种能捕食蚊蝇、对人类有益的动物,同时蝙蝠的"蝠"与"福"同音,也是幸福、吉祥、安宁的代名词,但在西方,蝙蝠却是一种丑陋的吸血动物,会给人带来厄运,是邪恶的化身(谢金领,2007)。在英语俗语中,bat 被解释为晚上出来的坏东西,即妓女。

Golden Cock(金鸡):雄鸡报晓,"鸡"与"吉"同音,所以"金鸡"在中国人心里能够引起好的文化联想。可是,在英语中,cock 则有"雄性生殖器"等粗俗不堪的意思。试问:使用 cock 一词作为出口商品的商标合适吗?据说,不懂西方语言文化的人先把"金鸡"牌鞋油直译成 Golden Cock 而致使该商品在国外市场上销路不畅,后经改译为 Golden Rooster 后才逐渐被西方人接受。

Tortoise(乌龟):中国人都把乌龟视为长寿的象征。我国海南有"椰岛鹿龟"酒,沈阳有"银龟"牌水泥防水剂。然而,西方一些国家把乌龟当作丑陋与令人不快的东西,所以带有"乌龟"商标的产品在欧美市场上不太容易畅销。

Rabbit(兔子)：中国人对兔子有特殊的感情，神话《嫦娥奔月》中就有一只白兔常伴嫦娥。上海冠生园的"大白兔"奶糖商标是我国的首批驰名商标之一。但是，俄国人看不起兔子，认为兔子胆小、没能耐。澳大利亚人恨兔子，因为澳大利亚是骑在羊背上的国家，兔子吃了草，羊就少了食物，羊毛产量就大受影响。所以，我国的"兔牌"樟脑丸销往澳大利亚、新西兰等国家便受到冷落。

Phoenix(凤凰)：在汉语中，凤凰象征富贵、吉祥，而在英语中 phoenix 却有着"死里逃生"的意思。

再者，我们将有些动物名称用作商标名称时应注意区别不同的外国文化联想意义。比如，Black Cat(黑猫)深受英国人、比利时人和西班牙人喜欢，因为他们视黑猫为吉利的动物，遇到白猫则预示着厄运的降临。英国的消费者，特别是英国的家庭主妇，是不会购买"White Cat"牌商品的。所以，很受中国人青睐的上海"白猫"牌洗衣粉到了英国可能就会无人问津。然而，美国人正好与此相反，他们视白猫为吉利的动物，认为黑猫预示着厄运的到来。

◆ 1.2　使用溢美之词的汉英商标语言文化对比

汉语商标或汉译商标中使用词义外显之词的情况大大多于英语商标，如"金凤"牌毛巾、"金鸡"牌闹钟、"金龙泉"啤酒、"瑞星"杀毒软件、"乐达"自行车、"雅致"女装、"红蜻蜓"皮鞋、"永久"牌自行车、"美的"电器、"康佳"电视、"肤美灵"(Skinice)化妆品、"雅芳"(Avon)化妆品等。这一点也可从许多西药药名中看出，如"速眠安""益保世灵""咳喘宁""利福平""快克"等。

相比之下，英语商标大多比较简明，较少使用词义外显之词，它们大多暗示意美之联想词义。LUX("力士"香皂)一词源自拉丁文，有"阳光"之意，使用者不禁由阳光联想到健康的肌肤，其词形与发音又可使人联想到 Luck，Luxury 等词语。

◆ 1.3　汉语商标仿造、自造"洋"名与英语商标创新词

随着市场经济的发展，一些中国本土的企业、商店在为品牌冠名时往往千方百计加以"洋化"。一些商品品牌、公司、商店往往先起英文名字，然后再用汉字去拟写这些名字，将其"英化"。例如，"雅戈尔"(Younger)、"亚细亚"(Asia)、"戈德"(Good)、"开普"(Cap)、"纳爱斯"(Nice)、"格力"(Gree)、"隆力奇"(Longlife)、"德芙"巧克力(Dove)、"万得福"烤鸭店(Wonderful)、"欧诗漫"化妆品(OSM／osmotic)、"汇德丰"照明灯(Way To Fund)、"美加净"牙膏(MAXAM)、"西格玛"自行车(Sigma)、"英克莱"自行车

（INCALCU）等"英化"品名,不是为了填补汉语语汇的空缺,而是为了迎合人们趋新求异的心理,从而美化、促销商品(戴卫平、裴文斌,2008)。

同样,为了使人产生好的联想和促销产品,英语商标大量采用创新词汇来命名。比如,Timex("天美时"手表)一词是由 time 和 excellent 两个词合成的,暗含 excellent 之意美;同类合成词还有 Rolex("劳力士"手表)、Earex(滴眼药品牌)、Kleenex("舒洁"面巾纸)、Windex(清洁剂品牌)等。再如,Uniball("三菱"牌圆珠笔)一词是由 universal 和 ball 两个词合成的,暗含 universal 之意美。

第二节 对汉英商标翻译的启示与警示

2.1 对汉英商标翻译的启示

基于汉语商标的语言文化特征,音译、音意兼译、回译、功能对等转换法和采用创新词是汉英商标翻译行之有效的译法。

2.1.1 传译积极文化义,避讳消极文化义

汉语商标或汉译商标较多使用词义外显之词,而英语商标较少使用词义外显之词。鉴于此,汉英转换可以采用音译或音意兼译法,传译积极文化义。

请对比分析以下汉英商标翻译实例:

① "美加净"(牙膏)

英译:MAXAM

对比分析:采用了音意双关翻译法。英译没有采用直译(如:beautiful and clean),原因是直译太过直白,并且不符合商标简洁的审美特征;而音意双关翻译构思巧妙,巧妙之处在于 MAXAM 在形式上类似于回文,在发音上接近于汉语原商标,而且其发音使人联想到 maximum 一词的"极致""最高"等积极词义。

② "昂立1号"(口服液)

英译:Only One

对比分析:汉语"昂立1号"这个商标寓意直白,取"高高在上、名列第一"之意。英译采用的音意双关翻译法用词简洁,其"独此一个"的寓意巧妙地传递了原商标的积极含义。

然而,有着积极文化联想意义的某些汉语商标若被直译成英语,可能会引起消极的

文化联想。

请对比分析以下汉英商标翻译实例：

③ "飞龙"（药品）

英译：Pharon

对比分析：为了跨越文化差异，商标汉英翻译可采用避讳消极文化词语的音译法。"飞龙"商标创造性的音译 Pharon 避免了因被直译成 Dragon 而带来的不好的文化联想。

④ "蝴蝶"（缝纫机、电子灶）

英译：Hudie

对比分析：蝴蝶在中国象征友谊和爱情，而英美国家的人则把蝴蝶当作轻浮之物。在英语中就有 social butterfly（交际花）一说。若用 butterfly 来译此商标，英语国家的消费者会产生什么样的联想呢？他们或许会对该产品的耐用性产生怀疑。此外，西方国家的人并不喜欢以鸟类或虫类作电子产品的商标名，虫鸟用作商标往往给人以质量低劣的印象。鉴于此，我们把"蝴蝶"商标音译成 Hudie 也无妨。

2.1.2 采用功能对等的译法，实现同样的商标功能

汉英两种语言均存在"词汇空缺"的现象。鉴于此，英译应灵活地进行对等转换。

请对比分析以下汉英商标翻译实例：

⑤ "鸳鸯"（枕套）

英译：Lovebird

对比分析：鸳鸯（Mandarin Ducks）在英语文化中根本就没有汉语所有的比喻义。但"鸳鸯"可以被灵活地套译成英语中有着同样引申义的 Lovebird 一词，这样就能引起同样的文化联想，并传达出汉语原商标"相亲相爱"的比喻义。由此可见，我们在进行商标汉英翻译时应思路开阔，把注意力转向商标在汉英两种语言中的形象效果的等效传递上。

2.1.3 采用创新词，传译积极词义

商标命名的一个宗旨是新颖独特，吸引人的注意。英译可以根据汉语原商标的寓意，采用创新词进行英译。

⑥ "新飞"（冰箱）

英译：Frestech

对比分析：一些词义肯定的汉语商标的英译可以采用创新词（意译+ex/tech 后缀）的译法，如"新飞"（Freshtech；Fresh+technology）、"心相印"（Hearttex；Heart+excellent）。

2.2 对汉英商标翻译的警示

因不了解汉英文化差异,一些汉语商标的英译有着文化上的失误、失当之处。比如,"小糊涂"(酒)的音译 Hutu 和谐音 Hootoo 在英语中有"厄运、不祥之物"的意思;再如"芳芳"牌婴儿爽身粉的音译"Fangfang" Baby Talcum Powder,就因译者不了解 fang 在英语中有"蛇的毒牙"这个不好的文化联想含义,而造成了误译。

请对比分析以下汉英商标翻译实例:

⑦"五羊"牌自行车

误译:"Five Rams" bike

改译:"Five Goats" bike

对比分析:"五羊"中的羊为中国传统的吉祥之物。广州有"五羊城""羊城"的别称,由此可知广州产的自行车以"五羊"为品牌的由来。其英译 Five Rams 中所用 Ram 一词在英语中用作名词表示"好斗的公羊",而用作动词的意思就是"碰撞"。可想而知,较少有人会购买并使用"Five Rams"牌自行车。所以,不妨将其译成 Five Goats(广州越秀公园内的五羊石雕的英文是 the Statue of Five Goats);如此这样,不良引申义就荡然无存了(顾维勇,2005)。

⑧"白象"牌电池

误译:"White Elephant" battery

改译:"Silver Elephant" battery

对比分析:白象因稀少而珍贵,所以选用这种稀有动物作为商标名称的用意就显而易见了。但是,把"白象"这个商名直译成 White Elephant 就有不妥之处。White Elephant 在英语中有"大而无用之物""累赘"等意思,所以标上 White Elephant 这个品名的电池出口到外国市场会无人问津。后来,有人意识到译名不妥就将"白象"改译成 Silver Elephant 或 Brown Lion。这样才解决了问题。同样,"白象"牌方便面也不能被直译成"White Elephant" Instant Noodles,而应被意译成"Bijoy" Instant Noodles。(成昭伟、周丽红,2011)。

⑨"紫罗兰"牌男装

误译:"Pansy" men's suit

改译:"Violetex" men's suit

对比分析:"紫罗兰"在汉语文化中有着"浪漫""高雅"等意义,而其直译 Pansy 一词在英语文化里是个带有贬义的口语词汇,其内涵之义为 effeminate man(女人气的男人)或 male homosexual(同性恋男子)。可想而知,以 Pansy 冠名的男装在英美等西方国家的销路是不会好的。如果换一种译法——Violetex,效果将大为改观。

⑩"西泠"牌电冰箱

误译:"Xiling"(refridgerator)

改译:"Serene"(refridgerator)

对比分析:误译采用了音译法,没有取得良好的市场效果。后经专家分析与精心设计,采用了音意结合的译法——Serene,市场效果大为改观,原因就是Serene一词有着"宁静""安宁"的美好寓意,能带给人静谧而美好的积极联想义。

以上几个商标的汉英误译实例表明,商标命名是一个十分重要的问题。因为消费者在购买商品时,不仅考虑其物值效用,而且更注重商品的文化内涵和文化品位。同样,商标的翻译转换也是一个十分重要的问题。商标的英译不好,就会影响商品的出口销售。

附表 常见商标翻译

日用消费品类常见商标	
Olay // 玉兰油(系列护肤品)	Unilever // 联合利华(护理护肤等日用消费品)
P&G // 宝洁(洗发洗涤等化学日用品)	L'Oreal // 欧莱雅(化妆品)
Quick // 快克(洗涤剂)	Kleenex // 洁净(纸巾)
Lucky // 乐凯(胶卷)	Tides // 汰渍(洗衣粉)
Gillette // 吉利(剃须刀)	Avon // 雅芳(化妆品)
Mininurse // 小护士(防晒霜)	Crest // 佳洁士(牙膏)
Pampers // 帮宝适(尿不湿)	Rejoice // 飘柔(洗发水)
Ariel // 碧浪(洗衣粉)	Boat // 船牌(洗衣皂)
West Lake // 西子(香皂)	Safeguard // (舒肤佳)
Pond's // 旁氏(洗面奶)	Johnson & Johnson // 强生(保健及护理品)
Cologne // 科隆(香水)	Orlane // 幽兰(爽肤水)
Colgate // 高露洁(牙膏)	MAXAM // 美加净(牙膏)
Lux // 力士(香皂)	Lancome // 兰蔻(化妆品)
Kiss Me // 奇士美(睫毛膏)	Maybeline // 美宝莲(唇膏等化妆品)
Pantene // 潘婷(洗发水)	Skinice // 肤美灵(洗面奶等化妆品)
Nice // 纳爱斯(洗涤用品)	Clean & Clear // 可伶可俐(护肤用品)
Bausch & Lomb // 博士伦(隐形眼镜)	Revlon // 露华浓(口红等化妆品)
Arche // 雅倩(化妆品)	OMO // 奥妙(洗衣粉)
Bluemoon // 蓝月亮(洗涤用品)	

续表

汽车类常见商标	
BYD // 比亚迪	Trumpchi // 传祺
Geely // 吉利	HAVAL // 哈弗
BMW // 宝马	Ford // 福特
Cadillac // 卡迪拉克	Porsche // 保时捷
Volvo // 沃尔沃	Rolls-Royce // 劳斯莱斯
Chrysler // 克莱斯勒	GM // 通用
Opel // 欧宝	Santana // 桑塔纳
Lincoln // 林肯	Fiat // 菲亚特
Chevrolet // 雪佛兰	Honda // 本田
Toyota // 丰田	Crown // 皇冠
Lexus // 凌志	Pontiac // 庞帝克
Buick // 别克	Mercedes-Benz // 奔驰
家用电器类常见商标	
HUAWEI // 华为	MI // 小米
Canon // 佳能	Konka // 康佳
Supor // 苏泊尔	Haier // 海尔
Hisense // 海信	Ricoh // 理光
Midea // 美的	Siemens // 西门子
Ericsson // 爱立信	Casio // 卡西欧
Epson // 爱普生	Nokia // 诺基亚
Whirlpool // 惠而浦	Motorola // 摩托罗拉
Serene // 西泠	Yamaha // 雅马哈
Philips // 飞利浦	Toshiba // 东芝
Triangle // 三角	Star // 实达
服装类常见商标	
YOUNGOR // 雅戈尔	Adidas // 阿迪达斯
Kin Don // 金盾	Goldlion // 金利来
Reebok // 锐步	Gucci // 古奇
Unisports // 优跑	Timberland // 天木兰
Rainbow // 彩虹	Umbro // 茵宝
Puma // 彪马	Robinhood // 罗宾汉
Peak // 匹克	Firs // 杉杉
FUGUINIAO // 富贵鸟	Guski // 古士旗
Giordano // 佐丹奴	Boss // 博斯

服装类常见商标	
Louis Vuitton //路易威登	Mickey //米奇
Senda //森达	Bosideng //波司登
Romen //罗蒙	Dar & Dar //达达
Menten //曼特	Hermès //爱马仕
Dunhill //登喜路	Bossini //堡狮龙
Nike //耐克	Elegance //雅致
SEPTWOLVES //七匹狼	Santa Barbara Polo & Racquet Club//圣大保罗
PLAYBOY //花花公子	Yves Saint Laurent //伊夫圣罗兰
手表类常见商标	
Omega //欧米茄	Fiyta //飞亚达
Rado //雷达	Swatch //斯沃琪
Longines //浪琴	Tempo //天霸
Seagull //海鸥	Hamilton //汉密尔顿
Cartier //卡地亚	BVLGARI //宝格丽
Rolex //劳力士	EPOS //爱宝时
MIDO //美度	DAVOSA //迪沃斯
IWC //万国	Paul Picot //柏高
Citizen //西铁城	Tissot //天梭
其他类常见商标	
Coca Cola //可口可乐(饮料)	7-Up //七喜(饮料)
Pepsi-Cola //百事可乐(饮料)	Carlsberg //嘉士伯(啤酒)
Camel //"骆驼"牌(香烟)	Kent //健牌(香烟)
Marlboro //万宝路(香烟)	Happiness //吉庆(香烟)
Golden Bridge //金桥(香烟)	Jade Flute //玉笛(香烟)
Hope //福牌(香烟)	Apollo //阿波罗(香烟)
Welcome //迎宾(香烟)	Heineken //喜力(啤酒)
Budweiser //百威(啤酒)	Holsten //好顺(啤酒)
Goodyear //固特异(轮胎)	

思考与练习

1. 思考题

（1）汉英商标命名在语言文化上有什么差异？对汉英商标翻译有什么启示与警示？

（2）请结合 Head & Shoulders 这个英语商标的成功汉译"海飞丝"实例，谈谈此商标翻译的成功之处。

2. 句子翻译

（1）下周末约翰将从西雅图驾驶别克轿车到温哥华度假。

（2）杰克花了四美元复印了《英语故事》一书的第一章。

（3）珍妮驾驶福特牌轿车去底特律旅游时，杰克却开着狩猎牌汽车去西雅图度假。

3. 请判断以下汉英商标的翻译是否恰当并说明理由

（1）"席而灵"牌小闹钟：Sailing Travel Clock

（2）"芳芳"牌口红：Fang Fang

（3）"金凤"牌毛巾：Golden Phoenix Towel

（4）"七匹狼"牌服饰：SEPTWOLVES

（5）"白翎"牌钢笔：White Feather

（6）"鹿王"牌服饰：King Deer

（7）"达芙妮"牌女鞋：Daphne

（8）"金鸡"牌闹钟：Golden Cock

（9）"旺德福"火锅店：WONDERFUL

（10）"回力"牌运动鞋：Warrior

第十一章

汉英商用名片对比分析与翻译

> **Identify the problems in the following translations**
> ① 油城二路8号
> 英译：8 Second Oil City Road
> ② 茂名市政总公司
> 英译：The City General Company of Maoming
> ③ 新福新村
> 英译：Xinfu New Village

何为商用名片？商用名片就是商务交往中以名字为主体、用以介绍自我身份的小卡片。它带有公司和个人的商业信息，包括持有者的姓名、身份、头衔、联系方式等有效信息。随着我国经济的不断发展和经济全球化的不断加深，社交和商务往来中商用名片（business card / visiting card / calling card / name card）的使用越来越普遍。因此，对于名片的翻译，我们必须采取严肃认真、积极负责的态度，分析中西方国家在政治、经济、文化、社会、语言等方面的差异，字斟句酌，力争使汉语名片英译符合国际惯例，让名片真正起到方便沟通、提高交流质量的作用。

第一节 汉英商用名片的语言文化差异对比分析

名片虽小，但涵盖的内容很多，涉及人名、地名、职务名称、单位名称、通信地址、邮政编码、电话、电子邮件地址等。下面就从人名、地名和职务名称三个方面来探讨一下如何跨越商用汉英名片中的语言文化障碍。

1.1 人名中的语言文化差异对比分析

汉语中姓在前、名在后,而英语则恰好相反。汉语的姓与名都有着丰富的文化外涵,名字还蕴含取名者所赋予的特殊含义。所以,汉英两种语言在文化上的差异就给姓名翻译带来了诸多困难。比如,汉语拼音名字就不能把原先名字所蕴含的意思准确地传译出来,如"程爱国"中"爱国"的含义十分清楚,但是英译成 Cheng Aiguo 后,其中的 Aiguo 就体现不出"热爱祖国"的含义。(翁凤翔,2002)

目前,商用名片上的人名英译除了完全按照汉语姓名的顺序进行音译之外,还有按照英美等西方国家的名在前、姓在后的顺序来英译汉语名字,但通常在姓的前面加上逗号,使其与名字分开,也可以缩写名字。比如,"王建军"可以被翻译成 Jianjun Wang 或 J. J., Wang。此外,人名中的姓可以全部大写,以此起到突出醒目的作用,以免外国人将姓与名搞错。比如,"张建军"可以被翻译成 ZHANG Jianjun,"武松"可以被翻译成 WU Song。

1.2 地名中的语言文化差异对比分析

汉英两种语言的地址写法不同,其顺序完全相反。例如,"青岛市黄岛区钱塘江路369号国际学院"可以被翻译为 International School, No. 369 Qiantangjiang Rd., Huangdao District, Qingdao。在名片上,地址应该保持一定的完整性,门牌号与街道名不可分开写,必须在同一行,不可断行,但各种名称可以断开。例如,英国加工与包装机械协会有限公司上海代表处的邮政编码和地址如下:

① 200135 中国上海浦东新区商城路 660 号乐凯大厦 1511 室

英译:

Room 1511, Lucky Mansions

No. 660 Shang Cheng Rd.

Pudong New Area

Shanghai 200135

China

对比分析:汉英地名的排列顺序恰恰相反:汉语地名是从大到小排列,而英语地名则是从小到大排列。

汉语地址中的"路""街""道/大道/林荫大道"一般被英译成 Road(Rd),Street(Str),Avenue(Ave);"里""弄""巷"的英语对应词都是 lane;而"胡同"有所不同,其英译是 alley。此外，还有一些地名已经有约定俗成的译法，如香港（Hong Kong）、澳门（Macao）、西藏（Tibet）、呼和浩特（Huhehot）、哈尔滨（Harbin）、内蒙古（Inner Mongolia）、新疆维吾尔自治区（Xinjiang Uygur Autonomous Region）、乌鲁木齐（Urumchi）等。这些约定俗成的地名不好采用拼音音译，原因是它们由来已久，早已被国际社会接受。这是历史文化的原因。

最后值得注意的一点是，地名中的"东""西""南""北""中""一路""二路"等的翻译转换必须合乎英语的表达习惯，不能一字一句地硬译。

请对比分析以下地名的汉英翻译转换：

② 茂名市茂南区光华北路

英译：North Guanghua Road, Maonan District, Maoming City

对比分析：汉英地名中的方位修饰词"东""西""南""北""中"的词序位置大不相同。英语地名所用方位词 East, West, South, North, Central 修饰整个路名；汉语地名中的方位词修饰"路"字。

③ 油城七路

英译：Seventh Oil-City Road

对比分析：汉语地名中所用数词为基数词，而英译地名表示"七路"所用数词则为序数词。

◆ 1.3 职务职称中的语言文化差异对比分析

小小的一张名片体现了两种文化的差异。中国人要求名片上尽可能多地体现出持有人的各种职务、头衔；而西方社会在名片设计上则注重名片的实效性，讲求实用，一般在名片上只列出最能代表持有人身份的头衔即可。比如，在欧美国家，没有人把"博导"头衔放在名片上。

由于历史、文化传统等方面的差异，汉英两种语言的职务职称称谓大不相同，特别是商贸企业等商务组织中惯用的职务职称有较大的差异。全球化与改革开放使中国的经济面貌发生了天翻地覆的变化，职务职称的叫法也随之国际化，manager（经理）的"帽子"满天飞，洋味儿十足的 CEO 早已不足为奇，"总工程师""总会计师""总设计师"的名号更是司空见惯。所有这些足以表明西方文化的影响力。

例如，汉语中"老总"常被下属用来称呼公司的总经理，即英语的 general manager 或 president。此外，在有总编辑的报社，在有总厂厂长的企业，下属也可能用"老总"来称呼他们的总负责人。但是由于中西方企业文化的不同，中国的"老总"（总经理）与美国的 General Manager 有时并不对等。在美国不设 president 的小公司里，general manager 就是日常事务总管，与我国的总经理对等，而在设 president 的大公司里，其地位介于

department manager(部门经理)和 president 之间。由此可见,汉语"老总"有时与 general manager 对等,有时又与 president 对等。

再如,汉语表示职务或职称的"副"字大多译自英语的 deputy, vice, associate, assistant, sub-等"副"词。由此可见,英语中这些"副"词大有讲究,有着复杂的文化内涵。

associate 一词一般与表示职称的名词搭配,如 associate professor(副教授)。

vice 一般用于称谓职位较高的副职人员,如 vice president(副董事长/副总裁)、vice premier(副总理)、vice chancellor(大学副校长)等。vice chancellor(大学副校长)在英国、澳大利亚、新西兰等国家或中国香港地区的大学里指的就是正校长,因为 chancellor 基本是不管事的"名誉校长"。vice 虽常与职位较高的名词连用,但这并不意味着 vice 不能与职位较低的名词连用,如 vice manager(副经理)。

deputy 一般与职位较低的名词搭配,如 deputy director(副厂长/副所长/副主任)、deputy headmistress(副女校长)等。但是,它也可以与职位较高的名词连用,如 deputy minister(副部长)、deputy attorney-general(副总检察长)。

sub-这个前缀一般表示"次"或"子",如 sub-title(子标题)。但是,当它用在表示"人"的名词前时,就是"副"的意思,如 sub-agent(副代理)、sub-head(副科长)。

上述种种搭配只是习惯罢了,也没有严格的界限,如 vice-director/ deputy-director(副主任/副处长)、associate professor/ vice-professor(副教授)等。

第二节 对汉英商用名片翻译的启示与警示

2.1 对汉英商用名片翻译的启示

2.1.1 职务名称的英译应跟上潮流

名片上所用职务名称有很多已与国际接轨,也有很多已经更新换代。比如,过去常用的"推销员"已经被"业务代表"(Rep)替代。

请对比分析以下汉英翻译实例:

① 财务总监

英译:Financial Director

对比分析:以前,我们习惯使用"财务处处长",而在当今这个职务名称已经不那么新潮。很多企业已经采用更加时髦的名称——总监,如技术总监(technical director)、市场营销总监(marketing director)等。

2.1.2 地名所用数词的英译应做到基序有别

汉语名片上的地名所用数词看不出基础词与序数词之间的区别,但英译就要加以区分。

请对比分析以下汉英翻译实例:

② 官渡二路 139 号

英译: 139 Guandu Second Road

对比分析:英语表示"一路""二路"等路名所用的数词为序数词,而门牌号所用数词就是基数词。

2.2 对汉英商用名片翻译的警示

2.2.1 不要死译、硬译地名

对于名片的英译,切记不要死译、硬译,应按照汉语原文的内涵义和英语的表达习惯做灵活处理以及词序调整。

请对比分析以下汉英商用名片翻译实例:

③ 祈福新村

误译: New Qifu Village

改译: Qifu Village

对比分析:地名中的"新村"不是 New Village,而仅仅是 Village 一词,原因是刚建成的居民住宅小区叫"新村",几年后还叫"新村"。所以,无论新旧,都只是居民住宅小区。

④ 新福三路 168 号

误译: 168 Third Xinfu Road

改译: 168 Xinfu Third Road

对比分析:英语表示"二路""三路"等路名所用的数词因有无门牌号,其词序位置大不相同。若无门牌号,表示路名的序数词就被放在整个路名前;若有门牌号,表示路名的序数词就被放在 Road 前。切勿放错位置!

2.2.2 名称"总""总"繁多,英译不要想当然

汉语公司、职务等名称中有许多带"总"的修饰语,不可一味地将"总"译为 general。

请对比分析以下汉英翻译实例:

⑤ 自来水总公司

中国轻工产品进出口总公司

总裁

误译：Running Water General Company

China Light Industrial Products Imp. & Exp. Corporation

General Manager / Managing Director

改译：Running Water Corporation

China National Light Industrial Products Imp. & Exp. Corporation

Chief Executive Officer

对比分析：名片上的公司名称、职务名称带"总"的有很多，如总经理、总公司、总裁、总监等。有些人总是把"总"字死译成 general，结果英译大错特错。

2.2.3 词汇空缺，英译不可死译

如果在英语中找不到与汉语原文对应的词，汉英翻译要灵活把握，不要死搬硬套。请对比分析以下汉英翻译实例：

⑥ 办公室主任

误译：Office Director

改译：Office Manager

对比分析：名片上的职务或职衔汉英有别，不能把"主任"一职简单地套译成 head 或 director。虽然 director 常常被汉译成"主任"，但它最常用的意思是"总监"。若用 director 来译，"主任"极易被人们误解成单位或部门的领导人。如果采用 manager 进行功能对等的英译转换，就不会引起误解。这是因为 manager 的基本词义就是"某个部门的负责人"。

附表　汉英名片翻译中的常用单词和表达

名片中的企业名称	
company //公司（BrE）	corporation //公司（AmE）；总公司
company limited（Co., Ltd.）//责任有限公司	public limited company（Plc）//股份有限公司
incorporated（Inc.）；Co., Inc. //股份有限公司	group //集团公司
holding(s) //控股公司	branch；branch office //分公司
share company //股份公司	subsidiary //子公司
associated company；associates //联合公司；联号；联营公司	union //联合公司

名片中的企业名称	
alliance //联盟公司;联合公司	joint company //联合公司
consolidated company //联合公司	affiliate; affiliated company //联营公司;分公司;附属公司
integrated company //联合公司	proprietary company //控股公司
firm //公司;商号	agency //公司;代理公司
line //公司;航空航运公司	enterprise(s); enterprise corporation //企业公司;实业公司
industries //工业公司;实业公司	store(s) //百货公司
products //用品公司;产品公司	services //服务公司
system //系统公司	laboratory //制药公司
assurance; insurance //保险公司	head office; headquarters //总公司;总部
joint venture //合资公司;合资企业	parent company //母公司
daughter company //子公司	freight forwarder //货运代理公司
shipping line //船运公司	joint stock limited liability company //股份有限公司
factory //厂	works //厂
mill //厂	plant //厂
paper mill //纸厂	flour mill //面粉厂
textile mill //纺织厂	steel works //钢铁厂
gas works //煤气厂	cement works //水泥厂
cotton mill //棉纺厂	printing & dyeing mill //印染厂
plastics factory //塑料厂	meter factory //电表厂
sewing machine factory //缝纫机厂	glass factory //玻璃厂
processing factory //加工厂	hardware factory //五金厂
radio factory //无线电厂	power plant //发电厂
machinery plant //机械厂	shipyard //造船厂
brewery //啤酒厂	winery //酿酒厂
distillery //酿酒厂	sugar refinery //制糖厂
名片中的职务名称	
MD (managing director); GM (general manager) //总经理	president //董事长;总裁
CEO (chief executive officer) //首席执行官;总裁	director //总监;董事;厂长;主任;主管
CFO (chief financial officer) //首席财务官;财务总监	financial controller //财务主任

续表

名片中的职务名称	
office manager //办公室主任	CMO (chief marketing officer); marketing director //首席营销官;营销总监;市场经理;市场部主任
director of personnel department //人事处处长	director of general services division //总务处处长
CTO (chief technology officer); technical director //首席技术官;技术总监	COO (chief operational officer); operational director //首席运营官;运营总监
vice president //副总裁	deputy director //副厂长;副主任
assistant manager //助理经理;副经理	manager's assistant //经理助理
sales manager //销售经理	manager of dispatch dept //发货部经理
manager of purchasing dept //采购部经理	manager of production dept //生产部经理
manager of product dept //产品部经理	director of R & D dept //研发部主任
manager of advertising dept //广告部经理	manager of after-sales dept //售后服务部经理
director of PR dept //公关部主任	director of planning dept //计划部主任
director of quality & control //质控部主任	director of training dept //培训部主任
manager of project dept //项目部经理	manager of engineering dept //工程部经理
service manager //服务部经理	administration manager //行政经理
human resources manager //人力资源部经理	lobby manager //大堂经理
chief engineer //总工程师	engineer //工程师
chief accountant //总会计师	accountant //会计师
secretary to general manager //总经理秘书	head waitress //领班
personal assistant //私人秘书;私人助理	business representative //业务代表
property consultant //置业顾问	executive secretary //行政秘书
account manager //客户经理	section head //科长
名片中的地址名称	
Road; Rd //路	Hubei Road //湖北路
Guanghua Bei Road; North Guanghua Road //光华北路	Sichuan Nan Road; South Sichuan Road //四川南路
Wenming Zhong Road; Central Wenming Road //文明中路	Second Zhongshan Road (S) //中山(南)二路
Changshou Feeder Road //长寿支路	Street //街;道
Jingzhou Street //荆州街	Chang'an Street //长安街
Main Street //大街	Inner Jianguomen Main Street //建国门内大街
Avenue //道;大道	Century Avenue //世纪大道
Riverside Avenue //滨江大道	Main Avenue //干道
Jinghua Main Avenue //锦华干道	Lane //里;弄;巷

续表

名片中的地址名称	
East Lane //东里	Tongde Lane //同德里
Lane 115；115th Lane //115 弄	Lane；Alley //胡同；里
Dongtiao Alley //东条胡同	Residential Quarter；Residential Area //小区
Room（Rm）//室；房	Floor（Fl）//楼；层
Building（Bldg）//楼；幢	Village（Vil）//村
Block（Blc）//街区	Unit //单元
Apartment（Apt）//寓所；公寓	Town //镇
District（Dist）//区	County //县
Dongjiang Residential Quarter //东江小区	Haiyuan Village //海苑新村
名片中的常用缩略词	
Rd（road）//路	St（street）//街；道
Av（avenue）//道；大道	Bldg（building）//楼；幢
Fl（floor）//楼；层	Rm（room）//室
Apt（apartment）//公寓；寓所	Co（company）//公司
Corp（corporation）//公司	Inc（incorporated）//股份有限的；股份有限公司
Ltd（limited）//责任有限的；责任有限公司	Co., Ltd（company limited）//责任有限公司
Plc（public limited company）//股份有限公司	MD（managing director）；GM（general manager）//总经理
CEO（chief executive officer）//首席执行官	Rep（representative）//业务代表
Exec（executive）//主管；经理	Dr.（director）//博士
Tel（telephone）//电话	H（home phone）//住宅电话
O（office）//办公电话	Telex（telegraph exchange）//电传
Fax（facsimile）//传真	E-mail（electronic mail）//电子邮件
Cable（cable address）//电报挂号	M. P.（mobile phone）//移动电话
P. C.（AmE：post code）//邮编	Zip（BrE：zip code）//邮编
P. O. B.（post office box）//邮政信箱	Add（address）//地址

思考与练习

1. 思考题

（1）汉英商用名片在语言文化上有什么差异？

（2）汉英商用名片在语言文化上的差异对汉英商用名片翻译有什么启示与警示？

2. 名片中的地名和职务名称翻译

（1）世纪大道 169 号

(2) 长寿支路5号

(3) 副经理

(4) 副董事长

(5) 营销总监

(6) 人力资源部经理

(7) 公关部经理

(8) 首席执行官,总裁

(9) 首席财务官

3. 名片翻译

(1)

> **上海外语教育出版社**
>
> 王强（编辑）
>
> 上海市中山一路295号
> 邮编:200083
> 传真:021-65425400　电话:021-65425300

(2)

> **中国轻工业产品进出口总公司**
>
> 李为民
>
> 进口部经理
> 中国北京市东城区广渠门街82号
> 邮编:100076
> 传真:021-65425400　电话:021-65425300

(3)

> **中国东方航空公司北京营业部**
>
> 马纯　总经理
>
> 北京王府井大街67号
> 电话:4665363
> 传真:4082694

第十二章

商务汉英信函对比分析与翻译

Identify the problems in the following translations

① 贵方在5月的第一天所写信函,我方已经收悉,谢谢!

英译:Your letter you wrote on the first day of the month of May has been received by me with many thanks.

② 你们答应一周内发货,但是你们却迟迟不发,给我们带来了极大不便。

英译:You promised to deliver the goods within a week, but you have brought considerable inconvenience to us through the long delay.

③ 随函附寄产品目录一份,请查收。

英译:I enclose a catalogue for your reference.

商务信函(business letters)是商务信息书面交流与沟通的主要手段之一,是公司或企业对外公共宣传关系中重要的途径,对于树立良好的公司形象有着极为重要的作用。商务信函贯穿商务活动的始终,内容广泛,涉及商务活动的各个环节,包括建立业务关系(establishing business relationship)、询盘(inquiry)、发盘(offer)、还盘(counter-offer)、受盘(acceptance of offer)、订立合同/下订单(placing orders)、保险(insurance)、包装(packaging)、装运(shipment)、索赔(claim)、代理(agency)、求职(application for jobs)等。

商务信函不仅有普通信函的一般性文体特征,还有其独特之处。商务活动和商务信函的种种特殊性要求商务信函在"斟词酌句、布局谋篇"上不仅要符合商务汉英信函语篇各自的篇章模式和言语程式,而且还要遵守商贸这个行业的语言规范与专业要求,做到言简意赅、专业地道。所以,具有政府部门公函的某些特点的商务信函也应被纳入公文之列(王佐良、丁往道,1997)。在英译时,我们有必要对商务汉英信函在语言文化上的差异进行对比分析,以便更加有效地指导对外商贸信函交际活动。

第一节　商务汉英信函语言文化差异的对比分析与翻译

一方面,作为一种正式的应用文文体,商务信函具有用词简练准确、行文专业客观、少文饰而重纪实(factual)等文体性、专业性较强的特点。商界的专业人士大都很忙,各种商务文书应当在涵盖需要传达的信息的基础上做到言简意赅、文字质朴。此外,国际商务信函涉及的专业范围较广,如进出口、海运、金融、财会、银行、保险等,必然涉及有关专业的知识、术语。国际商务信函比其他行业的应用文使用国际通用的专业术语更多,其行业规范程度更高。美国语言哲学家保尔·格赖斯(Grice,1975)认为,在所有的语言交际活动中为了达到特定的目标,说话人和听话人之间存在着一种默契,一种双方都应该遵守的原则,这种原则被称为会话的合作原则(Cooperative Principle,CP)。具体来说,合作原则要求每一个交谈参与者在整个交谈过程中所说的话符合这一次交谈的目标或方向。正是他们这种合作使得交谈者能够持续地进行有意义的语言交际。就国际商务信函而言,合作原则有四条准则,即数量(quantity)、质量(quality)、关联(relation)和方式(manner)。在公司对公司的旨在交流信息的国际商务信函写译中,"数量准则规定了国际商务信函交际时需要传递必要的信息量;质量准则规定了国际商务信函交际的真实性,所传递的信息应有根有据;关联准则规定了国际商务信函交际内容要切题,与主题无关的内容不要涉及;方式准则在表达方式上提出了要求,要求国际商务信函交际的语言要简洁,不用语义含糊的词语,避免啰唆"(梁玉茹、黄远鹏,2011:354)。所以,国际商务信函行文要专业地道、精确严谨、用语礼貌。总之,国际商务信函的写译要在语言文字上做到文本格式"尺牍"化;行文用字套式化;信文内容实用化;业务用语专业化(贾文波,2004)。

但是,商务汉英信函在"斟词酌句、布局谋篇"上存在较大差异。这就要求我们辨别商务汉英之间的异同,去异趋同,尽量在国际商务信函写译中遵照合作原则,满足国际商务信函写译的文体语言要求,使我们的国际商务信函写译更加规范、有效。

另一方面,作为人们传递信息和沟通业务的一种文体,"每一封商务信函在本质上都是一封促销信,每写一封信就是在推销一样东西:产品、公司形象、企划或是你自己"(许建忠,2002:269)。因此,商务汉英信函的礼貌用语或客套话比比皆是。但是,由于文化价值观的差异,不同国别、不同民族的人对礼貌的表达方式也有所不同。此外,为了维持交易双方之间的业务关系,我们须对汉英的语态进行转换,以便使语气委婉。

1.1 用词简练准确、行文专业规范上的汉英语言文化差异对比分析与翻译

1.1.1 文本格式"尺牍"化,商务汉英信函的言语程式不同

商务汉英信函的格式有显著的区别。比如,商务汉语信函的称呼语用"启者"或"敬启者",英译就是 To Whom It May Concern 或 Dear Sir or Madam。又如,汉语证明信或介绍信的开头一般都是"兹证明……"或"兹介绍……",英译就是"This is to certify … "或"This is to introduce … "。再如,汉语信函表达意愿的结尾段大多说"盼复",英译就是"We are looking forward to hearing from you."或其省略句"Looking forward to hearing from you."。

商务汉语信函"尺牍"化用语与对应的英语信函程式化套语对比见表12.1。

表 12.1 汉语"尺牍"化用语与英语信函程式化套语对比

汉语"尺牍"化用语	英语程式化套语
函悉	acknowledge receipt of your letter
今来函有关……	We are writing concerning …
兹复	In reply
请告之	Please let us know
特此奉告	We are pleased to advise/inform …
顺告	For your reference
特此函告	Notice is hereby given that …
提请注意	would like to draw / call / invite one's attention
如蒙答复,不胜感激	Your kind reply will greatly oblige us.
谨告之	Please be advised …
详见附表	as per list enclosed
随函附寄……请查收	Enclosed please find …
谨启/敬上	Sincerely yours / Faithfully yours

1.1.2 信文内容实用化,但汉英有别

作为以功利性为目的的实用性文体(贾文波,2004),商务汉英信函重在传递交流商贸信息,因此行文通俗、用词朴实、句法结构简明、段落层次分明,一事一段,带有较强的"公事公办的持重感",从不含糊啰唆。

请对比分析以下商务汉英翻译实例:

① 24 盒装 1 托盘,10 托盘装 1 整集装箱。

英译:Twenty boxes are on a pallet, and ten pallets to an FCL container.

对比分析：汉英信函用词无冗余。汉语原句无任何虚词,而英译因句法需要加上几个介词和一个连词。

此外,商务信函的另一特征就是,"为顺应'实用有效'的原则而不避章法雷同,篇章布局基本公式化"(贾文波,2004:269)。

请对比分析以下商务汉英信函翻译实例:

②
尊敬的麦克布瑞德女士:

有关第954号采购合同,条款列明交货日期为2020年6月。现欲提前至2020年3月交货。

本公司对于提早装运该货所引致的不便,深表歉意。然而,实因有急切需要,才做此要求,还望贵公司能加以谅察。

本着贵我双方长期良好的商业联系,相信贵公司定会尽力帮忙。

如蒙帮助,将不胜感激。

速复为盼。

埃里克·埃文斯敬启
经理
(签名)

英译:

Dear Ms. McBride,

We refer to our purchase contract No. 954.

Under the terms of the contract, delivery is scheduled for June 2020. We would now like to bring delivery forward to March 2020.

We realize that the change of delivery date will probably inconvenience you and we offer our sincere apologies. We know that you will understand that we would not ask for earlier delivery if we did not have compelling reasons for doing so.

In view of our longstanding, cordial commercial relationship, we would be very grateful if you would make a special effort to comply with our request.

We look forward to your early reply.

Yours sincerely,
Eric Evans
Manager

对比分析：汉英信函通篇无任何废话,用词朴实客观,无文饰;就事论事,公事公办,无任何虚礼客套之辞。

但是,汉语倾向于使用修饰语,中国人喜欢使用比喻等修辞手法而堆砌一些渲染之辞的语用修辞情结,这与英语简明扼要的修辞倾向产生了语言文化上的冲突,这一冲突导致在以"重纪实、少文饰"为主要文体特征的商务汉英信函写译中出现了大量语用失误问题。

请对比分析以下商务汉英翻译实例:

③ 我们<u>满怀信心地</u>认为,你们的交易额将<u>十分</u>可观,你们不用多久就会再次向我们订货。

误译:We <u>confidently</u> believe that you will have a good turnover, and that you will be able to place repeat orders with us in the near future.

改译:We are <u>confident</u> that you will have a good turnover, and that you will be able to place repeat orders with us in the near future.

对比分析:汉语原文很好地示例了汉语喜欢渲染的修辞倾向。误译使用了同义词语 confidently,而使文字啰哩啰唆。所以,只有删除这个重复之词,才能使改译的表达简洁经济。

1.1.3 业务用语专业化,汉英信函充斥专业术语

作为有着专门用途的实用文体,商务汉英信函的语言表达自然有其专业性。专业性的表现就是大量使用专业术语(technical terms),如唛头(shipping marks)、离岸价(FOB)、CIF(到岸价)、bulk pack(散包装/大包装)等。专业性用语是商务汉英信函有别于普通信函的最本质的区别。只有准确而恰当地使用专业术语,才能使商务信函行文地道。

请对比分析以下商务汉英翻译实例:

④ 对于所订货物的付款方式,我方要求凭装船单据,以保兑的不可撤销的即期信用证支付。

英译:For goods ordered, we require payment to be made <u>by a confirmed and irrevocable letter of credit payable on sight upon the presentation of shipping documents</u>.

对比分析:此例主要涉及付款方式,其特点是措辞严谨准确、信息量大、专业性强。其中,使用的专业术语集中,包括"装船单据""保兑的""不可撤销的""即期的""信用证"。此外,汉语对虚词使用也较多,如"所""凭""以"等。为了实现专业性较强与正式文体信息的等值转换,英译同样简洁严谨、准确地道、专业性强,堪称精确。(李明,2007)

1.2 礼貌用语上的商务汉英语言文化差异对比分析与翻译

在我国,"人无笑脸别开店""好言好语事事通";在英国,礼貌被看作"一封四方通用的自荐书"。无论是中国人的俗话,还是英国人的比喻,它们都说明了礼貌及礼貌用语(expressions of politeness)的重要性。礼貌用语是表示客气的一种礼貌语言,是约定俗成的客套话。然而,由于汉英语言与文化的差异以及东西方有关礼貌的思维表达习惯不同,商务汉英信函礼貌用语有着很大的区别。

除了使用敬辞敬语之外,汉语信函还通过使用"贬己尊人"的谦辞敬语表达对对方的尊敬。这些谦辞敬语大多是汉语文言词语,或者是常用的地道客套语,如贵公司(your company)、贵函(your letter)、惠顾(your patronage)、敝公司(my company)、敝人(I)、拜读(have the pleasure of reading)等。

以上所举汉语谦辞敬语就是"满招损,谦受益"的中国礼貌文化的具体体现。不同民族的礼貌用语或客套话有各自的习惯表达方式。如果不了解这些文化差异,就会出现语用文化失误。比如,我们就不能不顾表达习惯或文化差异而把"敝公司""拙见""贵函"等谦辞敬语直译成不符合英语文化习惯的汉式英语——our poor company, my humble opinion 或 your valuable letter。相比之下,规范得体的等值英译转换应删减那些"贬己尊人"之词,如 poor, humble 或 valuable。

请对比分析以下汉英翻译实例:

⑤ 兹确认贵公司 8 月 12 日的订单。承蒙惠顾非常欣慰。

英译:We have much pleasure in confirming herewith the order which you kindly placed with us on August 12.

对比分析:原文虽未使用"贬己"之谦辞,但使用了"敬人"的语言表达方式"贵公司"。"敬人"的礼貌用语"贵公司"在当代英语环境下只需要被翻译成 you 或 your company/corporation 即可。

1.3 语气和语态使用上的商务汉英语言文化差异对比分析与翻译

俗话说得好,"和气生财"。不管是面对面交谈,还是电话交谈,或是书面交流,商务人士都应本着客气、礼貌的原则。写信人有着明确的为了自己利益的目的,但收信人最关心的是他本人或他所代表的公司的利益。写信人应该让收信人读信时感到心情舒畅,这对交易的达成会起到很大的促进作用。所以,商务汉英信函写译非常注重委婉语气的使用。但是,汉英两种语言在委婉语气的表达方面存在着语用文化上的差异,因此我们必须充分重视这种文化差异,按照不同的语言与文化习惯,更加有效、恰当地进行跨文化商务交流。

由于汉英文化的差异,中国人可能在某些方面表达得更加间接;而英美等西方国家的人可能在另一些方面表现得更加委婉。比如,中国人在拒绝别人的请求时通常不会直接说"不",而是使用"让我考虑考虑"之类的委婉之辞;与中国人偏爱使用祈使句提出比较直接的请求方式不同的是,英美等西方国家的人可能选用语气较委婉、意思较间接的陈述句和疑问句提出请求。究其原因是,"在西方文化里,实施'命令''建议''劝告''批评''要求'等指示性言语行为都被当作对个人主义的侵扰"(黄勇,2007:146)。所以,人们往往选择比较间接、比较委婉的得体语气来表达上述语言功能。例如:

⑥ 烦请贵方尽快报纽约离岸最低价。(祈使句)

英译1:We shall be very grateful to you if you would quote us your lowest price FOB New York ASAP.(陈述句)

英译2:Would you please quote us your lowest price FOB New York ASAP?(疑问句)

除了使用不同功能的句式表达不同的语气之外,在商务英语信函中,被动语态也常被用来表达较委婉的批评、责备、埋怨、索赔等负面的消息或消极的思想观点,以便顾全对方的面子,避免触犯对方。相比之下,汉语倾向于使用主动语态。汉英之间这种语态上的差别极有可能造成中国学生使用主动语态较多而使表达出现语用失误。所以,为了"和气生财",我们在进行商务汉英信函写译时应注意汉英在语态上的差异,并进行汉英语态的必要转换,以便表达间接、礼貌一些。

请对比分析以下商务汉英翻译实例:

⑦ 你方在装船发货过程中由于马虎而弄错了。

英译:A careless mistake was made during the course of shipment.

对比分析:汉语原句所用主动语态似乎有责备抱怨之意,可能会伤害读信人的感情。英译所用被动语态使语气缓和了许多,也委婉了一些。这有利于交易双方之间的业务关系的维持。

第二节 对商务汉英信函翻译的启示与警示

◆ 2.1 对商务汉英信函翻译的启示

通过对商务汉英信函语言文化差异进行对比分析,我们发现,商务汉语信函英译须注意以下几点。

2.1.1 英译要准确规范

卡耐基指出,书信是人们传递信息、交流感情的一种文体。因此,商务信函所传递的信息是信函这种文体最为重要的内容。

准确规范是商务汉英信函翻译必须遵循的原则。准确是指在翻译转换过程中做到信息的准确无误。"规范"是指译文应合乎不同商务专业领域的行文规范。国际商务涉及许多领域,在长期实践中已经形成了独特的专业术语、行话、套语等。在翻译过程中,我们首先必须准确理解这些专业术语表达的含义与其固定译法。在此基础上,我们应该在译文中使用专业地道的英语,努力做到翻译规范准确。

请对比分析以下商务汉英翻译实例:

① 我方在传真中已报实盘 250 长吨钢管拉各斯成本加保险费加运费每长吨 620 英镑。

英译:You must have noticed from our fax that we are in a position to make you a firm offer on 250 L/Ts Steel Tubes at £ 620 per L'T CIF Lagos.

② 一份可转让提单连同一张汇票及其他装运单证已寄给你方银行,以收取货款。

英译:One copy of negotiable bill of lading together with a draft and other shipping documents has been forwarded to your bank for collection of the payment.

对比分析:在例①中,译文将汉语原文所用价格术语和重量单位"成本加保险费加运费"和"长吨"准确而专业地转换成同样专业地道的 CIF 和 L/T。在例②中,汉英专业术语的翻译也是非常地道规范的。

2.1.2 在功能对等的基础上照顾读者的语言文化语境

正如前文所说的"4Es"翻译原则,商务汉英信函的翻译同样要做到对等。具体来讲,信函翻译对等是指语义信息、文体风格信息、专业文化信息和读者反应上的对等。但是,汉英两种语言的读者有着不同的语言文化语境,为了使读者反应尽量一致,英译可以从语言形式上进行改写。

请对比分析以下商务汉英翻译实例:

③ 这是我们的包装设计图纸,请交给制造商,供他们参考。(祈使句)

英译:This is our design for the packing. Could you possibly give it to the manufacturers for their reference?(疑问句)

对比分析:汉语原句属于祈使句,汉语读者习惯于"祈求""要求""命令""建议"等指示性言语行为,而英语读者会认为这些言语行为是对个人的侵扰,所以英译将汉语祈使句转换成了语气委婉一些的疑问句。

2.2 对商务汉英信函翻译的警示

2.2.1 英译不能浮夸

汉语偏爱浮夸渲染之辞,一些言辞无太大实际意义,但这已经成为汉民族的一种修辞倾向。在进行商务汉英信函翻译时,我们应大胆删除那些言之无物的空洞之辞。这也是遵守"质量准则"的具体体现与要求。

请对比分析以下商务汉英翻译实例:

④ 本公司对市场有着绝对的垄断地位。

误译:The company has a complete monopoly of the market.

改译:The company has a monopoly of the market.

⑤ 贵方在五月的第一天所写信函,我方已经收悉,谢谢!

误译:Your letter you wrote on the first day of the month of May has been received by me with many thanks.

改译:Thank you for your letter of May 1.

对比分析:此例因死译汉语原文而导致英译啰唆冗余。

2.2.2 英译语气不能太冲

以礼待人有利于业务关系的维护与发展,礼貌委婉的语气在商务沟通中非常重要。英译不要受汉语主动语态的负面影响,应做变"态"处理,或改用其他语气委婉一些的表达方式。

请对比分析以下商务汉英翻译实例:

⑥ 贵方未能在新的价格实施前将订单寄给我们。

误译:You failed to send your order to us before the new prices were introduced.

改译：Unfortunately, we did not receive your order before the new prices were introduced.

⑦ 鉴于你方违约给我方造成的不应有的损失，我方遗憾地撤销了此合约，并保留对我方损失的索赔权。

误译：In view of the fact that your violation of the contract has caused us undeserved losses, we regret to say that we have canceled the contract, and we reserve the right to claim damages.

改译：In view of the undeserved losses caused by your violation of the contract, we regret to say that we have canceled the contract, and we reserve the right to claim damages.

对比分析：例⑥中的误译属于语气生硬的直译，对方不易接受；改译则转换主语，变直接的指责为间接委婉的表达，使对方比较容易接受。在例⑦中，汉语原文使用了汉语常见的主动语态，语言表达比较直接，充满怨气和不满，极有可能伤害双方的感情。误译未对汉语原句所用主动语态进行变"态"转换，所以语气同样伤人；而改译所用被动语态使语气得到了缓和，意思表达间接多了。

2.2.3 英译语气不能不近人情

被动语态的使用给人以"公事公办"的不近人情的感觉。相比之下，主动语态的使用可以塑造比较亲切自然的语气，这样就能拉近彼此之间的距离。

请对比分析以下商务汉英翻译实例：

⑧ 若贵方价格至少降低8%，我们会非常高兴继续订货。

误译：If your price could be reduced at least by 8%, we would be very happy to place further orders with you.

改译：If you could reduce your price at least by 8%, we would be very happy to place further orders with you.

⑨ 随函附寄我方产品宣传册和价目表，请查收。

误译：Enclosed herewith are a brochure and a price-list.

改译：I enclose a brochure and our price-list for your reference.

对比分析：误译采用了被动语态的译法，给人一种不近人情的感觉，不利于营造亲近自然的气氛，而改译采用的主动语态则有益于建立友好和谐的业务关系。

附表　商务汉英信函常用语和相关表达

商务信函开头常用语	
We are writing to … //我方写信的目的是……	With regard to；With reference to；Regarding … //关于……
We are in receipt of your letter … //贵方……来函收讫。	Thank you for your letter. //来函收悉,谢谢。
We have received your letter of … //……的来函已经收悉。	We acknowledge receipt of your letter of … //贵方……来函已经收悉。
I am contacting you for the following reason. //因下述事由,兹联系贵方。	We are pleased to tell you that … //我方很高兴地告知贵方……
商务信函结尾常用语	
Looking forward to hearing from you. //盼复!	I look forward to receiving your reply. //盼复!
I hope that this information will help you. //希望这个信息将对贵方有所帮助。	Please contact me if you need any further information. //若需了解更多情况,请与我联系。
Please feel free to contact me if you have any further questions. //若有问题,请随时联系我,不要客气。	Please let me know if you need any further information. //若需了解更多情况,请告知。
Thank you so much for … //非常感谢……	Thank you again for … //对……再一次致谢。
建立业务关系常用语	
business relationship //业务关系	build；establish；set up；enter into (trade relationship) //建立(贸易关系)
Commercial Counselor's Office //商务参赞处	the Chinese Embassy in London //中国驻伦敦大使馆
Chamber of Commerce //商会	import and export //进出口
firm //商号	importer //进口商
exporter //出口商	with a view to building trade relations //旨在建立贸易关系
询盘常用语	
for your reference；for your information //仅供参考	In a position to do … //能够做……
general inquiry //一般性询价	specific inquiry //具体询价
current price；ruling price //现行价格	competitive price //优惠价
rock-bottom price //底价	market price //市价
in urgent need of the goods //急需此货	mini fair //小型交易会
price-list //价目表	sample book //样品簿
inquiry note //询价单	We enclose … //随函附寄……

续表

询盘常用语	
Enclosed please find … //随函附寄……请查收。	attachment //附件
catalogue //产品目录	comply with //依照
inquire about //询问	make an inquiry about … //对……进行询价
报盘常用语	
offer //报盘	quotation //报价
firm offer //实盘	non-firm offer //虚盘
proforma invoice //形式发票	cash discount //现金折扣
quantity discount //数量折扣	subject to our final confirmation //以我方最后确认为准
subject to prior sale //以先售为准	subject to goods being unsold //以货未售出为准
subject to change without notice //以变价不予通知为准	effective (valid, firm, open) for ten days from 15 January //自1月15日起有效,有效期为10天
还盘常用语	
counter-offer //还盘	the difference in price //差价
the market is declining //行市疲软	be fully booked; be fully committed //订货已满
out of stock //缺货	be on the high side //偏高
be unable to entertain your counter-offer //无法接受贵方还盘	revert to sth. //重谈某事
成交常用语	
conclude a transaction; close a transaction; finalize a transaction //成交	Let's call it a deal. //成交!
accept your offer //接受你方报盘	confirm your order //确认你方订单
place an order with …; register an order with …; file an order with … //向……下订单;订货	repeat order //再订货
regular order //经常订货	trial order //试订货
SC (sales confirmation) //售货确认书;售货合同	PC (purchase confirmation) //购货确认书
包装及装运常用语	
packing //包装	large packing //大包装
small packing //小包装	transport packing //运输包装
sales packing //销售包装	outer packing //外包装
inner packing //内包装	neutral packing //中性包装
shipping marks //装运标志;唛头	warning marks //警示标志
directive marks //指示标志	carton //硬板纸箱
seaworthy packing //适于海运的包装	bulk cargo //散装货

包装及装运常用语	
shipment //装运	transshipment //转运
partial shipment //分批装运	container ship //集装箱船
FCL (full container load) //整箱货	LCL (less than container load) //拼箱货
shipping advice //已装船通知	shipping note //托运单
shipment note //装船通知单	consignment //托运的货物
carrier //承运人	consignor //发货人;托运人
consignee //收货人	shipping instructions //装船须知
shipping documents //装运单证	shipping order //装货单
shipping agent //装运代理人	freight forwarder //货运代理人;货代
book shipping space //预订舱位	charter //整船包租
付款常用语	
terms of payment //付款条件	Documentary L/C //跟单信用证
Irrevocable L/C //不可撤销信用证	Clean L/C //光票信用证
Usance L/C //远期信用证	Confirmed L/C //保兑信用证
Transferable L/C //可转让信用证	Revolving L/C //循环信用证
Sight L/C //即期信用证	Cash & Carry //一手交钱,一手交货
deposit //定金	advance payment //预付款
payment //货款	commission //佣金;提成
allowance;discount //折扣;回扣	draft/ bill of exchange //汇票
collection //托收	remittance //汇兑
opening bank //开证行	advising bank //通知行
negotiating bank //议付行	confirming bank //保兑行
paying bank //付款行	debit note //借项清单;付款通知书
credit note //贷项清单	invoice //发票
保险常用语	
insurer //保险商	insurance company //保险公司
effect insurance //投保	premium //保险费
insurance policy //保单	insurance coverage //保险范围
Ocean Marine Cargo Insurance //海洋运输货物保险	insurance claim //保险索赔
insurance indemnity //保险赔偿	insurance clause //保险条款
survey report //检验报告	surveyor //检验员

续表

索赔理赔常用语	
complaint and claim //申诉与索赔	lodge a claim //提出索赔
entertain a claim //答应索赔	accept a claim //接受索赔
withdraw a claim //放弃索赔	force majeure //不可抗力
arbitration //仲裁	consultation //协商
without recourse //无追索权	reserve the right to claim on you //保留向你方索赔的权利
商务信函常用缩略词	
'Cause(because)//因为	wf(wharf)//码头
Ad/advert(advertisement)//广告	Int'l(international)//国际
w'hse(warehouse)//仓库;货栈	EC(electronic commerce)//电子商务
asap;ASAP(as soon as possible)//尽快	a/c bks(account books)//账本
B/L;Blading(Bill of Lading)//提单	telecon(telephone+conference)//电话会议
X WKS(ex works)//工厂交货价	XXL(double extra large)//超特大号
FOB(Free On Board)//船上交货价	CFR(Cost and Freight)//成本加运费价
CIF(Cost,Insurance and Freight)//成本、保险加运费价	L/C(Letter of Credit)//信用证
D/P(Documents against Payment)//付款交单	D/A(Documents against Acceptance)//承兑交单
CAD(Cash Against Delivery)//凭单付款	PICC(the People's Insurance Company of China)//中国人保
T/T(Telegraphic Transfer)//电汇	M/T(Mail Transfer)//信汇
D/D(Demand Draft)//票汇	4 SALE(For Sale)//出售
s.s.Qingdao(steamship Qingdao)//青岛号轮	m.v.Guangzhou(motor vessel Guangzhou)//广州号轮
商务信函基本构成部分的名称	
letterhead //信头	reference number //文号
date //日期	inside name and address //封内姓名与地址
attention line //经办人姓名	salutation //称呼语
body of the letter //信函正文	subject line //主题行
complimentary close //信尾客套语	signature //签名
Encl(enclosure)//附件	C.C.(carbon copy)//副本抄送
P.S.(Postscript)//附言	Per Pro(Per Procurationem)//由……代理;由……代表

思考与练习

1. 思考题

(1) 商务英语信函有什么语言特征?

(2) 商务汉英信函翻译应该采取什么策略?

2. 句子翻译

(1) 我们对贵方样品展览室里陈列的男式衬衫很感兴趣。

(2) 请尽早寄来最新目录五份。

(3) 如果交易条件和交货日期合意的话,相信我们会定期向贵方订货。

(4) 如果贵方尽早寄来交易条件优惠的样品,我们将不胜感激。

(5) 谢谢你方来函表示愿意提供服务,我方愿与你方就扩大贸易的可能性进行讨论。

(6) 请注意,我们与发展中国家做生意只接受信用证付款方式。

(7) 一旦收到贵方订单,我们将立即发货。

(8) 关于我方提供压缩机一事,一俟我方有进一步消息,即电告你方。

(9) 如果你们订购这种商品,我们可以按你们所需要的数量供应。

(10) 我方可接受交单付现的付款方式。

(11) 相关信用证将通过雅加达第一国家银行开出。收到后请立即安排装运,我方非常感谢。

(12) 如果你方能满足我方的需要,答应提前交货,我方就接受你方的价格。

(13) 你方价格远低于我方成本,我方不能按你方价格成交。

(14) 贵方须更换受损的货物。

3. 语篇翻译

● 语篇1

敬启者:

关于第1234号合同的第一批到货,其中部分货物的质量不符合合同规定,对此我们已经于本月7日函告,并要求贵方做出解释和提出处理办法,但迄今尚未得到答复。

所以我们很遗憾地说,我们不能接受第二批货物。我们只好要求贵方暂时缓装该批货物。自不待言,我方对此不负任何责任。

候复。

谨上

- 语篇 2

敬启者：

我方第 U89 号订单

　　我公司第 U89 号订单项下 100 套咖啡具昨天交到，但遗憾的是，其中 15 套损坏严重。咖啡具外包装状态良好，故我方接受了到货并予以签收，未提任何问题。在开包时，我们十分小心，可以认为，损坏只能是在装箱前某个阶段搬动不慎所造成的。

　　希望你公司能对这 15 套咖啡具尽快全部予以调换。我们已将损坏的咖啡具保存，以备你方向供货单位索赔时使用。

　　此致

敬礼

2019 年 9 月 18 日

- 语篇 3

敬启者：

　　今冒昧来信做自我介绍。我们担任你天津分公司陶瓷部门代理已有一段时间。我们的努力令双方都很满意。这一点贵方可向你天津分公司查询。

　　我们专营家用物品和装饰品，如瓷器、漆器和水晶饰品，所以我们希望担任贵公司的独家代理，在温哥华推销贵公司的产品。

　　如果贵公司同意我们的建议，请告知贵方签订独家销售协议的条款。

　　此致

敬礼

2019 年 10 月 12 日

第十三章

商务汉英合同对比分析与翻译

Identify the problems in the following translations

① 供方应保证自己是所提供的技术的合法拥有者,并且保证所提供的技术具有完整性、准确性、有效性,能够达到合同规定的目的。

英译:The supplier shall ensure that it is the lawful owner of the technology to be provided, which is complete, accurate, effective and capable of attaining the technical targets specified in the contract.

② 合同自签字之日起6个月仍不能生效,双方均有权解除合同。

英译:In case the contract cannot come into force within SIX months after the date of signing the contract, both parties shall have the right to cancel the contract.

③ 上述合同由于双方的良好配合,得以顺利执行,双方甚为满意,贵方要求继续合作,我方表示欢迎。

英译:Because of both parties' good cooperation, the above-mentioned contract has been carried out smoothly. Both parties are very satisfied. We welcome your requirements for the continuation of the cooperation.

商务合同是具有法律约束力的文件。合同类文件包括合同、契约、协议、意向书等,是双方当事人就某一经济或商业活动经过协商达成的协议,对当事人具有法律效力。我们这里讨论的合同是指正式的涉外商务合同。这种合同因有涉外交易性质,需要汉英两种版本,所以大多需要翻译。

众所周知,一份规范、贴切的合同"也许就带来了业务的提高、收益的增加"(邹海峰、赵耀、Manvel Lunes,2003:前言)。但在我国对外经贸快速发展与涉外经贸合同数量不断增加的同时,涉外经贸纠纷也越来越多。其中,不少涉外纠纷在很大程度上是由合同文字引起的。合同的措辞不当、词义含糊不清、文义松散宽泛等,致使合同一方有意或无意地利用合同漏洞,逃避应该承担的责任和义务,就导致合同纠纷的产生。我国涉外经贸交往中采用的合同大多为英文本,而英文经贸合同对语言有严格的要求,强调措辞准确、结构严谨、格式规范。因此,为了避免纠纷,法律文书必须词义准确、文义确切,既不能因词义模棱两可而产生歧义,也不能因句子缺乏严密组织而任意歪曲。

总体而言,商务汉英合同具有篇章结构程式化与表述结构条目化、句式结构复杂、用词正式规范、内容完整、具有针对性等法律文献的语言文化特征。

第一节　商务汉英合同语言文化差异的对比分析与翻译

商务合同集专业性、实用性、规范性于一身,在长期的实践过程中,汉英合同文本已形成自己特殊的风格、惯用的格式和专用的词汇与语句,这些特点使其有别于其他文体。对于商务合同中的许多专业词汇,汉英两种语言都有一一对应的特点,我们在翻译时必须按照其表达的专业意思进行翻译,要不折不扣地反映出合同语场中原文的语言面貌和内涵。比如,promissory note 指"本票";instrument 在商业上多表示"正式的单据或文件",而在结算业务中表示"票据"的总称;合同中的"清偿、补偿"用 satisfaction;"损害"则用 prejudice 表示。这些专业、半专业语汇在汉英合同中都能一一找到对等词。因此,译者要根据专业知识和英语语言知识去"选用对应的商务合同专业术语,不得盲目搭配或随意创造"(胡亚红、李崇月,2009:371)。"在商务合同语场中,其焦点就是指向信息,译者必须提高与普通词汇同形的词汇在合同中的理解与辨别能力,确保译文与原文达到概念意义的对等。"(王盈秋,2011:92)下面将从精确、庄重、严谨三个合同语言特征方面对比分析商务汉英合同的共同点与不同点。

◆ 1.1　商务合同都力求精确,但汉英各有其道

合同语言的一大特征就是精确无误。"精确就是恰如其分地表达当事人的要求,不使用歧义、多义、含糊的词句,标点符号都不能用错。"(黎运汉,2005:350)

合同语言表达要做到精确,用词造句必须规范,数量、时间、地点的表达尤其要精确无误,不能模棱两可。例如:

① 在正常情况下,乙方拒不交货,则每天处以货物总额 20% 的罚金;质量不合,则重新酬价;如逾期交货,则每天处以货款 5% 的滞罚金。

分析:这里的"正常情况""质量不合""逾期交货"都是罚款的前提条件,不能被遗漏,"20%""5%"的表达非常精确。我们既不能笼统地说"处以罚金",也不能

在"20%"和"5%"之后加"以上""以内"之类的词语,否则难以执罚。(黎运汉,2005:350)

② On the date of coming into force of this Lease, the Lessee deposits with the Lessor the sum equaling three months' rent (=USD 6,000) as security for the faithful performance of the provisions of this Lease, and to be returned to the Lessee without interest when the Lessee surrenders the premises and all the equipment are in good condition on expiration November 24, 2008 of this Lease or based on the condition of this Lease for sooner termination. [本租赁合同生效日起,承租人应向出租人支付相当于3个月租金(6 000美元)的押金,作为忠实履行本租约的担保金。本押金将于2008年11月24日租约到期时,在承租人交还租房,并且所有设备完好的前提下,归还承租人,不计利息,或者,在租约提前终止时,按本租约规定办理。]

分析:这里的"相当于3个月租金(6 000美元)的押金""于2008年11月24日租约到期"都必须准确无误,不得笼统模糊,否则就会引起经济上的纠纷。

商品的数量在交易中至关重要,必须写得精确。合同中不能出现笼统含糊的数字,如"一堆"(a heap of)、"一套"(a set of)等,交货数量也不能使用"约"(about/approximately)字。计量单位也要明确,是"斤"(*jin*)还是"公斤"(kilogram),是"吨"(ton)还是"公吨"(metric ton),是"长吨"(long ton)还是"短吨"(short ton),是"打"(dozen)还是"罗"(score),是"尺"(*chi*)还是"米"(meter),这些不能写错,也不能含糊,否则就容易产生纠纷。双方履行的时间界限也必须写得具体、准确。例如,财产租赁合同、借贷合同的起止时间,都不能含糊。如果不是实际日期的,其界定应用"以前"(not later than)、"以内"(within),而不能用"以后"(after),也不能用"尽可能在……"(as possible as you can),否则可能招致很大损失。交货、运货地点也必须写明。

为了确保合同语言的精确性,商务汉英合同常用语义相对固定单一的法律、商贸等专业术语,每一个专业术语都表示一个特定的法律或商贸概念,任何人在任何情况下都必须对它做同一解释,如下列英语法律术语:alibi(不在犯罪现场)、appeal(上诉)、bail(保释)、burden of proof(举证责任)、cause of action(案由)、damages(损失赔偿金)、defendant(被告)、due diligence(审慎调查)、remedy(补偿,赔偿)、felony(重罪)、lessor(出租人)(潘红,2004);其结构与组词(structure and components)约定俗成,通常无法用其他词语替代。由于涉外经贸合同主要涉及国际贸易及国际投资方面的内容,因此我们在起草或翻译经贸英语合同时经常会用到许多国际经贸、国际结算、国际投资等领域中的专业语汇,如negotiable instrument(流通票据)、bill of lading(提单)、shipping marks(唛头)、neutral packing(中性包装)、factoring(保理)等。考虑到特定场合的需要,有时合同会对一些关键术语的定义做明确的限定和说明。此类释义一般可分为两种,即扩展性解释和限缩性解释。例如,"'Trademark' here means registered trademark"(本合同中的"商标"系指注册商标)这一句就对商标做了限定性解释,因而排除了普通商标,即非注册商标。

其次,商务汉英合同还常使用套话,如 and for no other purposes, shall not operate as a waiver, shall not be deemed a consent, including but not limited to, or other similar or dissimilar causes, without prejudice to, nothing contained herein shall 等。此外,为了防止所涉及的条款出现片面性解释,商务汉英合同通常会用特定的套语,如"Words in the singular include the plural and vice versa; words used in the masculine gender include every gender."(文字上之单数包括复数在内,反之亦然;文字上之男性包括女性在内,反之亦然。)。

再者,为了强调其庄严性,追求准确效果,普通词汇中有不少同义词叠用现象。"这种同义词叠用,从一份合同中看,数量并不多,从合同的总体来讲,这种现象不可不谓之多。"(杨一秋,2003:40)这种以 and /or 并置的同义词或近义词分为以下几种:

- 名词:clause, covenant, or agreement(条款、约定或协议);loss or damage(损失或损害);negligence, fault or failure(疏忽、过失或未履行规定的责任和义务);duties or obligations(责任或义务);terms and conditions(条款/条款及细则);the complication of the contract or the expiration of the contract(合同履行完毕或合同到期)
- 动词:made and signed(签订);alter and change(变更);bind and obligate(约束);make and enter into(签订)
- 形容词:sole and exclusive(独家的);final and conclusive(最终);null and void(无效的/无束缚力的)
- 从属连词:when and as(当……时候)
- 介词:by and between(由……);over and above(在……之外);from and after(从……之后)

1.2 商务合同都力求庄重典雅,但汉英各择手段

商务汉英合同常常涉及经济利益或法律权利、责任等,所以合同所用语汇和行文往往庄重典雅,表现出严肃规范的文体风格。例如:

③ 本合同经各方签章之日起生效。本合同一式三联,借款人、保证人各持一联,贷款方持一联。

④ 本协议用中、英两种文字缮制,两种文字具有同等法律效力。协议双方各执一份。

分析：带有下划线的字词为语体正式的书面语汇，大多用于极正式的文体。

⑤ At the request of Party B, Party A agrees to send technicians to <u>assist</u> Party B to install the equipment.

分析：商务合同要求使用文体正式的语汇，assist 就比 help 正式多了。相比之下，assist 的文体色彩较浓，一般用于像法律文体这样的正式文体之中。

⑥ In processing transactions, the manufacturers never have <u>title</u> either to the materials or to the finished products.

分析：title 一词属于法律词汇，专门用于法律文体之中，而与之语义近似的 ownership 的文体语义就没有 title 那么庄重典雅。

庄重典雅、严肃规范是所有合同语言追求的文体风格，但是汉英合同为达此目标而各择手段。汉语大多采用文言或半文言语汇，如"本""兹""其""于""之""在此""特此""自此""随附""鉴于"等。此外，为了达到庄重严肃的效果，汉语合同常用文体极正式的书面语汇，如"未了债务""协商未果""不得""终止合同""续约""履约""违约"等。相比之下，英语合同为使语言庄重典雅而往往采用典雅的古体词，如 hereafter（after this time, in the future）、hereby（by this letter or in this way）、herein（in this document）、hereinafter（later in this contract）、hereinbefore（in a preceding part of this contract）、therefrom（from that）、therein（in that / in that particular）、whereto（to which）等。此外，英语合同常采用正式、庄重的法律和书面词语，如 shall, in accordance with, termination, liquidation 等。例如：

⑦ 合同自签字之日起6个月仍不能生效，双方均有权解除合同。

In case the contract cannot come into force within SIX months after the date of signing the contract, the contract <u>shall</u> be binding neither to Party A, nor to Party B.

⑧ 本合同期限届满时，双方发生的未了债权和债务不受合同期满的影响，债务人应向债权人继续偿付未了债务。

英译：The outstanding claims and liabilities existing between both parties on the expiry of the validity of the contract <u>shall</u> not be influenced by the expiration of this contract. The debtor <u>shall</u> be kept liable until the debtor fully pays up his debts to the creditor.

◆ 1.3 商务合同都力求严谨，但汉英各有不同

作为法律语言，合同所用词句的词义、语义必须严密，没有歧义。只有如此，才能保证法律的严肃性、权威性和强制性。

汉语是意合型语言，词与词、短语与短语、句子与句子之间的联系大多靠的是意义内

部的关联,而不像英语那样必须使用衔接词语加以衔接,以表明它们之间的层次及逻辑关系。

请对比分析以下商务汉英翻译实例:

⑨ 甲、乙方合作经营的目的是:本着加强经济合作和技术交流的愿望,采用先进而适用的技术和科学的经营管理方法,提高产品质量,发展新产品,并在质量、价格等方面具有国际市场的竞争能力,提高经济效益,使合作各方获得满意的经济利益。

英译:The goals of the parties to the cooperative venture are to enhance economic cooperation and technical exchanges, to improve product quality, to develop new products, and to gain a competitive position in the world market in terms of quality and price by adopting advanced and appropriate technology and scientific management methods, so as to raise economic results and ensure satisfactory economic benefits for each cooperator.

对比分析:汉语中,动宾搭配的使用非常频繁,本例中就有"本着……愿望""采用……技术和方法""提高……质量""发展……产品""具有……竞争能力""提高……效益""获得……经济利益"。由于汉语是意合型语言,这些动宾搭配在汉语中以线性的方式排列而不需要明确它们之间的逻辑关系,但在将它们翻译成英语时则不能像汉语的行文方式一样不考虑它们之间的层次关系和逻辑关系,即有些动宾搭配要以介词短语译出,有些需要用动词不定式进行翻译。本例中的"采用先进而适用的技术和科学的经营管理方法"就是"提高产品质量,发展新产品"的前提,故将它译为 by adopting advanced and appropriate technology and scientific management methods 比较恰当。而"提高经济效益,使合作各方获得满意的经济利益"是前面几个并列动宾搭配的最终目的,故将它以 so as to …译出。(李明,2007)

第二节 对商务汉英合同翻译的启示与警示

◆ 2.1 对商务汉英合同翻译的启示

2.1.1 行文精确,避免歧义

商务合同中有很多专业术语、数字、货币名称等,涉及交货时间、交货条件、价格、付款等

方面的内容。翻译的时候必须做到准确无误,否则将会给双方当事人造成难以估量的损失。

请对比分析以下商务汉英翻译实例:

① 货款由乙方于<u>一周内</u>付清。

英译:Payment shall be made by Party B <u>within a week after taking the delivery</u>.

对比分析:从汉语字面上看,"一周内"似乎可以被译为 in a week,但是这只是其中一个意思,in a week 还可表示"一周后"。所以,为了避免出现因歧义而发生误解的情况,英译准确无误地将汉语原文"一周内"翻译转换成了 within a week after taking the delivery。这样就不会因发生误解而导致经济纠纷。

2.1.2 合句调序,确保严谨

由于汉英两种语言在思维表达方式上存在较大的差异,商务汉语合同大多使用流水句,短句居多;而商务英语合同因行文要求准确严密,一个句子含有几个分句的情况随处可见,长句较多。因此,商务汉英合同翻译不能照句直译,而应在充分理解汉语原文流水句之间的逻辑关系的基础之上,按照英语句法和"主—谓"框架机制对汉语原文的短语、短句等进行重组。这样做的另一个客观原因是英语合同行文为了表达严谨而常使用长句。

请对比分析以下商务汉英翻译实例:

② 合同价格是以现行运费计算,装运时运费的增减均属买方。卖方则承担至交货地的全部运费。

英译:The prices stated are based on current freight rates, any increase or decrease in freight rates at time of shipment is to be the benefit of the buyer, with the seller assuming the payment of all transportation charges to the point or place of delivery.

对比分析:三个汉语短句共传达了三层意思:合同价格的计算、买方对运费的责任和卖方对运费的责任。这三层意思密切相连,一层紧接一层。按照英语表达习惯,英译用了一个 with 引导的介词结构把第三层与前两层意思紧密地连在一起,可谓结构严密。

2.2 对商务汉英合同翻译的警示

2.2.1 宁可略显烦琐,也不留疏漏

合同翻译在词汇和句法上或许都是最有限制性的。为了使译出的文件能有效和有约束力,译者必须遵守一些传统的特殊形式和惯例。"尽管英语有同义重复的忌讳,讲究行文简洁流畅,但在经贸文件中,对一些事关重大的内容和细节表达则应尽量做到详尽精细,以避免含混不清或表述不明。"(贾文波,2004:250)鉴于此,为了表述精确严密,该

重复时还得重复,该啰唆时还要啰唆,宁可略显烦琐,也不留下半点疏漏。

请对比分析以下商务汉英翻译实例:

③ 双方受本合同明确规定的专门条款的约束,如果任何一方因不可抗力如地震、风暴、洪水、水灾或其他自然灾害、瘟疫、战争、暴乱、敌对行动、公共骚乱、公共敌人的行为、政府或公共机关的禁止、劳资纠纷或其他双方无法控制、不可预见的事件,这些事件的发生为不可预防和避免,而无法履行本合同规定的义务时,受妨碍的一方如果可能的话,应在这类不可抗力事件发生后的 8 天内书面通知另一方,并应在 15 天内,提供事件的详细情况和由有关部门签署的证明及一份解释不能履行其按本合同规定应履行的全部或部分义务的说明书。

误译: Subject to special provisions explicitly provided for in this Agreement, if either party has been prevented from performing its obligations under the Agreement because of an event of force majeure such as earthquake, storm, flood, fire, other acts of nature, epidemic, war, riot, hostility, public disturbance, acts of public enemies, prohibition or acts by a government or public agency or labor disputes, or other unforeseeable events beyond the control of the parties, and their occurrence is unpreventable and unavoidable, the party so prevented shall notify the other party in writing within eight (8) days after the occurrence of such event of force majeure, act to mitigate damages, if possible, and within fifteen (15) days thereafter provide detailed information of the event, a certificate of evidence thereof issued by the relevant authorities and a statement explaining the reason for its inability to perform all or part of its obligations under the Agreement.

改译: Subject to special provisions explicitly provided for in this Agreement, if either party has been prevented from performing its <u>duties or obligations</u> under the Agreement because of an event of force majeure such as earthquake, storm, flood, fire, other acts of nature, epidemic, war, riot, hostility, public disturbance, acts of public enemies, prohibition or acts by a government or public agency or labor disputes, or other unforeseeable events beyond the control of the parties, and their occurrence is <u>unpreventable and unavoidable</u>, the party so prevented shall notify the other party in writing within eight (8) days after the occurrence of such event of force majeure, act to mitigate damages, if possible, and within fifteen (15) days thereafter provide detailed information of the event, a certificate of evidence thereof issued by the relevant authorities and a statement explaining the reason for its inability to <u>fulfill and perform</u> all or part of its <u>duties or obligations</u> under the Agreement.

对比分析: 改译所用同义重复(juxtaposition)的语言手段虽显啰唆,但是它们在商务英语合同中已经约定俗成,不可去掉其中任何一个词。否则就会像误译那样,可能因删减其中某个词而发生误解。由此可见,并列的两个同义词(如:duties or obligations, unpreventable and unavoidable, fulfill and perform)虽显冗余,但其共核意义可以避免产生歧义。

2.2.2 英译不要马虎

商务汉英合同翻译转换的信息涉及经济利益,牵扯到合同当事人的责任与义务。所以,英译容不得半点马虎,否则就会给当事人带来经济损失。

请对比分析以下商务汉英翻译实例:

④ 买方须凭复验证书向卖方提出索赔(包括换货),由此引起的全部费用应由卖方负担。

误译:The Buyer shall make a claim against the Seller (including replacement of the goods) by an inspection certificate and all the expenses shall be borne by the Seller.

改译:The Buyer shall make a claim against the Seller (including replacement of the goods) by the further inspection certificate and all the expenses incurred therefrom shall be borne by the Seller.

对比分析:误译并没有准确地译出"复验证书"和"由此引起的全部费用",而只是笼统地将其译成了 inspection certificate 和 all the expenses。相比之下,改译就增译了 further 一词和修饰限定语 incurred therefrom,这样就准确严密多了。

2.2.3 避免不地道的英译,大胆套用

汉英两种语言在合同的行文格式上大不相同(事理顺序也不一样),因此我们进行汉英翻译时就需要跳出汉语行文的条条框框,用英语语言表达习惯和思维逻辑顺序重新组合。否则,英译就会不地道,不符合英语的逻辑顺序。

请对比分析以下商务汉英翻译实例:

⑤ 本协议由双方各自全权代表在上述首签之日起亲自签订,一式两份,双方各执一份,各自具有同等效力。立此为证。

误译:Two copies of the agreement shall be signed by the representatives of the parties hereto, duly authorized for the purpose, on the day and year first above written. Both of the agreement shall be authentic, each party retaining a copy thereof.

改译:IN WITNESS WHEREBY, the parties hereto have caused their representatives, duly authorized for the purpose, to set their hands and seals to two copies of the agreement, both of which shall be authentic, on the day and year first above written, each party retaining a copy thereof.

对比分析：原译没有套用英语合同约定俗成的言语套路，译者完全凭自己的理解进行翻译转换，结果英译有失行文规范。而改译的译者完全以英语习惯行文用字，基本上是一种"填入式"的操作，压倒一切地采用了归化的手法，多了不少原文没有的尺牍用语，却都是英语合同文本不可或缺的、带有鲜明语域特征的固定表达，与信息型文本的翻译要求刚好切合。（贾文波，2007）

附表　商务汉英合同常用语及相关表达

合同名称及序文常用语	
SC（Sales Contract）//售货合同	PC（Purchase Contract）//购货合同
SC（Sales Confirmation）//售货确认书	PC（Purchase Confirmation）//购货确认书
Sales Note //售货单	Purchase Note //购货单
Sales Agreement //售货协议	Purchase Agreement //购货协议
Export Contract //出口合同	Import Contract //进口合同
Consignment Contract //寄售合同	Agency Contract //代理合同
The undersigned Sellers and Buyers have agreed to close the following transaction//本合约签字的买卖双方同意达成以下交易	This contract is made by and between Party A and Party B//本合约由甲方与乙方签订
According to the terms and conditions stipulated below //按以下规定条款	On the terms and conditions as below //根据下列条款
合同结尾常用语	
IN WITNESS WHEREOF //特此为证	in duplicate //一式两份
in quadruplicate //一式四份	in triplicate //一式三份
in two originals //正本两份	duly authorized representatives //授权代表
execute the contract //执行本合同	equally valid //同等有效
品质条款常用语	
Sales by Sample //凭样品买卖	Quality as per Seller's Sample //质量以卖方样品为准
Quality as per Buyer's Sample //质量以买方样品为准	Sales by Specification, Grade or Standard //凭规格、等级或标准买卖
F. A. Q.（Fair Average Quality）//良好平均品质	G. M. Q.（Good Merchantable Quality）// 上好可销品质
Sales by Trademark or Brand //凭商标或牌号买卖	Sales by Specification //凭说明书买卖

续表

品质条款常用语	
be identical to the sample; be equal to the sample //与样品一致	to be final //为准
to be binding upon both parties //对双方均有约束力	to be taken final //为最后依据
数量条款常用语	
gross weight //毛重	net weight //净重
tare //皮重	actual tare; real tare //实际皮重
average tare //平均皮重	customary tare //习惯皮重
computed tare //约定皮重	5% more or less //百分之五溢短装
conditioned weight //公量	theoretical weight //理论重量
landed net weight //到货净重	any shortage or excess within one percent of B/L weight //提单货物重量增减不超过1%
合同组成部分的名称	
Title //合同名称	Preamble //前文
Definition Clause //定义条款	Basic Conditions //基本条款
General Terms and Conditions //一般条款	Witness Clause //结尾条款

思考与练习

1. 思考题

（1）商贸英语合同有什么语言特征？在商贸合同汉英翻译中，如何塑造庄重典雅的文体风格？

（2）商务汉英合同语言文化差异对商贸合同汉英翻译有什么启示与警示？

2. 句子翻译

（1）本合同用英文和中文两种文字写成，一式四份。双方执英文本和中文本各一式两份，两种文字具有同等效力。

（2）本合同由双方代表于2019年12月9日签订。合同签订后，由各方分别向本国政府当局申请批准，以最后一方的批准日期为本合同的生效日期，双方应力争在60天内获得批准，用电传通知对方，并用挂号信件确认。

(3) 本合同有效期从合同生效之日起共10年,有效期满后,本合同自动失效。

(4) 本合同期限届满时,双方发生的未了债权和债务不受合同期满的影响,债务人应向债权人继续偿付未了债务。

(5) 运输契约中任何条款、约定或协议,凡解除承运人或船舶由于疏忽、过失或未履行本条款规定的责任和义务,而引起货物或关于货物的丢失或损害责任的,或在本公约外减轻这种责任的,都应作废或无效。

(6) 承包商应负责按工程师书面提交的有关点、线和水平面的原始参数如实准确地进行工程放线,且如上所述,负责校准工程各部分的方位、水平、尺寸和定线,并负责提供一切必要的相关仪器、装置和劳力。

(7) 一旦顺利完成这些测试,买方须签署一张工厂验收证,证明测试已经完成,并列出将由CAE在买方同意的期限内校正的任何经认可的缺陷。

(8) 买方须随时能对专利软件的拷贝做出解释,拷贝的目的只在于提高其预期功能的使用效力。

(9) 在实施分包工程期间,分包商应随时向承包商提供有关已完成工程、在建工程、计划完成工程和影响施工事件方面的精确完整的资料,同时应向承包商提供所有相关的计划和报告文件(每日、每周和每月的进度报告、事故及安全报告、计算报告和劳务职员与外籍人员名单)。

(10) 经销商储存并运输经销产品的设施应保证经销产品处于良好状态,并应符合供应商关于产品储存和运输条件的合理要求。

3. 语篇翻译

● 语篇1

售货合同

合同号码:
签订日期:
签约地点:
卖　　方:
地　　址:
电　　话:
电报挂号:
买　　方:
地　　址:
电　　话:
电报挂号:

（1）兹经买卖双方同意由卖方出售、买方购进下列货物，并按下列条款签订本合同：商品名称、规格及包装。

商品名称、规格及包装	数量	单价	金额
总价：			

（允许卖方在装货时溢装或短装5％）

（2）唛头：　　　　　　由卖方指定：

（3）保险：由卖方按发票总值的110％投保一切险，按中国人民保险公司条款（不包括罢工、暴动、民变险）。如买方欲增加其他险别或超过上述额度保险时须事先征得卖方同意，其增加费用由买方负担。

（4）装船口岸：

（5）目的口岸：

（6）装船期限：

（7）付款条件：买方须开出保兑的、不可撤销的、可转让的、可分割的、无追索权的、支付全部货款的即期信用证，以卖方为受益人凭货运单据向中国的议付银行议付。信用证须于……前到达卖方，议付有效期延至装运期后15天在中国到期。

（8）商品检验：由……签发的品质数量/重量检验证。作为品质数量/重量的交货依据。

（9）不可抗力：由于人力不可抗拒事故，卖方不能在合同规定期限内交货或者不能交货，卖方不负担责任，但卖方应立即以电报通知买方，如果买方提出要求，卖方应以挂号函向买方提供证明上述事故存在的证件。

（10）异议索赔：如果卖方不能在合同规定期限内把整批或一部分的货物装上船，除非人力不可抗拒原因或者取得买方同意而修改合同规定外，买方有权在合同装船期满20天后撤销未履行部分的合同。如果货到目的口岸买方对品质有异议，可以凭卖方同意的公证机构出具的检验报告，在货到目的口岸30天内向卖方提出索赔，卖方将根据实际情况考虑理赔或不理赔，一切损失凡由于自然原因或属于船方或保险公司责任范围内者，卖方概不负赔偿责任。如果买方不能在合同规定期限内将信用证开到或者开来的信用证不符合合同规定，卖方可以撤销合同或延期交货，并有权提出索赔要求。

（11）仲裁：凡因执行本合同或有关本合同所发生的一切争执，双方应协商解决。如果协商不能得到解决，应提交北京的中国国际贸易促进委员会对外贸易仲裁委员会，根据该仲裁委员会的仲裁程序暂行规则进行仲裁，仲裁裁决是终局的，对双方都有约束力。

（12）责任：签约双方，即上述卖方及买方，应对本合同条款全部负责履行，凡因执行本合同或者有关本合同所发生的一切争执应由签约双方根据本合同规定解决，不涉及第三者。

（13）其他条款：

①信用证内应明确规定卖方有权可多装或少装所注明的百分数，并按实际装运数量议付。

②信用证内容须严格符合本售货合约的规定,否则修改信用证的费用由买方负担,卖方并不负因修改信用证而延误装运的责任,并保留因此而发生的一切损失的索赔权。

③除经约定保险归买方投保外,由卖方向中国的保险公司投保。如买方须增加保险额及/或须加保其他险可于装船前提出,经卖方同意后代为投保,其费用由买方负担。

④买方须将申请许可证副本寄给卖方,俟许可证批出后再即用电报通知卖方,假如许可证被驳退,买方须征得卖方的同意方可重新申请许可证。

卖　　方:　　　　　　　　　　　买　　方:

本合同由买方签署后,正本一份航寄还卖方。

- 语篇2

签约全职高级关税管理员任命书

甲方:中国北京A公司(以下称"本公司")与乙方:来自英国伦敦的史密斯先生(以下称"签约人")于2019年9月1日签署本服务协议。

双方达成协议并声明如下:

(1) 本公司将……

(2) 本协议自……起执行

(3) ……

(4) ……

作为证明,双方于上述日期签字。

签署人姓名:

签名:

代理人签名:

签约人姓名:

签名:

代理人签名:

• 语篇3

合同

合同编号：

日　　期：

买方:丹麦安德森贸易公司

卖方:广东土特产品进出口公司

按照以下规定条款，买方同意购买，卖方同意出售下述货物，特立约如下：

(1) 商品名称:武夷花生

(2) 规格:2018年产良好平均品质

(3) 数量:100公吨

(4) 单价：CIF丹麦奥胡斯到岸价每公吨500美元

(5) 总金额:50,000.00美元(50万美元)整

(6) 包装:用三层麻袋装,每袋50公斤

(7) 唛头：

(8) 保险:卖方按发票金额加10%投保一切险

(9) 装运条款:2019年7月装运,哥本哈根转运

(10) 装运港:中国黄埔港

(11) 目的港:丹麦奥胡斯港

(12) 支付条款:以不可撤销信用证,凭即期汇票议付。信用证须在装运前30日开到卖方手中,有效期应为装运期后15天在中国议付有效。

本合同于2019年4月20日在广州签署。

买　方
（签名）
（头衔）

卖　方
（签名）
（头衔）

第十四章

汉英商业广告对比分析与翻译

> **Identify the problems in the following translations**
> ① 不同的肤色,共同的选择。(青岛啤酒广告)
> 英译:The same choice for different colors.
> ② 仁者近山,智者近水。(房地产广告)
> 英译:The good are close to the mountain, the wise are close to the water.
> ③ 要想皮肤好,早晚用大宝。
> 英译:Good skin comes from Dabao.

　　在商品经济社会里,有人的地方就有广告(advertisement, ad)。那么,什么是广告呢？在汉语中,"广告"就是"向公众介绍商品、服务内容或文娱体育节目的一种宣传方式"。英语中 advertisement 一词来自法语,意为"通知""报告""广告"。但 advertisement 一词最早源于拉丁语的 advertere,其意思是"唤起大众对某种事物的注意,并诱于一定的方向所使用的一种手段"(翁凤翔,2002)。由此可见,语言是一种社会现象,是社会生活的反映。"社会文化影响并制约广告语言及其表达,广告语言则蕴含或反映社会文化。语言是民族的语言,广告存在于一定的社会之中。一个民族的哲学思想、思维模式、文化心理、道德观念、生活方式、风俗习惯、社会制度、宗教信仰等都必然会对广告语言产生作用。所以,任何一个社会的广告语言不可避免地反映社会文化的各个方面"(谭卫国,2003:107)。因此,广告的制作及其翻译"需要研究语言、地域文化、消费心理和审美价值的差异,绝不是将一种语言文字转换成另一种语言文字的机械翻译活动,它涉及语言学、经济学、营销学、消费心理学、美学等多种学科知识"(包惠南,2001:273)。

　　下面就汉英商业广告语言文化对比分析与翻译的问题进行一些粗略的探讨。

第一节　汉英商业广告语言文化差异对比分析

　　语言表达及文化背景的差异使得汉英各有自己的广告撰写规范与特色。在符合译语文化背景的同时，广告译文也应符合译语广告的写作特色及编排习惯。如果译者过多地受源语广告写作手法的束缚和干扰，一味考虑源语语言因素，则有可能使一则优秀的广告变得不伦不类，让译文读者难以理解与接受。例如，有一段时间，我国广告大都以标榜"国优""部优"为荣，常使用四平八稳的广告套语，行文拖沓，缺乏新意。如果直译为英文，译文则有可能不能被称为广告。(李明，2007)鉴于此，广告的制作与翻译须注意汉英的不同语言规范与文化特色，努力实现汉英广告语言与文化的转换。

◆ 1.1　汉英商业广告语言及思维表达方式差异对比分析

1.1.1　浮夸的渲染话语与简洁的含蓄言辞

　　成功的商业广告应能实现以下功能：提供信息功能、诱导争取功能、美感功能、表情功能等。但是，"英语表达客观具体，突出信息功能，而汉语讲究以言感人，偏重呼唤功能"(顾维勇，2005：44)。例如：

　　　① 日日创新，步步领先，年年夺冠。("皇冠"牌手表)
　　　② 三十年纺织品和服装出口经验。质量第一，信誉第一，友情第一。重合同、守信用、始终如一。

　　分析：在例①中，"皇冠"牌手表的广告词"日日创新，步步领先，年年夺冠"都是浮夸之辞，并无多少具体信息。例②的广告"质量第一，信誉第一，友情第一"纯属"王婆卖瓜，自卖自夸"式的自我评述，毫无实际意义。诸如"第一""最佳""一流""首家""独创""誉满全球""无与伦比""天下第一""举世无双""包治百病""药到病除"之类自夸虚浮之辞在汉语广告中比比皆是。由此可见，汉语广告行文公式化，语气夸张。

　　与汉语广告的浮夸之风不同的是，英语广告"简洁明快，含蓄不露"(蔡基刚，2003：337)。"西方广告经历了数百年的发展阶段，从文字到插图都十分讲究，显得较成熟。众多的英语广告注重摆事实、列数据，采用纵横比较对照等方法，以明白具体的语言描述产品或服务的特点和优点，同时注意创造商品的形象，给人一种真实可靠的感觉。"(谭卫国，2003：111)例如：

③

Olympus（Camera）

Congratulations! Olympus youth series has reached 20 million cameras sold. Within the promotion period, get a special free gift with every purchase of a selected Olympus camera or digital recorder. Distributed by the Hongkong Sole agent. Don't miss it!

分析：Olympus Camera（奥林巴斯照相机）的广告并无渲染浮夸之辞；其本质是讲事实，以事实服人。

1.1.2 螺旋式思维表达方式与线性思维表达方式

民族文化是通过某个民族的活动而表现出来的一种思维和行动方式。不同民族的思维与语言表达有着不同的逻辑系统（logical system）。汉语的语言思维表达倾向于螺旋式（spiral mode），而英语的语言思维表达则偏爱线性方式（linear mode）。倾向于螺旋式（spiral mode）思维表达的中国人喜欢使用较间接的语言表达方式，而偏爱线性思维表达方式的英美等西方民族则倾向于较直接的语言表达方式。如果中国产品要打入国际市场面向西方消费者，那么广告的表达方式应该符合他们的线式思维习惯，在一开始就要点明产品的名称及特点，以引起消费者注意。如果按照汉语的广告内容照字面直译，西方消费者则会犹如坠入云里雾里，可能因不知所云而失去阅读的兴趣。这样就达不到广告宣传的效果。例如：

④

嘉士利，为你珍藏童真的滋味……

那一年，我和妹妹去乡下姥姥家，我们在田野上奔跑，在小河里钓鱼，在收割过的麦地里拾麦穗，空气里尽是迷人的清香！现在很难找到那种感觉了。田野变成了厂房，小河也不见了……咦？这是什么？味道真特别，让我想起乡下麦地里那迷人的清香。

嘉士利饼干，为你珍藏童真的滋味！

分析：例④是嘉士利饼干的汉语广告，但它的第一个句子并没有提及"饼干"，而是谈起了对童年的回忆。正是这种对过去的回忆触发了东方人念旧的情怀，引起一种感情上的共鸣，其制作意图是用诗一般的语言来描绘出一个意境，似乎与主题没有关系，其实是想以情动人，找到感觉后才转到主题。

与迂回的汉语思维表达模式不同的是，说英语的西方人倾向于开门见山，直接点明文章的主题，以便他人对此做出反应（Scollen & Scollon, 2000），然后，广告接下来就将围绕这一主题展开。例如：

⑤ "Lucky" Brand Chocolates are made of choice materials by up-to-date scientific method. The product is allowed to leave the factory only after strict examination of its quality. Owing to the influence of tropical climate on raw materials used, white spots may occasionally appear on the surface of the product, but the quality remains unchanged in that event. Please send particular to our distributors concerned.

⑥ Sharp Z-20 Smallest Plain Paper Copier. It's more than just new. It's smaller, and it's lighter. And it fits almost anywhere. It starts automatically. "Goes to sleep" automatically. Even sets exposure automatically. And it's not only affordable to buy. Economical to run. It's also simple to maintain. It uses replaceable cartridges. For copies in red, blue, or black. And it has copy quality that's truly unsurpassed. In fact, it's the plain paper copier that's anything but plain. It's the new Sharp Z-20. So incredibly small, it's the only plain paper copier that makes any place, your workplace.

1-800-BE SHARP

from sharp minds come sharp products

（翁凤翔，2007b）

分析：广告⑤开门见山地介绍商品名称及制作原料，在强调质量的同时毫不隐瞒食品表面可能因为气候而会有些美中不足，这就很容易以其直言坦诚的特点吸引西方人的注意。从整体来看，英语广告的语言组织结构紧密，表达直接，没有多余无用的虚浮之辞，符合西方人的思维特点。广告⑥同样是开门见山，直接说产品的特征与优势，没有多余的浮夸渲染之辞。

▍1.2 汉英商业广告语折射出的不同文化心理和价值观念对比分析

曹志耘（1992：135）指出，"每个民族都拥有一些深植于本民族传统文化的心理特征。这些心理特征影响着人们的日常生活和风俗习惯，也制约着人们的语言活动"。比如，汉民族崇尚权威，英美民族较尊重事实；中国人重视群体取向的文化价值观念，西方人则崇拜具有强烈个人主义色彩的文化价值观。

1.2.1 崇尚权威与尊重事实

"广告里的承诺和保证通常都要有可靠的依据，中英文广告在选择依据方面略有不同。"（韦钦，2005：104）中国传统文化提倡绝对的权威，并对这种权威表示极大的尊重。权威指的是在某种范围里最有威望、最有地位的人或事物，直到现在它还是多数中国人进行判断决策的依据。西方文化稍有不同的是它更强调以经验事实为依据。在西方，人们热衷于搜集事实和数据，看重经验和观察的方式。以下这个调研结果很能说明汉民族对于"厂家调研"的广告信息的态度：加拿大多伦多约克大学的莱斯等两位广告和市场营销专家曾经运用内容分析法对中国杂志广告的信息进行了分析，并对14类信息出现的频率做了统计，得出的结论是含有"厂家调研"信息的广告数据小于1%。这多多少少表现出"以中国文化为主流的东方文化和以英语文化为主流的西方文化在广告创作中有着较大的差异"（周晓、周怡，1998：166）。

汉语广告里通常都会引用各种权威对产品的评价。所以，我们经常会听到或看到广告用"协会推荐品牌""上榜品牌""国家保护品牌""国家免检产品""中国消费者协会推荐产品""昔日宫廷秘方""国宴饮料""用科学方法""获得某某金奖""省优""部优"等评述性话语作为承诺的依据。这些广告词显然在暗示产品都有"权威"做后盾。例如：

⑦ 省优、部优、葛优（国优）。（双汇火腿肠）

⑧
"东风"牌手工编织地毯

"东风"牌手工编织地毯以其工艺精湛、色彩鲜艳、图案丰富多彩、经久耐用而闻名于世。

该地毯曾于1965年荣获莱比锡国际竞赛的金质奖章，1979年荣获国家优质工业产品金质奖，接着，在国家首届工艺品"百花奖"大赛上又获金杯。

"东风"牌地毯在同类产品中始终名列前茅。

广州贸易公司

分析：例⑦的广告语用形象代言人的姓名"葛优"来替代"国优"，令人在忍俊不禁而对产品印象深刻的同时，也不知不觉地接受了有关双汇火腿肠的产品质量的评述性话语。例⑧的产品广告简介使用了反映中国传统文化心理的评述性话语——"于1965年荣获莱比锡国际竞赛的金质奖章""1979年荣获国家优质工业产品金质奖"和"在国家首届工艺品'百花奖'大赛上又获金杯"，无外乎是在用这些奖项往自己脸上"贴金"。

虽然"英语国家里广告宣传也使用权威，但广告撰稿人更注重事实的权威。比如经过多次试验得出的实验数据，多次调查的最后结果以量化的数据去说服消费者，并以此作为承诺的依据"（汪滔，2001：87）。例如：

⑨ They are subjected to 16,000 inspections. They are driven the equivalent of 3 miles on a special test stand.

⑩ For her deepest dive—1,250 feet down to the floor of the pacific—Dr. Earle relied on a massive cast alloy diving suit to protect her from such an alien environment. In just such a way, the Rolex that Dr. Earle wears relies on its massively strong case to protect the delicate movement within. Indeed, so rugged is the case that sculpting it from a solid block of metal requires pressures of up to sixty tons.（韦钦，2005）

分析：例⑨的大众汽车广告寥寥数语，却提到了两个具体的可靠数据，即

16,000 inspections 和 3 miles on a special test stand,使消费者对产品质量深信不疑。在例⑩的劳力士手表广告中,厂家通过令人信服的准确数字说明了外壳的坚固。

1.2.2 群体取向与个人取向

群体取向的中国人提倡凡事以家庭、社会和国家利益为重。这在一定程度上反映了"家国天下"的佛教文化影响。在这种以群体取向为特征的文化影响下,中国人在商务交往中十分"看重人际关系、集体和睦和对集体的忠诚"(肖青云,2005:95);有着从众心理的中国人总是相信大多数人都去做的事情就不会错,因此当看到商店里或大街上有很多人在抢购一件商品时,人们往往会蜂拥而至,这就是典型的从众心理的表现和羊群效应。在广告中,中国广告商充分利用从众文化心理,大肆渲染群体趋向文化。例如:

⑪ 海尔,中国造。(海尔集团)

⑫ 中国人的生活,中国人的美菱。("美菱"牌电冰箱)

分析:两则广告均表达了一种以国为荣的感情。广告商运用心理学原理,定位好产品的消费群——本国人民,巧妙运用"中国""中国人"等词语来宣传产品,以此激发本国消费者心中的爱国情,继而唤起大众的购买欲望,最终达到其推销目的。

与中国文化相反,西方人(尤其美国人)崇拜个人主义。个人主义是指在社会的大环境里个人是一个重要的独立体,每一个人的独立是最有价值的。霍夫斯泰德(Hofstede,1998)的调查结果表明,个人主义取向在美国社会中占第1位,而在中国香港占第32位,在中国台湾占第36位。由此可见,中国和西方在个人主义取向方面的差异较大。这一维度在广告中得到很好的反映。西方广告中经常出现诸如 independence/independent, equal, uniqueness/unique, privacy/private 之类的用词。比如,日本的三菱汽车公司向美国市场销售产品时创制了"Not all cars are created equal."这则广告。熟悉美国历史的人一见这则广告,立即会想起《独立宣言》中"All men are created equal."的名句。日本商人套用了美国人家喻户晓的名句,就是利用了美国人追求个性、追求差异的特点。再如:

⑬ Fit you well. (Reebok)

⑭

What Sort of Man Read Playboy?

He's his own man. An individualist. And he can afford to express himself with style — in everything from the girls he dates to the way he dresses.

分析:例⑬的广告语展现了西方文化展露个性和追求个性的个人取向的价值观。例⑭的广告通过对自我个性的强调,诉诸英语民族追求自我独特魅力的文化心态,达到预期的宣传促销效果。

1.2.3 企业至上与用户至上

从汉英两种语言文化的角度考虑,广告的语言表现形式大相径庭,读者的期待和关注点不尽相同。"英语广告强调用户至上,消费者利益高于一切,突出 You-attitude,因而,语言形式上多用 You-form;汉语广告突出企业至上,以"我"为中心,但惯用第三人称进行自我评述,以树立其自我形象。"(顾维勇,2005:44)

从广告宣传的主题或广告对象来看,汉语广告大多以宣传的企业或产品为对象,习惯使用第三人称进行介绍,以此树立企业或产品的形象(顾维勇,2005)。例如:

⑮
    茅台一开,满室生香;
    国酒茅台,源远流长。

（贵州茅台酒广告）

⑯
凯歌凯歌,凯旋电视,名振山河。凯歌设计,富有特色,图像清晰,音色柔和。
家有凯歌,增添欢乐,家有凯歌,人人快活。

（上海"凯歌"牌电视机广告）

分析:茅台酒和"凯歌"牌电视机的广告宣传无一不是以其自身为中心,突出自我,以此博得用户或消费者的信赖。

与汉语广告采用第三人称不同的是,英语广告往往以用户为中心,采用第二人称,强调消费者利益至上的企业文化。这是值得注意的汉英商业广告评述角度的不同之处。例如:

⑰ When the wind has a bite … and you feel like a bite … then bite on a Whole Nut.

（原装果料 Whole Nut 的广告语）

⑱ You don't just rent a car. You rent a company.

（Heze Car Renting Company 的广告语）

分析:这两例英语广告无不以用户为中心,采用第二人称,处处为消费者着想,突出了"顾客就是上帝"(Customers are God)的企业文化。

第二节 对汉英商业广告翻译的启示与警示

◆ 2.1 对汉英商业广告翻译的启示

不管采用什么方法进行广告翻译,译者首先要牢记的是广告语言的特殊风格和广告的功能与目的。此外,译者还必须考虑英语作为广告译入语的接受者的语言文化语境。任何翻译都不能抛开译作的接受者,翻译作品离开了读者,就失去了翻译的意义。广告的目标就是要通过各种途径去打动读者,使他们采取行动——掏钱购买广告中的商品或接受广告中提供的服务。由此可见,为达此目标,汉英商业广告翻译需要在语言与文化上实现地道而灵活的功能对等转换。下面是汉英商业广告翻译可采取的行之有效的策略和技巧。

2.1.1 去繁就简,删除浮夸之辞

汉语广告偏爱堆砌大量的并无多少实际内容的修饰词(程镇球,2002),借此大肆渲染,以求打动人,取得人们的共情。而在以"客观精确"为主要特征的英语广告中,这些汉语惯用的自我评述性的浮夸之辞就显冗余。鉴于此,汉英商业广告翻译须"去繁就简"。

请对比分析以下汉英商业广告翻译实例:

① 随着我国汽车工业的迅速发展,汽车家庭化、大众化已成事实,人车一体化的生活逐渐成为时尚,爱车养车理念已渐入人心。所以,汽车美容养护势如破竹,前景一片光明。

英译:With the rapid development of domestic auto industry in China, it's become a fashion for people to enjoy a life with their own cars, which, therefore, brings about a good opportunity to develop the auto beauty and maintenance service.

对比分析:汉英企业说明均采用了煽情的文字。比如,汉语原文所用"大众化已成事实""爱车养车理念已渐入人心""势如破竹"等文字意在增强感染力。相比之下,英译删减了汉语原文中的那些言之无物的文字,使其行文符合英语通用的文体规范。

如上所述,造成汉语广告浮夸的渲染效果的一大原因就是,汉语喜欢连续使用四字结构。四字结构是汉语的一大语言特色。连用几个四字结构,就会使言语节奏鲜明、朗

朗上口、便于记忆。但是,连用四字结构的一个可能后果就是,其中一些四字结构或四字结构中的一部分言辞可能无多大实际意义。在此情况下,译者必须辨明虚实,去虚存实,以求信息量的最大转换。

请对比分析以下汉英商业广告翻译实例:

②
人无我有,人有我优;
电话订餐,送货上门;
备有快餐,欢迎品尝。

英译：The restaurant offers varieties of food of better quality. The services include telephone reservation and free delivery. Fast food is also available. We are always at your service.（翁凤翔,2002）

对比分析：汉语四字结构连用的格律和韵味铿锵有力,在英译中是不可能再现的。但是,英译将名词短语和简短句加以并列使用,这多多少少也给了译文一些节奏和对称上的美感。最值得注意的是,译文抛开了汉语广告的语言形式,进行转换时舍弃了汉语原文的虚浮之辞,如"欢迎品尝"。

2.1.2 辨明虚实,突出事实

汉语总是喜欢在对产品进行广告宣传时大吹一通、自我评述一番：不是获得金奖就是银奖,不是第一就是最好,等等。在以英语为译入语的广告接受者听起来,此类广告词实在过于虚浮,没有多少实质信息的传达。在广告效果上,这将适得其反,不利于产品的推广销售。由此可见,有必要辨明虚实,删除空洞无物之辞,以便突出事实或真实情况。

请对比分析以下汉英商业广告翻译实例:

③ ……经几代技术人员的努力,吸取现代先进工艺之精华……

英译：The natural flavor is improved by years of researched state-of-the-art technology …

对比分析：中国的许多广告常用"先进的设备和技术""引进国外先进技术""高科技技术""科学的方法"等字眼来强调产品制造过程的科学性。这些词语听起来空洞无物,并无多大实际意义。如果我们把上述汉语广告词译成"It's the result of many years of intensive studies done by the technical personnel of our factory and is refined with modern advanced technology."就很显然不符合西方人的文化心理。"对于处于科技发达背景下的西方人们,物质产品的科学性是不言而喻的,人们更崇尚的是自然和返璞归真。"（来东慧,2005:94）

2.1.3 转换主题,突出消费者

汉语广告大多以企业为主题进行宣传,而英语广告往往从用户或消费者出发,把他

们作为广告宣传的主题。所以,汉英商业广告翻译需要实现广告对象的转换。

请对比分析以下汉英商业广告翻译实例:

④ 宾至如归,热诚服务。(天津市旅游公司广告)

英译:A home from home with our cordial service.

对比分析:原来有人将汉语广告误译成"Offering a home for the wanderer, a heaven for the connoisseur.",则显得不妥,原因是 wanderer 表示"流落他乡之人",对国外游客来说是不合适的。再者,"第三人称的表述流露出高高在上的态度,容易让人不悦"(张敬,2009:221)。这也有悖于西方广告突出消费者的文化价值观念。所以,改译符合西方"以顾客为上帝"的价值观,将消费者置于中心位置。

⑤ 出手不凡钻石表。

英译:Ask for a Diamond brand watch, if every second counts for you.

对比分析:汉语广告的主题是产品本身,即钻石表。如果直译的话,其英译"Our Diamond brand means excellent wrist watches out of your hand."就显得生硬、含混不清,读起来令人费解。为了使译文符合英语广告的语言文化习惯和规范,英译广告需要变换语气,采用与汉语第三人称不同的第二人称——You-attitude(李明,2007)。

2.1.4 转变价值取向,突出个人

对于 individualist 一词,中西方文化有着不同的理解:在中国文化里,"个人主义"或"个人主义者"有着贬抑的含义,即自私自利和损人利己;而在西方文化中,individualist 一词却含有褒美的积极语义,即珍视个人权利、乐于张扬个性和敢于自我表现(潘红,2004)。由此可见,中西方的人们对于"个人主义"的文化价值观念的不同理解与态度。在进行汉英商业广告翻译时,我们需要突出个人取向的文化价值观,以迎合英语读者的文化价值观念。

请对比分析以下汉英商业广告翻译实例:

⑥ 五谷香酥片配以麻辣、五香、奶油、巧克力、芝麻、咖喱、海鲜等各种佐料,方便即食,营养丰富,老少皆宜。

英译:Crisp Cereal Chip is nicely flavored with condiments such as hot pepper, spices, cream, chocolate, curry, and seafood extract. It is nutritious and ready to serve.(刘法公,2004)

对比分析:如果我们把"老少皆宜"硬译成 suitable for both the old and young,显然就忽略了"老"在西方文化中的忌讳性。因为"老少皆宜"是汉语的套语,其指称是笼统而广泛的,英语中无特殊情况绝少使用这种表达,所以省略不译为好(刘法公,2004)。或者,按照英语广告的习惯表达,我们可以将"老少皆宜"中的"老少"译

为 for grownups and children, for both sexes of all ages 或 for growing children and the whole family。

2.2 对汉英商业广告翻译的警示

2.2.1 灵活对等,避免死译

广告是一种艺术语言。在商务文体中,商业广告作为一种另类,有着不同于商务信函、商务合同或商务报告的呼唤型功能和移情功能。商务汉英广告创作有不同的语言文化,所以商务汉英广告翻译不能囿于语言形式而死译、硬译。为了达到与汉语原广告同样的产品促销效果,译者最需要做的就是在充分理解并掌握了原文意思的基础上,不拘一格,创造性地使用各种语言手段进行灵活对等的翻译转换。比如,"I am yellow."这则美国出租车广告所用 yellow 一词就具有独特的美国文化内涵,即用颜色词指称不同类型的交通工具。因此,它不能被死译成"我是黄色的",而应被意译成"我是出租车"。

请对比分析以下汉英商业广告翻译实例:

⑦ 眼睛是心灵的窗口,为了爱护您的眼睛,请给窗户装上玻璃吧!

误译:Eyes are windows of our hearts. To protect your eyes, please fix glass to your window!

改译:A bright world with our glasses on!

对比分析:这是一则眼镜广告。汉语原文因使用了比喻修辞手法而形象生动,但篇幅过长。误译错在对原广告一字一句地硬译,结果译文令人啼笑皆非。而改译抛弃了汉语原广告虚浮的比喻,使用了一个简短的名词短语,与一个具有汉语动词功能的介词短语连用,整体看来前后平衡、言简意赅。

⑧ 爱您一辈子。("绿世界"化妆品)

误译:Love you for a lifelong time.

改译:Love you tender, love you true.

对比分析:这是一种化妆品的促销广告。汉语原文是一句通俗用语,而英译不能毫无情趣地直译。所以,套用了"猫王"歌词的仿译就使人有着情趣非凡的感受,可以吸引广大消费者,并能够达到"广为流传"的绝佳广告效果。

⑨ 世界首创,中国一绝。天然椰子汁。

误译:The pioneer of the world. The most delicious in China. Natural Coconut Juice.

改译:Natural Coconut Juice: a world special with an enjoyment beyond all your words.

对比分析：汉语广告原文过于自夸，令人生厌。误译完全套用汉语的表达形式，生硬死板，不符合译入语消费者的欣赏习惯。虽然改译也渲染产品的成分，但在表述方式和渲染程度上不同于误译。所以，"翻译这一类广告时，在不忽略原文信息的前提下，可以增加一些产品本身的实用信息，适当去掉不必要的'夸大'部分，以免西方消费者觉得夸夸其谈"（张敬，2009：220）。

2.2.2 英译不可务"虚"

汉语多实景虚写，借助虚化之笔赋予描写对象以诗情画意。相比之下，英语多实景实写，力求直观再现自然景象，遣词造句以朴实见长，不太追求繁缛、华丽。（冯庆华、刘全福，2011）汉英两种语言之间的这种差异在旅游广告中表现得尤为突出。所以，在汉英翻译转换过程中，英译千万不可务"虚"。

请对比分析以下汉英广告翻译实例：

⑩ 这里三千座奇峰拔地而起，形态各异，有的似玉柱神鞭，立地顶天；有的像铜墙铁壁，巍然屹立；有的如晃板垒卵，摇摇欲坠；有的如盆景古董，玲珑剔透……神奇而真实，迷离而实在，不是艺术创造胜似艺术创造，实令人叹为观止。

误译：Three thousand crags rise in various shapes. They are like whips or pillars propping up the sky; or huge walls, solid and sound; or immense eggs piled on an unsteady boarder; or miniature rocky or curious … Fantastic but actual, dreamy but real! They are not artistic works, but more exquisite than artistic works.

改译：Three thousand crags rise in various shapes—pillars, columns, walls, shaky egg stacks and potted landscape … conjuring up fantastic and unforgettable images.

对比分析：这是一则旅游景点的广告宣传。原汉语广告行文优美，文采四溢，尤其是四字格的连续使用，更是将汉语表达优势推向了极致，读来如行云流水。误译不顾汉英之间的行文差异，试图一字一句地对译。结果，行文累赘，语义虚幻，尤其是后半部分，更显空洞无物；像 immense eggs piled on an unsteady boarder 这样的译文还会产生意想不到的语用问题，即可能令人联想到不安全的因素。相比之下，改译的行文直观可感，"素面朝天"，理性之美由此而生。就汉语旅游广告的英译而言，如改译那样，译者应稍就理性之范，在保留必要信息及描写成分的同时，尽量采取避"虚"就"实"的手段，去掉某些过分渲染的溢美之辞"（冯庆华、刘全福，2011）

附表　汉英商业广告常用单词及相关表达

商业广告常用语	
advertising agency //广告公司	advertising contract //广告合同
advertising license //广告许可	billboard //广告牌
roadside poster //路边广告牌	public-welfare advertisement //公益广告
body copy //广告正文	caption //广告标题；解说词
C. D.（Creative Director）//创意总监	classified advertising；classified //分类广告
double spotting //插在节目中的广告	exclusivity //独家广告
film commercial //电影广告	hitchhike //插播的短篇广告
commercial advertising；commercial //商业广告	institutional advertising；corporation advertisement //企业形象广告
estimate //广告预算	zoned campaigns //某地区的广告攻势
golden time //（电影、电视的）黄金时间	copyright //版权
incentive //刺激销售	in-and-out promotion //促销
key account //主要广告客户；主要零售商	push money //推销奖金
a great variety of models//款式多样	a complete range of specifications //规格齐全
attractive and durable //美观耐用	at moderate price //价格适中
choice materials //选料考究	dependable performance //性能可靠
courteous service //服务周到	durable in use //经久耐用
economy and durability //经济耐用	elegant appearance //美观大方
excellent in quality //品质优良	exquisite in workmanship //做工讲究
fine quality //质地优良	prestige first //信誉至上
general wholesale //百货批发	selling well all over the world //畅销全球
with a long-standing reputation //久负盛名	goods genuine and price reasonable //货真价实
Quality first, customers first. //质量第一，用户第一。	unparalleled both in beauty and in art //制作精良，外观华美，无与伦比
Our product wins a high reputation and is widely trusted at home and abroad. //产品深受国内外用户的信赖与称赞。	Inquiries are welcome. //欢迎垂询。
Local sales agents are invited. //诚征各地区代理商。	Sincerity is forever. //真诚到永远。
Inquiries and orders are warmly welcome. //竭诚欢迎客户惠顾。	Please order now. //欲购从速。

思考与练习

1. 思考题

(1) 商务英语广告有什么语言文化特征?

(2) 如何跨越商务汉英广告之间的语言文化差异来实现有效的汉英翻译转换?

2. 对比分析

请对比分析美国 AKAI 公司针对不同交际对象,分别在《新闻周刊》(Newsweek)和《音响评论》(Stereo Review)刊登的同样内容的两则广告。

● 刊登在《新闻周刊》(Newsweek)上的广告:

Big Name Recording Star AKAI cassette decks are known worldwide for quality sound and state-of-the-art features. Including AKAI's exclusive GX Heads—guaranteed for 150,000 hours, over 17 years of play. See our wide selection of cassette decks at your AKAI dealer …

● 刊登在《音响评论》(Stereo Review)上的广告:

Good Sound Is in Your Hand. AKAI's GX Head is guaranteed for over 17 years.

What you're looking at is AKAI's exclusive GX Head.

A technical departure from any other recording/playback head design on the market today. Its composition: glass and crystal ferrite.

Imagine, if you will, a virtually wear-free head with a smooth glass face that doesn't allow dust to collect. A head that AKAI guarantees to perform for over 150,000 hours. That's 17 years of continuous, superb play.

It's a head that many audiophiles feel has set the industry's performance and durability standards. And you'll find it exclusively in AKAI cassette and reel-to-reel decks.

All of which means that to get the clean, crisp sound your head deserves, use ours.

3. 句子翻译

(1) 气垫软底鞋,穿着舒适,价格合适。

(2) 百事可乐,冷饮之王。

(3) 橙汁饮料,天然纯正,无与伦比。

(4) 道路不沾水,司机更安全;司机不沾酒,道路更安全。

(5) "白翎"系列滋润霜给您水般滋润。

(6) "上宝交通"驰名世界,让世界遍布"声佳电器"。

(7) 一夜之中,每时每刻,玉兰油晚霜使您的皮肤始终保持湿润,增加皮肤的自然再生能力,舒展细微皱纹,让您的皮肤显得更柔软、更年轻。

(8) 把握天时地利,开拓源源商机。
　　参展良机就在眼前,请立即报名参加。
　　创新科技及设计博览!

(9) 不同凡响的宜兴大理石的奇迹。

(10) 第一流的产品,为足下增光。(皮鞋油的广告语)

(11) 要想皮肤好,早晚用大宝。("大宝"护肤霜的广告语)

(12) 为您提供美,为您提供乐,为您提供爱,为您提供趣。(《故事会》杂志的广告语)

(13) 非常可乐,非常选择。("非常可乐"饮料的广告语)

(14) 北京欢迎你。(2008年北京奥运会的广告语)

4. 语篇翻译

- 语篇1

在这个世界的某个地方——在热带丛林中,在酷热难挨的沙漠里,抑或在极地的荒原上,一位探险家可能正借助仪器测定方位。这时,绝对可靠的计时器可是生命攸关的啊!

自从1926年问世以来,劳力士一直颇受探险家和勘探人员的青睐。它坚固耐用,计时准确,曾帮很多人走上了成功之路。

而这些曾走遍天涯海角、上天入地的劳力士表,正是您在任何劳力士表行中常常见到的那一种。

日内瓦出产的任何一块劳力士表,都将成为主人的忠实伴侣。

您将戴着您的劳力士在何方创造辉煌呢?

- 语篇2

"银行就是晴天借你雨伞、雨天向你索回的地方。"

芝加哥北方信托公司庆幸并非我们激发罗伯特·弗罗斯特写出这句惊世名言。弗罗斯特曾四次获得普利策诗歌奖,他的每句话展示出辛辣的新英格兰式的讽刺感。

然而,96年来,我们一贯在雨天呵护人们,而今我们又服务于新的一代。我们推出了像"净值信用额"这样的个人金融服务,它可以让您用自己的房屋来获得个人贷款的最高额度。我们想和您谈谈这个方案,谈谈您所需要的其他银行服务。

如果不想在雨天淋湿,请与我们联系。

电话:(312)630-60000。

北方信托公司

我们有话要说,到时您可以引用我们的名言。

- 语篇3

立顿草本袋泡茶

立顿茶并不一定乏味。

因为立顿推出了全新的美味系列产品。

有果味的、浓香的、咸味的……就让它们的名称来告诉您这些草本茶美妙无比的口味吧。

香醇橘子、清新薄荷、舒心柠檬、幽香甘菊、玉桂苹果。

口味纯美,不含咖啡因。

您可以随时享受立顿草本茶。

立顿品牌

草本茶

不含咖啡因

- 语篇4

"雪山"牌羊绒衫色泽鲜艳,手感柔滑,穿着舒适,轻软保暖。其品质优良,做工细致,花型、款式新颖,尺码齐全,深受国内外消费者青睐。

第十五章

汉英商业说明书对比分析与翻译

Identify the problems in the following translations

① 快速反应、马上行动、质量第一、信誉至上是公司的宗旨。我们将以客户的需求为发展动力,为用户提供满意的产品及优质的服务。

英译: Our tenet is "Quick reflection, immediate action, quality first, reputation first". We will be always pursuing what you need and provide you with satisfactory products and top-notch service.

② 十多年来,中国出口商品基地建设总公司在工业、农业、贸易、科研、金融等行业开展了跨系统、跨地区、跨所有制的多方位横向经济联合,兴办合营、联营、中外合资企业400多家,逐步培养出一批质量好、适销对路、深受群众欢迎的出口骨干产品,涉及粮油食品、土畜、纺织、轻工、五金矿产、机电、化工、医保等大类。

英译: Over the past decade, the China National Export Bases Development Corporation has developed trans-system, trans-regional, trans-ownership cooperation and horizontal economic links in the fields of industry, agriculture, foreign trade, scientific research and finance, etc., and established more than 400 jointly operated enterprises and Sino-foreign joint ventures which have turned out a great number of key export products in high quality, in ready market and very popular with the public, such as cereals, oils & foodstuffs, native produce & animal by-products, textiles, light industrial products, metals & minerals, machinery & electronics, chemical products, medicines and health products.

③ 地处风景秀丽的江南名城常熟,占地133 400平方米,公司拥有先进的生产设备,拥有经验丰富的技术人员,常熟市无缝钢管有限公司值得您的信赖。

英译: Located in International Garden City—Changshu, Jiangsu Province, with an area of more than 133,400 square meters, advanced equipments and skilled technicians. Changshu Seamless Steel Tube Co. Ltd is your wise choice.

商业说明书是企业介绍自己或说明产品情况的应用文文体。"商业说明书具有很高的使用频率和良好的公关宣传功能。"(黎运汉,2005:357)商业说明书包括两类:企业说明书和产品说明书。企业说明书(company introductions)旨在介绍本组织的历史与现状、组织机构、实力地位、经营特色、经营业绩等,其基本格式包括标题、正文和附页。产品说明书(product descriptions/instruction/direction)是生产厂商为销售其产品而附在产品包装外部或内部的一种宣传说明,是用于识别产品及其特征的各种表达和指示的统称。产品说明书主要用文字、符号、标志、标记、数字、图案等来表示,旨在向销售者、购买者提供有关产品的信息,帮助他们了解产品的性能、质量状况,说明产品的使用、保养条件,起到引导消费的作用。此外,一份好的商业说明书还起着向公众或广大消费者宣传介绍企业或产品的重要作用,力争人们对企业的信任支持,激发人们对产品的购买欲望。

"经调研发现,如今的说明书的译文存在各种各样的问题,如存在语法错误、翻译痕迹明显等。如不能很好地解决这些问题,势必影响顾客对说明书的印象,进而影响产品或服务的销售。"(冯克江,2010:161)同样,若旨在对外宣传的企业简介英译不符合英语语言文化要求或行业规范,不够准确客观,或错误百出,也会引起公众误解,并严重影响企业的对外形象。

以下就从专业规范与客观准确两方面简略地探讨一下有关汉英商业说明书语言文化差异对比与翻译的问题。

第一节　汉英商业说明书语言文化差异对比分析与翻译

◆ 1.1　力求客观准确,但汉英有别

客观准确是汉英商业说明书的第一要求。比如,产品说明书旨在对产品的性能、特征、用途、用法等进行介绍说明,以便消费者购物时做出正确的选择。所以,产品说明书不能夸大其词,对产品及企业的宣传应客观、准确。

请对比分析以下商务汉英翻译实例:

①

蒙牛纯牛奶
净含量:250毫克

超高温(UHT瞬间)灭菌
保鲜包装,无须冷藏,可直接饮用

请勿带包在微波炉中加热

开启后请储藏于0℃~4℃之间

产品标准号:Q/NMRY31

蒙准印:HH3584-1999

保质期:8个月

产品类型:全脂灭菌纯牛奶

生产日期:见盒底部

配料:鲜牛奶

营养成分:每100毫升内含

脂肪≥3.3克　非脂乳固体≥8.1克

蛋白质≥2.9克　钙≥115毫克

钾≥145克

制造商:中国内蒙古蒙牛乳业股份有限公司

厂址:中国内蒙古呼和浩特市和林格尔盛乐经济园区

销售热线:(0471)7390171　7390164

消费者热线:(0471)7390333

传真:(0471)7390166

邮编:011500

请勿乱扔空包　保持环境清洁

英译:

Mengniu Pure Milk

Net Content：250ml

UHT treated

Keep fresh without refrigeration.

Use directly.

Do not heat the package in a microwave.

Please keep cool after opening.

Standard code of product：Q/NMRY31

Printing number：MZY HH3584-1999

Shelf life：8 months

Product type：UHT treated full cream milk

Production date：Bottom of pack

Ingredients：Fresh milk

Average nutrition composition (per 100ml)

Fat：≥3.3g

Non-fat milk solid：≥8.1g

Protein：≥2.9g

Calcium：≥115mg

Potassium：≥145mg

Manufacturer：Inner Mengolia Mengniu Dairy Industry Co., Ltd., China

Address：Shengle Economy District, Helingeer Hohhot, Inner Mengolias, China

Sales line：(0471)7390171　7390164

Customer line：(0471)7390333

Fax：(0471)7390166

Postcode：011500

Please dispose properly.

对比分析：汉英产品说明书均无任何文饰或虚浮之辞，所用文字客观准确。这正是产品说明书有别于商业广告之处：产品说明书的主要功能就是向消费者提供产品特点和使用信息。

但是，汉英商业说明书在力求准确客观方面的语言表达形式与尺度有所不同。汉语行文虚浮夸张，语言较为堆砌，特别是企业简介中的"四言八句口号"多。相比之下，英语行文客观通俗，表达直截了当，信息功能突出。（贾文波，2004）

请对比分析以下汉英企业简介：

② 中国人民保险集团股份有限公司是一家综合性保险(金融)公司，注册资本为155亿元。自1949年10月20日成立至今，中国人保已发展成为旗下拥有人保财险、人保寿险、人保健康、人保资产、人保投资、人保香港、中盛国际、中人经纪和中元经纪等9家专业子公司的大型保险金融集团。集团现共有正式员工9万余人，营销员10万余人，经营范围涵盖非寿险、寿险、健康险、资产管理、保险经纪等多个领域，建立起了保险产业集群，<u>在海内外具有深远影响力</u>。

③ American International Group, Inc. is a holding company which through its subsidiaries provides a varied range of insurance and insurance-related activities in the United States and abroad. The Company's main activities include both general insurance and life insurance & retirement services operations as well as financial services and asset management.

对比分析：同样属于保险公司的宣传介绍，中国人民保险集团股份有限公司简介的最后一句"在海内外具有深远影响力"就是典型的自夸式评语，而American International Group, Inc(美国国际集团股份有限公司)的简介就没有在段尾附加没有实际内容的渲染之辞。

请对比分析以下企业简介的汉英翻译实例：

④ 我司经营的品种中有举世闻名的贝雕工艺品；色彩艳丽、种类繁多的人造花卉；令人爱不释手的小工艺品；体态生动活泼的各式玩具；款式新颖、穿着舒适的各种工艺鞋；稀有名贵的钻石珠宝；技艺精湛、巧夺天工的玉石雕刻；格调高雅的抽纱工艺品。

英译：Our famous products include carvings, a variety of colorful artificial flowers, small arts and crafts articles, lively toys, fashionable and comfortable shoes, rare jewelry, meticulus jade carvings and sophisticated embroideries.

对比分析：本例中，汉语原文是汉语中的典型表达方式，而英译也是英语中惯用的表达方式。将汉语原文同英译对比不难发现，英译对原文进行了简化处理，尤其是其中的四字短语。汉语中喜欢使用四字短语，构成排比结构，读来抑扬顿挫、铿锵有力，但英文中则在绝大多数情况下很难找到与汉语四字短语相对应的表达方式。其实，进行汉英翻译时，对这些汉语中的四字短语，完全可以使用英语中的某一个词语来表达，因为汉语四字短语中有些信息是冗余信息。如果将这些冗余信息翻译出来反而会因形害义。例如，"色彩艳丽"以 colorful 译出即可，这里的"色彩"就是冗余信息，同样"种类繁多"中的"种类"、"体态生动活泼"中"体态"、"款式新颖"中的"款式"、"穿着舒适"中的"穿着"、"技艺精湛"中的"技艺"、"格调高雅"中的"格调"等都是冗余信息，翻译时大可不必将它们一一翻译出来。这是汉英翻译中我们一定要好好把握的重点所在。

◆ 1.2 在说理与移情功能上的语言表现有异

汉英商业说明书应该分门别类，采用与功能相匹配的语言手段和行文方式。为了使说明简明易懂、客观具体，汉语说明书在文字说明上追求对企业和产品的具体感受与描写。同时，为了使文字说明具有感召力和可读性，汉语说明书经常采用文学上"雅"的语言。在描写过程中，字里行间常见两字词语、四字短语、三字或五字或七字结构等夹叙夹议的渲染之辞，而这种语言特征或偏爱往往给人以虚浮夸张的负面印象。

由于思维表达的模糊性特征，中国人倾向于"说大话，说空话，说废话"。前驻法大使吴建民所说的一段话很有代表性："很多中国官员不大懂得交流。他们万里迢迢到国外招商，请了很多人，介绍自己的省份或者城市，结果一上台先说天气，'在这个春暖花开的季节，我来到美丽的巴黎，巴黎人民有光荣的革命传统……'好不容易到正题了，又是一大堆让人云里雾里的话语，比如'我们的对外开放是全方位、多渠道、宽领域的开放'

之类。这些代表团在给国内的报告中无一不说'获得了圆满成功',但我作为一个大使,坐在旁边却感到很不自在。"(摘自《羊城晚报》)很多人说话全凭主观判断,而不是靠数字和事实。相比之下,精确性是近代西方思维方式的一大特征。"西方人崇尚科学和理性,注重活动的严格性、明晰性和确定性,注重思维程式的数学化、形式化、公理化、符号化和语言的逻辑性,思维方式也必然带有精确性。"(连淑能,2002:45)

请对比分析以下企业简介的汉英翻译实例:

⑤ 新的世纪,总部将"×××定位于发展百年企业,争做中国汽车美容养护<u>第一品牌</u>"写入公司的发展计划之中,计划3年内发展直营店100家、中心店300家、加盟店突破2 000家,6年内冲进中国连锁百强行列,实现"<u>有车就有弛耐普</u>"。

让我们紧紧"连锁"起来,共同打造这一响亮的品牌。

英译: In the new century, based on the scheme laid down by the headquarters, xxx aims to develop into an enterprise to be well-established for century with a <u>name-brand</u> at the top of Chinese auto beauty and maintenance trade, planning to develop further 100 selling stores, 300 center stores and more than 2,000 franchises within 3 years and determined to strive in 6 years into the 100 tops of China franchise. (贾文波,2004)

对比分析:汉语企业宣传资料使用了一整段的响亮口号作为结尾,其实并无多大实际意义。所以,英译略去了结尾处的口号,将"第一品牌"译成 a name-brand at the top of 就较贴切适当。

◆ 1.3 在专门性、行业性上各有表现

汉英商业说明书作为正式的应用文文体,行文具有专门性的特点(李明,2007),即简洁规范、合乎行业要求。

请对比分析以下产品说明的汉英翻译实例:

⑥ <u>一经使用</u>本品,<u>便</u>能随意梳理成型,秀发硬挺,使您更加美丽。

英译: The product is used <u>for creating your own hair style special</u>, <u>for creating your look and shaping beautiful hair</u>.

对比分析:汉语用词正式、精练,如"一经使用本品,便……";英语用词也同样简洁、正式,比如,连用的三个名词化短语 creating your own hair style special, for creating your look and shaping beautiful hair 在提高文体正式程度的同时可以大大地节约篇幅。此外,三个具有创意的 creating 一词的搭配在结构上形成前后排比,在气势上非同凡响,可以烘托出产品的好效果。

汉英产品说明书"殊途而同归"。为了突出文体正式和行文专业的特点,汉语产品

说明书常用文言词、书面语汇和惯用句型,如"本""此""即""若""切勿""少许""须知"等。同样,英语产品说明书则选用长词、名词化短语、介词短语等。

请对比分析以下产品说明书的汉英翻译实例:

⑦ <u>如在使用本产品过程中</u>,有强烈刺激感、红肿或灼痛现象发生,请立即用温水<u>冲洗</u>干净。

英译: In case of a reaction <u>during the application</u> such as intense stinging, rash or a burning sensation on the scalp, <u>rinse</u> immediately with lukewarm water. (李明,2007)

对比分析:汉语说明书所用语汇属于书面语汇,语体正式。这就是产品说明书措辞专业地道的特点。如果把"在使用本产品过程中"译成口语体的 in the process of using this product,就显得不够正式,也不具有专门性、行业性。此外,译文采用 rinse 一词,而没有使用文体等级较低的 wash,这同样为译文增添了行业性、专门性和权威性。

此外,因对不同行业或专业的产品或企业进行说明,说明书对普通英语词汇的词义加以引申,而赋予普通英语词汇以特定的专业词义。比如,在普通英语中分别表示"老鼠"和"班长"的 mouse 和 monitor,其词义在专业性较强的说明书中被引申为分别表示"鼠标"和"监视器"。这些半专业词汇与专业词汇的大量使用就使得说明书的专业性和行业性特征更加突出。相比之下,因词义范围较窄,汉语就没有英语词义如此灵活多变。

第二节 对汉英商业说明书翻译的启示与警示

◆ 2.1 对汉英商业说明书翻译的启示

2.1.1 产品说明书的英译要做到"信、达、雅"

产品说明书语言结构严谨,用词精确,专业词汇较多,具有较强的科学性和严密性。比如,"生铁浇注机"和"残夜泵"这些专业性较强词汇的英译分别是 pig caster 和 tail pump。其次,说明书具有较强的实用性,为了能够使用户一目了然,说明书的英译需要简洁明快、浅显易懂。再者,说明书是广告的一部分,其英译应该与原文一样具有感召力和可读性。

请对比分析以下产品说明书的汉英翻译实例:

① 早晚两次,用温开水洗脸后取本品少许,均匀搽遍面部即可收到满意效果。

英译：Wash the face with lukewarm water and evenly rub a little amount all over, twice daily, one in the morning and the other in the evening, and the satisfactory effect will soon be obtained.

对比分析：英译通俗易懂、简洁明了，做到了翻译所要求的"达"。

② 是夏季消暑保健之佳品。

英译：It makes a delightful and wholesome drink in summer.

对比分析：英译行文优美，使用了两个形容词修饰语，具有与汉语原文一样的感召力与可读性。

2.1.2 渲染适度，突出信息

纽马克认为，早期翻译理论对翻译的讨论忽视了翻译与意义、思维和语言普遍性的关系，如何翻译应取决于三个因素：文本功能类型、读者身份和翻译目的。因而，他提出应根据不同文本功能分别采用"语义翻译"和"交际翻译"。语义翻译是指"在译入语语义和句法结构允许的前提下，尽可能准确地再现原文的上下文意义"，而交际翻译是指"译作对译文读者产生的效果应等同于原作对原文读者产生的效果"（Newmark, 2001）。纽马克明确提到"语义翻译法"适用于"表达型"文本，而"交际翻译法"适用于"信息型"和"呼唤型"文本（Newmark, 2001）。商业说明书不只有单纯一种功能，它以一种功能为主而其他功能兼而有之。这就要求采用灵活的翻译手法及策略，使说明书的英译达到预期效果。（冯克江，2010）

为了激发消费者的购买欲望，有些产品说明书也会根据功能类别适当地采用煽动性文学语言，来增强说明书的可读性和感染力。为了在公众心目中塑造好的形象，企业的宣传资料同样如此。但是，译文既要再现原文的文学色彩，又不能夸大其词，力求在语气风格上与原文保持一致。这就要求英译渲染适度，对汉语原商业说明书中的浮夸之词做适当删减。

请对比分析以下产品说明书的汉英翻译实例：

③ ××特区工业发展总公司作为××集团的下属公司及××集团的对外窗口，背靠工业，立足国内，拓展海外，既建立了全国范围的销售网络，同时在美国、欧洲、菲律宾、巴西等国家和中国香港、澳门地区建立了分支机构，积极参与国际市场竞争，促进集团国际化。

英译：Affiliated with ×× Group Corp., ×× Industrial Development Corporation has, based on its industrial operation in China, developed its business with its sales net not only in Chinese mainland but also in the United States, Europe, the Philippines, Brazil and other districts such as Hong Kong, Macao of China.（贾文波，2004）

对比分析：中国人喜欢使用大段的评述性话语，这并不符合英语语言表达习惯。所以,在保留原汉语企业简介实质内容的前提下,英译删掉了汉语原文的炫耀性(并不说明公司的实际情况的)口号和语汇。

④ 愿美好的艺术和独具匠心、精湛的牙雕技艺使您满堂生辉。

英译：We are sure our supreme artistry will make your house more luxurious and beautiful.

对比分析：汉英产品说明均采用了煽情的文字。比如,汉语原文用了"美好""独具匠心""精湛""满堂生辉"四个修饰词;英语用了 supreme, luxurious, beautiful 三个形容词。由此可见,汉语有堆砌修饰词的倾向,像"独具匠心"和"精湛"这样的近义词并列使用的现象非常普遍。

2.1.3 语篇重构

目的论认为,言语交际是一种有目的、有意图的活动。由于文化背景、思维方式、表达习惯上的差异,源语作者意图及采用的语篇形式与译语读者的接受能力可能存在差异。因此,翻译的重点是根据目的语的语言文化和语用方式去传递信息,而不是尽量忠实地复制原文的文字。译者在翻译过程中有较大的自由度去解释原文,调整结构,排除歧义,甚至是修改原作者的错误。

请对比分析以下企业宣传说明材料的汉英翻译实例：

⑤　　　　　　　西苑饭店

西苑饭店是一座具有国际四星级水准的大型涉外饭店,位于北京三里和路,与进出口谈判大楼、北京图书馆、首都体育馆等毗邻,环境优美,交通便利。

饭店共有客房 1 300 余套,房间舒适、宁静,配有全套现代化设施。饭店共设餐厅酒吧 12 个,中餐经营粤、鲁、川、淮扬及清真风味菜肴;西餐主要经营俄式、法式及英式大菜。饭店还设有传真、电传、国际直拨电话等现代通信设施及各种综合服务设施和娱乐设施,为每位宾客提供尽善尽美的服务。

英译：

Xiyuan Hotel

Luxuriance, Convenience and Reassurance.

The four-star Xiyuan Hotel boasts of easy transportation, quiet and elegant environment as well as first-class service.

Located at Sanlihe Road and adjacent to the Negotiation Building, the Beijing Library and the Capital Gymnasium, Xiyuan Hotel is within your easy reach.

In any of the 1,300 guest rooms and suites, you can enjoy the opulent comfort of the modern facilities and courtesy service.

The twelve restaurants and bars offer you both Chinese food including Cantonese,

Shandong, Sichuan, Huaiyang and Muslem cuisine, and Western food featuring Russian, French and British dishes.

The up-to-date communication facilities, the recreational appliances and other comprehensive services are sure to win your appreciation.

When in Beijing, make your choice of Xiyuan Hotel.

Xiyuan Hotel: Service is all and all for you.

对比分析：英译进行了语篇重构，即充分考虑英语读者的审美、文化和接受差异，充分考虑他们的思维方式和价值观念，不受汉语原文思维表达和篇章结构的束缚，采用了译语读者喜闻乐见的表达方式和行文方式。此外，通过第二人称的使用，译文适度凸显了人际意义，极大地拉近了"我"（西苑饭店）与可能的客人之间的距离，语气无疑显得亲切友好，具有极大的感染力和吸引力。

2.2 对汉英商业说明书翻译的警示

根据目的性原则，翻译的过程应以译文在译语文化中实现其预期功能为标准。商业说明书要实现的功能正是在一个新的文化环境中再现原文在源语文化中所具备的各种功能：一是信息功能（informative function），即译文如实地传达商业说明书上所包含的全部信息，即准确介绍商品的成分、特点、用途及使用方法，或企业的性质、地位、经营规模及宗旨；二是美感功能（aesthetic function），即读者从译文的文字描述中获得美的享受，产生愉悦美好的感觉；三是祈使功能（vocative function），即通过在译文中再现原文的祈使功能，使译文读者做出与原文读者同样的反应。因此，译文应"成功地移植原文的各种功能，使译语文化中的受众能够受到译文的感召和吸引"（胡丽霞，2007：71），最终能够促销产品，扩大企业宣传，有助于企业树立良好的形象。但是，说明书英译若照本宣科，译语读者就可能因语言文化差异而不明白译文的信息、美感，这就不能达到有效交流的目的。如果不负责任而胡翻乱译，译文可能因错误百出而贻笑大方，严重损害产品或企业形象。

2.2.1 英译不得照本宣科

如果不顾汉英商业说明书在思维模式和行文方式上的差异，而照（汉语原文）本宣科（直译），那么译文就可能会不符合英语语言规范与文化语境，读者就可能生厌，或者完全不理解说明书的意思，甚至产生误解。

请对比分析以下企业宣传资料的汉英翻译实例：

⑥ 桐庐丹霞笔业有限公司是一家初具规模的专业生产圆珠笔的厂家，力量雄厚，设备先进，主要生产各种高、中、低档圆珠笔。

误译：As a producer specializing in making ball-pens, Tonglu Danxia Pen Co., Ltd.

enjoying strong technical power and advanced equipment, with the main products of series of high, middle and low quality.

改译：With strong technical power and advanced equipment, Tonglu Danxia Pen Co., Ltd. has begun to take shape. As a manufacturer specializing in ball-pens, it mainly makes various types of ball-pens of high, middle and low grade.

对比分析：误译不仅是一个没有谓语动词的病句，而且存在漏译（如：初具规模）和错译（如：high, middle and low quality）。误译结构混乱，逻辑不清，并显得啰嗦。

2.2.2 英译不得胡翻乱译

产品说明书事关产品的出口外销，企业简介关乎企业的对外形象。企业不能不负责任地对其进行翻译。韶关家园网网友在论坛发帖说，最雷人的汉英翻译莫过于某外企超市对"大米"和"面粉"的英译——Big Meters 和 Face Powder。这种胡翻乱译的说明书除了事与愿违之外，也起不到别的什么效果。

请对比分析以下产品说明书的汉英翻译实例：

⑦ 乐陵金丝小枣说明

乐陵金丝小枣的品质位于全国三大产区的小枣之首，以品质优异和营养丰富闻名于世。乐陵金丝小枣体形小、色红、核小、皮薄、肉质丰满。乐陵金丝小枣含有果胶维生素，蛋白质，脂肪，丰富的铁、钙、磷和维生素 AP 等营养物质，对人体有增热补血、滋肝、健脾功效，可益气养肾、润肤延寿，是历史悠久、中外驰名的高级补品。

误译：

SPECIFICATIONS

Leling Golden Silk Small Dates is produced in the biggest area of three big production areas. It is famous in the world for its small body, small pit, thin skin, rich of pulp, good quality and rich of nutrition. It contains Pectin Vitamin, Protein, Fat and rich of Fe, Calcium, Phosphorus and Vitamin AP etc. nutritious materials. It can add heat and blood to the people's body, nourish liver, invigorate the function of pleen, nourish kidney and prolong life of the people.

It is high-grade notic of having a long history and well known both in China and abroad.

改译： **INTRODUCTION**

Leling Small Sweet Dates are the best in quality in China's three big date-growing areas. They are well known for their small bodies, tiny pits, thin skin, rich pulp, good quality and rich nutrients. The date contains various nutritious elements such as pectin vitamin, protein, fat and rich ferrum, calcium, phosphorus and vitamin AP. It serves to improve your health by tonifying the blood to promote the production of heat, nourishing the liver and invigorating the spleen, supplementing qi and the kidney, so as to prolong your life.

It is a high-grade tonic with a long history and well known both at home and abroad.

对比分析："乐陵金丝小枣"说明书的原译文错误非常多。比如，把"脾"英译成 pleen（正确的用词是 spleen）的错误令人痛恨，将"补品"译成 notic（正确的用词是 tonic）的错误实在可笑。如此这般低劣的英译把中国优质的乐陵金丝小枣描绘得面目全非。可以肯定的是，这样的英文说明书对小枣的促销起不到好作用。（刘法公，2004）

附表　说明书常用语

产品说明书常用语	
name of product // 品名	main ingredients; main composition // 主要成分
propertiy // 性质；特性	specification // 规格
material // 材质	customized; custom-built // 定制
function // 功能	performance 性能
operating procedure // 操作程序	side effect // 副作用
precaution // 注意事项	expiry date; period of validity // 使用期限
shelf life // 保存期；保质期	usage 用法
warning // 警告	storage; preservation method // 储存；储存方法
ratification number; license number // 批准文号	guarantee time; warranty time // 保修期
maintenance // 维护；保养	production date // 生产日期
packaging; packing // 包装	directions for operation // 使用说明
manufacturer; producer // 制造厂商；生产商	artistic in appearance // 外形美观
place of origin // 产地	type // 类型
reliability, cost-effectiveness and various features // 性能可靠，经济划算，特色众多	The product has been well received by customers and sells well in Southeast Asia. // 本产品深受消费者欢迎，远销东南亚。
The product has won high praises from the users. // 本产品深受用户好评。	The product enjoys a good reputation at home and abroad. // 本产品在国内外享有很高声誉。
医药产品说明书常用语	
pharmacology // 药理作用	actions // 主治
indication // 适应证	adverse reaction // 不良反应

续表

医药产品说明书常用语	
contraindication //禁忌	side effect 副作用
symptom //症状	headache //头痛
stomachache //胃痛	influenza //流感
pneumonia //肺炎	cancer //癌症
rhinitis //鼻炎	hepatitis //肝炎
inflammation //炎症	sequel //后遗症
heal //愈合	cure //治疗
食品说明书常用语	
snack //点心；小吃	dessert；sweet //甜点
roast //烤	bake //烘
ingredient //配料	mustard //榨菜
appetizer //开胃菜	main course //主菜
starch //淀粉	preservative //防腐剂
sugar //白砂糖	condiment //调味品；佐料
chilly oil //辣椒油	sesame oil //芝麻油
protein //蛋白质	vitamin //维生素
edible after opened //开袋即食	suitable for all ages //老少皆宜
nutritious //营养丰富	organic food //有机食品
机电产品说明书常用语	
automatic //自动	easy to operate //易于操作
manual //手动	not easy to rust //不易生锈
processing range 加工范围	power //功率
output //输出功率	overall dimension //外形尺寸
frequency //频率	power supply //电源
installation //安装	breakdown；stoppage；fault //故障
volume //容量	appliance；equipment //设备
apparatus //仪器	electrical appliance //电器
household appliance //家用电器	electronic goods //电子产品
gear //齿轮	protection equipment //保护装置
convenient for operation and maintenance //便于操作，易于维修	after-sale service //售后服务

思考与练习

1. 思考题

(1) 汉英商业说明书在语言文化上有什么差异?

(2) 汉英商业说明书语言文化差异的对比分析对翻译有什么启示与警示?

2. 句子翻译

(1) 冰箱的额定电压为交流220V,额定频率为50Hz,允许电压波动范围为180V～220V。

(2) 本品适于四季饮用,是老少皆宜的营养饮料,也是馈赠亲友之佳品。

(3) 本机采用齿轮变速传动结构,串联组成多模连续拉丝机,可拉拔钢、铝、黄铜等金属线材。

(4) 加入适量的牛奶和糖,味道更佳。

(5) 结构简单,操作容易,维修方便,生产率较高。

(6) 配料:优质鲜牛肉、白砂糖、辣椒油、芝麻油、盐、调味料。

(7) 本表需要用英语填写。可附加寄达国所接受的其他一种语言,细节可从邮局进一步获悉。

(8) 勿向食物和餐具喷洒。勿在近火源处存放或使用。勿敲撬。宜放在阴凉、儿童不易碰到的地方。

(9) 请仔细阅读说明书,以便使本机发挥其最佳性能、经久耐用、不出故障。

(10) 工作时请注意不要经常把脚放在踏板上,以免不慎踏动,引起事故。

3. 语篇翻译

● 语篇1

保修期内,用户送修时必须持有购买送修产品的有效发票和厂方指定的相关三包凭证,三包有效期自发票开具之日起算。用户应妥善保存保修卡和购机发票,送修时必须同时出示保修卡和购机发票。用户遗失购买发票时,应按出厂日期推算三包有效期。

● 语篇2

潘婷PRO-V营养洗发露

使用潘婷PRO-V,能令头发健康、加倍亮泽。潘婷PRO-V营养洗发露现在含有更多维生素B5,营养能由发根彻底渗透至发尖,补充养分,令头发健康,发出耀眼光泽。洗发露兼含护发素,在洗发的同时护发。

用法:洗湿头发,以潘婷PRO-V营养洗发露轻揉,再以清水冲洗即可。每次洗发后,使用潘婷PRO-V营养护发霜,能加倍滋润头发,预防头发开叉。

- 语篇3

北京全聚德烤鸭店

全聚德创业于清同治三年(1864),距今已有130多年历史,是中外闻名的老字号风味饭庄。

全聚德烤鸭店主要经营挂炉烤鸭和山东风味菜肴,以及独具风味的"全鸭席"。全聚德具有雄厚的烹调技术力量,拥有一大批著名的烹饪高手。

全聚德烤鸭店坐落在北京和平门大街路口东南侧。这幢七层大楼建成于1979年,总建筑面积15 000平方米,共有大小餐厅40余间,可同时接待2 000余宾客,是目前中国,也是世界上专营烤鸭的最大饭庄。餐厅环境更加优雅、舒适、富丽堂皇。

全聚德烤鸭店全体员工,热情欢迎中外宾客前来品尝全聚德名优烤鸭、风味佳肴,并以热情服务、优雅环境竭诚为您服务。

- 语篇4

密码锁使用说明

出厂时,密码锁所设密码为三个零(000)。您可以保持三个零不变,也可以按照以下步骤设置新的密码:

第一步,按箭头方向顶进调码套按钮,保持其状态直到完成以下步骤。

第二步,转动字轮设定你想要的个人密码。

第三步,松开调码套按钮,再转动字轮隐藏你的个人密码。

第四步,现在您个人的新密码已经设定。

第五步,如果您想要更改密码,请重复上述步骤。

思考与练习答案

第一章 功能语境制约下的商务英语及其翻译

1. 思考题（略）

2. 句子翻译

(1) Should either party to this contract suffer damages because of any wrongful act or neglect of other party, claim shall be adjusted by agreement or arbitration.

(2) The bank in Ecuador will instruct its agent bank in the United States to establish a letter of credit. Price：RMB 30 per yard, C. I. F., C. 5%, Lagos. Payment：by confirmed, irrevocable L/C payable by draft at sight to be opened 30 days before the time of shipment.

(3) We have learned by courtesy of Mr. Greenhow that you are one of the leading importers of Chinese chemicals and pharmaceutics in your country.

(4) We look forward to your favorable reply.

(5) We shall be grateful if you would reply at an early date.

(6) Cultural events pave the way for trade activities.

(7) About 10 business centers will be formed on the Pedestrian Street for catering, entertainment, tour, leisure and shopping.

(8) Would you kindly quote us your lowest price FOB London ASAP?

(9) This is Cussons' newly acquired factory in Poland.

(10) In 1990, the Province approved a total of 99 foreign-invested enterprises (the three types of companies with foreign elements, i. e. sino-foreign joint ventures, sino-foreign cooperative businesses and wholly foreign-owned enterprises), with the aggregated total reaching 284.

3. 语篇翻译

- 语篇1

A joint venture is a venture that is jointly owned and operated by two or more firms.

Many firms penetrate foreign markets by engaging in a joint venture with firms that reside in those markets. Most joint ventures allow two firms to apply their respective comparative advantages in a given project. For example, General Mill Inc. joined in a venture with Nestlé SA, so that the cereals produced by General Mill could be sold through the overseas distribution network established by Nestlé.

Xerox Corp. and Fuji Co. (of Japan) engaged in a joint venture that allowed Xerox Corp. to penetrate the Japanese market and allowed Fuji to enter the photocopying business. Sara Lee Corp. and Southwestern Bell have engaged in joint ventures with Mexican firms, as such ventures have allowed entry into Mexican markets. There are numerous joint ventures between automobile manufacturers, as each manufacturer can offer its technological advantages. General Motors has ongoing joint ventures with automobile manufacturers in several different countries, including Hungary.

● 语篇2

Nike is one of the most powerful marketing companies in the business world today, but it had very small beginnings. The global giant company started in the 1960s with the company's founders selling cheap Japanese sports shoes to American high school athletes at school track meetings, using a supply of shoes they kept in their cars.

● 语篇3

Investors must understand that the current changes in economic geography, wealth and geopolitical power, while associated with greater geopolitical risks, also offer huge opportunities in emerging economies. They are the prime beneficiaries of the demise of Utopian socialism, the invention of instant and free communication, and efficient transportation and distribution, as well as easy US monetary policies. Investors would do well to have a significant overweight position in countries as diverse as Thailand, Malaysia, Vietnam, and Singapore, which are likely to significantly outperform the US over the next few years.

第二章　商务汉英语言文化对比分析与翻译

1. 思考题(略)

2. 请将以下汉语外来词译成英语,并做适当的解释说明

(1) 盎司:ounce

"盎司"是对 ounce 这个英制常用重量单位的音译。1磅等于16盎司(1 pound = 16 ounces),这种十六进位制很像我国过去使用的"1斤等于16两"的旧制。

此外,an ounce of 一般表示"少许"。

(2) 芭比娃娃:Barbie doll

"芭比娃娃"是十分畅销的金发碧眼玩具娃娃的商标名,是对 Barbie doll 的音译。芭比娃娃的模样为迷人的年轻女子,像一个艳丽的女模特儿。男玩具娃娃肯(Ken)是芭比(Barbie)的男朋友。此外,还有许多专为芭比(Barbie)和肯(Ken)设计的各式时髦服装、汽车、家具等。

如果一位女子长相迷人,喜爱打扮,但不是十分聪明的话,人们有时会将她比作"芭比娃娃"。

(3) 玻璃天花板:glass ceiling

"玻璃天花板"是一个外来词,是对 glass ceiling 的直译。glass ceiling 是指阻止人才在机构内部升迁并充分发挥潜能的无形人为障碍。这个词起初是指女经理和女主管职位升迁的最高点。其实,现在很多职位对女性来说都存在"玻璃天花板"和"玻璃墙"(glass wall)的问题。

(4) 西红柿:apple of love / love apple

"西红柿"的英语翻译为 tomato,这是大家熟知的,但是因为误解、误译,"西红柿"还有另一种浪漫的说法,即 apple of love / love apple(爱情的苹果)。16 世纪时,西班牙从南美洲引进了西红柿,后来西红柿传入摩洛哥,意大利商人再把西红柿带入意大利。意大利人把西红柿叫作"摩尔人的苹果"(pomo dei Moro)。法国种植者引种时,误以为意大利文 dei Moro(摩尔人的)是法文 d'amour(爱情的)的意思。这样,"摩尔人的苹果"就被误译成了"爱情的苹果"。

(5) 洗钱:money laundering

"洗钱"属于俚语和比喻性说法,又叫"洗赃款",意思是把非法掠取的巨额钱款通过一定的手段使其合法化;其英译是 money laundering。"洗钱行"往往被译为 laundry。

3. 句子翻译

(1) You will find it profitable to buy from us because the quality of our products is far better than that of other foreign makers in your district.

(2) It is estimated that their stock price will exceed $15 per share.

(3) Our commodities are reasonable in price and excellent in quality.

(4) Deals made across the dinner table are just as many as those made across the conference table.

(5) This house CNY 2,000,000 o. n. o.

(6) Our products are sold in Britain, America, Japan, Italy and Southeast Asia and well appreciated by their purchasers.

(7) One of the "Three Uniques"—three snacks—of Tianjin located by the Haihe River is the big mahua (fried dough twists), which was first developed by a Liu family operating in the Shibajie (the 18th Street) in the early 1900s. Now the proprietor

and operator of the food is the Guifaxiang Company, Tianjin.

(8) Keep off the Grass!

(9) No Smoking in Bed!

(10) Warm welcome to all honored guests from home and abroad to attend the Trade Talks!

(11) Nonrefundable, nontransferable, and good only on dates validated on tickets.

(12) Through contacts with overseas businessmen, Chinese companies can conduct overseas market surveys. This will help them to understand which commodities to produce and in what quantity, as well as which products to improve in terms of quality. They will also find out how to increase their range of products and how to improve the packaging of their commodities. All these will no doubt help promote China's export trade.

(13) Established in 1982, Guangzhou Clothing Factory specializes in the manufacturing of clothes with both domestic and export sales ranking first in Guangdong. Thanks to the unique design, its Xinxing brand jackets are sold in more than 30 countries and regions in the world, enjoying increasing popularity among end-users both at home and abroad.

(14) As China's overall national strength has grown in the course of reform and opening-up over the last two decades, more and more countries, international organizations and people have come into contact with China and have taken interest in Chinese culture.

4. 语篇翻译

- 语篇1

Mr. Vice President,

Our American friends,

My colleagues,

Ladies and Gentlemen,

On behalf of all the members of our mission, I would like to express our sincere thanks to you for inviting us to such a marvelous Christmas party.

We really enjoyed the delicious food and excellent wine. Also, the music was perfect. I enjoyed meeting and talking to you, and sharing the time together. As we say, well begun is half done. I hope we will be able to maintain this good relationship and make next year another great one together.

Thank you again for the wonderful party, and we had a great time.

In closing, I would like to invite you to join me in a toast.

To the health of Mr. Vice President,

To the health of our American friends,

To the health of my colleagues and,

To all the ladies and gentlemen present here,

Cheers!

- 语篇2

Negotiating can be a very stressful affair, and there will be moments when it hardly seems worth the effort. A CNO (Chief Negotiator Officer) must be equipped with a highly developed sense of humor in order to weather persistent storms. Some of the negotiating delays, logistical problems, and social settings may seem like exercises in absurdity, and many of the discomforts of travel can be downright demeaning. Viewing such problems with a humorous eye and avoiding the syndrome of taking yourself too seriously can make all the difference in keeping negotiations on track.

- 语篇3

Shaanxi Dark Horse Honey Biological Development Co., Ltd. is on the north slope of Qinling Mountain.

Qinling Mountain, located in central China, has a varied climate and grand landscapes. It is a place where visitors can enjoy blue skies and white clouds. The region abounds with living things. There are 1,988 different species of vegetables and 510 species of medicinal herbs. World famous quality honey is also produced here.

第三章 商务汉英翻译的标准及存在的问题

1. 思考题(略)

2. 句子翻译

(1) Many domestic franchised enterprises are never asked for any franchised fees in order to ensure a rapid growth in quantity, inevitably resulting in the fact that those who invest in foreign brands feel unpleased.

(2) The adjustment of economic structure results into a comparatively large number of laid-off workers.

(3) As the Chinese people are getting more and more wealthy, they will eat at restaurants more and more frequently.

(4) A lot of people have turned to business and made a very big fortune since the practice of the reform and opening up policy to the outside world.

(5) The three faithful friends are an old wife, an old dog and ready money.

（6）Usually, consumer packs are more costly than unpacked goods.

（7）It was also disclosed that he had set up a slush fund that contained at least CNY 600,000.00. He has yet to give a satisfactory explanation as to its origin.

（8）In China, cars with displacement less than 1.0 L can be classified as small-displacement cars.

（9）Exchange is the core concept of marketing. For an exchange to take place, several conditions must be satisfied. Of course, at least two parties must participate, and each must have something of value to the other. Each party must also want to deal with the other party and each party must be free to accept or reject the other party's offer. Finally, each party must be able to communicate and deliver.

（10）Western Europe has been hit harder than the United States and Japan. Some countries, such as Malaysia and Thailand, have been partly insulated.

3. 语篇翻译

- 语篇1

The field of consumer behavior covers a lot of ground: It is the study of the processes involved when individuals or groups select, purchase, use or dispose of products, services, ideas, or experiences to satisfy needs and desires. Consumers take many forms, ranging from an eight-year-old child begging her mother for Pokémon cards to an executive in a large corporation deciding on a multimillion-dollar computer system. The items that are consumed can include anything from canned peas, a massage, democracy, hip-hop music, or hoopster rebel Dennis Rodman. Needs and desires to be satisfied range from hunger and thirst to love, status, or even spiritual fulfillment. Our attachment to everyday products is exemplified by our love affair with colas. The World Coca-Cola in Las Vegas draws a million visitors a year. Exhibits ask, "What does Coca-Cola mean to you?" Many of the responses tell of strong emotional connections to the brand.

- 语篇2

The development of information technology and internet has accelerated economic globalization, removed the boundaries between countries and regions, and brought about the international flow and reasonable allocation of capital, commodities and technologies. As a result, commerce, finance and services of countries are increasingly linked together, and international cooperation and multinational operations have become a common practice. A slight change may influence the regional or even global economy, which means that the world is becoming an inseparable whole.

- 语篇3

Today, Nanjing University consists of two campuses, one in Gulou and the other in Pukou. It is one of the top universities in China, with beautiful campuses and modern teaching and research facilities.

With an elegant environment featuring green hills, fresh air, and a flowing creek with small bridges across it, the university is an ideal place for study.

第四章 商务汉英语体修辞对比分析与翻译

1. 思考题(略)

2. 句子翻译

(1) If by reason of delay on the part of the Purchaser, CAE reserves the right to apply a late payment charge of one and one-half percent per month.

(2) When you're sipping Lipton, you're sipping something special.

(3) Thank God! It's Friday! I'm off now. Have a good weekend!

(4) For more information, please ask for a leaflet.

(5) Quality of the goods is superior and prices are reasonable.

(6) Quality to be strictly as per sample submitted by the Seller on February 15, 2008.

3. 语篇翻译

- 语篇1

PRESS RELEASE

March 16, 2020

PUBLICATION DATE: March 22, 2020

Reorganization of ABC Company

Just as a person has to learn new skills to do more complex work, so a company sometimes has to find new ways of doing things as the work load grows. It's a nice kind of problem to have!

In order to handle the rapidly growing number of franchises and accounts with better service and quicker response, ABC Company is reorganizing its regional sales force, effective April 1, 2020. The ABC Company is dividing the nation into four Marketing Regions: Eastern, Southern, Central, and Western. Each region will have a Regional Manager: Margaret Olson (Eastern), Harry Baines (Southern), Rolf Johnson (Central), and Barry Jones (Western). To coordinate the entire national sales effort, Mark Vinson will be National Sales Manager. By May all the kinks would be worked out throughout the whole company, and the four regions would do business as the normal way. The company is confident that the end result will be well worth the effort as will be seen in the greater sales during the months ahead.

—END—

CONTACT: Mr. G. L. Sender, Public Relations Manager
Tel: 6654388

- 语篇2

May 5, 2007

Dear Mr. Lee,

Thank you for your letter of 15 April regarding payment terms.

We agree to your proposal, the terms of which are as follows.

(1) Payment will be made by confirmed, irrevocable letter of credit with draft at sight instead of direct payment at sight.

(2) The price quoted to us is with no discount.

The above payment terms have been approved by our Managing Director and will be acted on accordingly.

The order is being prepared and will reach you in the next ten days.

I would like to take this opportunity to inform you that our representative, Mr. John Green, will attend the forthcoming Canton Fair. He will be writing to you shortly.

We sincerely hope that future discussions between our companies will lead to further mutually beneficial business.

Yours sincerely,
Denis Thorpe

- 语篇3

Rongshan Hotel, situated in the beautiful central district of Fuzhou, Fujian Province, is ideal for business travelers and tourists, with convenient transportation, attractive décor and modern facilities.

The over 300 luxury suites are clean, quiet and private. Six lovely restaurants serve a variety of Chinese and Western cuisine, offering courteous service and a relaxed atmosphere. The complete leisure and fitness facilities provide the fun of exercise and a proper break from the day's stress.

The hotel's modern commercial center, with advanced telecommunication facilities and multifunctional conference halls, will make doing business away from the office efficient and easy.

The Internet services provided by the hotel link you with the world no matter where your business lies.

第五章 商务汉英词义对比分析与翻译

1. 思考题(略)

2. 句子翻译

(1) Most little shops have been absorbed into big business.

(2) Follower countries can just borrow the latest technology cheaply without having to bear the cost of research, invention and development.

(3) The accountant was found to have cooked the books.

(4) I think that the house will fetch at least US $5,600 per square meter.

(5) We are now long on steel.

(6) Upon receipt of the seller's delivery advice, the buyers shall, 15-20 days prior to the delivery date, open a transferable, divisible, irrevocable letter of credit in favor of the sellers for an amount equivalent to the total amount of the shipment.

(7) We are an important firm dealing in textiles in substantial quantities.

(8) We can raise the loan for this investment.

(9) We wish to cover the goods against All Risks.

(10) We are able to quote you very advantageous terms.

(11) Keep this passageway clear.

(12) There is no rule but has exception.

(13) You were, you are, and you remain to be the consumers of our products.

3. 语篇翻译

- 语篇1

Carrying out Localization Actively

It is of great importance for MNEs to carry out localization, a strategic policy to kill two birds with one stone. Not only can localization effectively lower costs of highly-qualified managing personnel appointed by home country, but also it can make full use of cheap human resources in host country. For a long-run term, it is a wise choice to promote excellent local managers to the level of decision-making, for they get familiar with laws and regulations of their own country, have a better knowledge of their market, have no cultural barriers and can effectively communicate with local departments. In short, they are more familiar with the rules set by the government of their home country. However, in order to attract and keep excellent talents, MNEs must take a practical measure, creating opportunities for those talents to develop their own abilities and get promotion. Take China, an emerging market, for example. The investment there made by MNEs is on the increase day by day and the total amount of foreign investment in China just ranks behind the most developed country nowadays—the United States. Therefore, there is fierce competition for excellent local talents in China among different MNEs. All of them are aware that the competition for market is the competition for talents. Those who attract more talents will get the upper hand in this fierce competition. Besides, equipped with sufficient capital, advanced technology, effective managerial expertise and operation, MNEs will hold an overcoming magic power to combat fluctuations in the market.

- 语篇2

The Role of China's Economy in the World Economy

With the advent of the 21st century, and especially after China's accession to the WTO by removing all kinds of the obstacles in its way, the role of China's economy in the world economy has attracted global attention. Thanks to the re-division of labor and transference of world production chains, China has become a big manufacturing country, promoting the advancement of the economy of many developing countries, which export to China resources, farm produces and semi-manufactured goods in the manufacturing industry, and at the same time China provides industrial products of low price and high quality for the entire world.

The UK *Economist* on July 30, 2005 gave an analysis of the status and role of China's economy in the world economy, believing that "China is almost the engine of the world economy" and "China's policies are exerting an increasing impact on the global inflation rate, interest rate, bond yields, prices of the real estate, incomes, profits and prices of commodities, which may turn out to be the most profound economic change in the world for at least half a century".

Since it adopted the policy of reform and opening up 28 years ago, China has kept an increase of 9.4% in its economy and has gained great achievements in many sectors. Moreover, China has strengthened its socialist system, as it has appropriately combined the basic social system of socialism with the market economy system. Its production capacity has had an unprecedented development, while the living standard of the people has achieved a conspicuous improvement. Its overall national strength has been notably enhanced and the economic structure has been properly adjusted. Therefore, China has improved its status in the world economy, becoming an impetus to its development.

- 语篇3

June 6, 2020

Dear Sirs,

We have received your Quotation No. TY678 but regret to find the price irrelevant to current market trend.

Right now in Europe, there are more Asian sellers and more material from Eastern Europe. The chief sellers, worrying about their market shares, are again lowering their prices. In the circumstances, the FH Group must have good reasons to be ready to accept last year's price level.

According to our information, the FH Group's tactic is to buy as much Chinese material as possible and pay a good price for it. Then they sell the Chinese material along with their own at the lower market price in Europe. Since their purchase from China is only a small part of their total sales, the cost of doing so is absorbed by the large profit margin of their own material. This means that when other competitors withdraw, Chinese suppliers will find it more difficult to sell and have to bow to the FH Group's pressure to let it to dominate the market.

We hope you will reconsider the matter and send us a new offer.

Yours sincerely

第六章 商务汉英词类用法对比分析与翻译

1. 思考题（略）

2. 句子翻译

(1) The failure of the firm was caused by bad management.

(2) These trade-liberalizing measures were intended to promote the more efficient use of resources in the country.

(3) In the memorandum, our readiness is indicated to provide technical service to your end-users.

(4) Aiming at the promotion of the bilateral trade, SINOCHEM and a big American corporation have come to the following agreement.

(5) Due to its total unawareness of the sales push, the home office had no plans to ship the products.

(6) Besides, this is essentially a stock picker's game.

(7) The application of plastics in automobile industry has brought about great increase of the consumption.

(8) The adoption of our company's new set of equipment will greatly reduce the percentage of deceptive products.

(9) Prompt payment is appreciated.

(10) Economists are confident that this trend is inevitable.

(11) He asked me for a full account of our products.

(12) Formality has always characterized their relationship.

(13) We have to make sure that the remittance of commission made as such is not

against local regulations.

(14) Light industry and textile products are now available in better designs with improved quality and in richer variety.

(15) A strong, prosperous and developed China will pose no threat to any country.

3. 语篇翻译

- 语篇1

We learn from your letter of September 20 that case of our shipment under your Order No. 43 arrived in badly-damaged condition. As the goods were packed in new strong wooden cases suitable for long distance ocean transportation, we can only conclude that the case has been stored and handled carelessly.

On receipt of your letter under reply we immediately appointed a surveyor at your end to inspect the damaged case with one of your staff members on the spot where the case was lying. On October 3 came the surveyor's report stating that to all appearance the case in question had been either left out in a heavy shower of rain, or else dropped into some water, and your staff member being impartial and friendly, on seeing the condition, admitted that it was the case.

We then instructed our forwarding department to further investigate the matter. The carrier has been communicated with, and informs us that the whole shipment arrived in good condition. They can be certain that the damage occurred during the time the goods were in your hands. In such circumstances, we regret having to say that we are not liable for the damage.

As we know, that case contains some important spare parts of our knitting machines, without which the machines will not work, we shall therefore be pleased to put in hand a repeat of the supply of the spare parts at the prices invoiced if you think it necessary, and we shall do our best to deliver them to you within a fortnight.

We await your reply.

- 语篇2

We have for acknowledgment your letter of 29 last month, and thank you for giving us the first opportunity to take up your agency here.

Our firm has a long history in dealing in chemical products as you know. We firmly believe that with our reputation and connections we can serve you well. With these advantages we do not think there is any difficulty either in pushing the sales or in extending the market for your products. We are interested in your proposal and should be pleased to accept it, if the terms of your agency agreement are acceptable. We request you to airmail us your terms at your soonest possible convenience.

Best regards and looking forward to receiving your early reply.

- 语篇3

Japan's once enviable jobless rate will soar to double-digit levels if—and the warning is a big one—firms opt for drastic Western-style layoffs to boost profits. While Japan's lifetime employment system is visibly unraveling, many economists still doubt whether a scenario of soaring joblessness will occur, given that economic incentives to slash payrolls clash with social and political pressures to save jobs. A kinder, gentler approach to restructuring would soften the social instability many people fear would result from doubling the jobless rate, already at a record high.

Critics believe it would also cap gains in profit margins and stifle economic vitality, especially in the absence of bold steps to open the door to new growth industries. Some economists believe different methods of counting mean Japan's jobless rate is already close to 7 percent by United States standards, not that far from the 7.8 percent peak hit in the US in 1992 when it began to emerge from a two-year slump.

第七章 商务汉英句法对比分析与翻译

1. 思考题（略）

2. 句子翻译

(1) The boom was created by several factors that worked together.

(2) You will notice that every single one of our products is made from 100% natural ingredients.

(3) People spent money as quickly as it was gained. The motor industry was greatly benefited by the Boom as the amount of car sales, and so cars on the roads rose. This meant jobs were created in building cars, building roads, building roadside diners and advertising.

(4) After the said import license is approved, we shall establish an irrevocable letter of credit in your favor.

(5) We deeply regret the inconvenience this delay has caused you and other established customers.

(6) We have been in touch with our legal advisers on this matter, and they have informed us that we are not legally responsible for any claims you might bring against us.

(7) The quality of your Ginseng Wine is fine, but its packing is rather poor. Bottles are subjected to breakage and paper boxes are very thin. Please put each bottle in a foam plastic casing and then in a thicker paper box for our future orders.

Otherwise, we shall be compelled to give up this business.

(8) The exporter has to give due consideration to the packing of the goods to be shipped abroad, and try his best to pack the goods in accordance with the instructions of the buyer.

(9) In the construction of an export package, the important factors of efficiency and economy must be taken into consideration. The exporter should bear in mind that the goods should be packed in a manner which ensures their safe arrival at destination and facilitates their handling in transit.

(10) Our cotton prints are packed in cases lined with craft paper and water-proof paper, each consisting of 30 pieces in one design with 5 color-ways equally assorted.

(11) The biannual Guangzhou Fair is attended by almost all foreign trade companies in China and presents a great number of export commodities to buyers from abroad. Many business transactions are concluded at the fair. As sellers and buyers can all gather in one place to conduct trade talks, the fair apparently saves them a great deal of time and money. This explains why the Guangzhou Fair has long been popular among overseas traders.

(12) Responding to client expectations in a changing world market strengthened its efforts in developing its market.

(13) Our Machine Tool Plant, founded in 1935, has gong through large-scale innovation and expansion after the founding of New China in 1949, and has become the biggest lathe manufacturer in China. It has a strong technical force with advanced technical craftsmanship, modern equipment and up-to-date management, supplemented by well-equipped measuring, inspecting and testing apparatus. It manufactures machines which are superior in quality and reliable performance.

(14) More to the point is France's failure to win an important place in the market for what they call "point forte" products, namely knockout products, especially those which are in greatest demand such as machine tools, cameras and computers.

(15) Elegant and up-to-date in designs, attractive and delightful in shades, the Zhejiang printed pure silk fabrics are elaborately printed by hand, and are really an ideal high-quality material for noble-looking garments and ceremonial dresses in various styles.

3. 语篇翻译

- 语篇1

As a result of the productivity survey carried out in the factory, more rapid and more efficient ways of operating are now being applied. In the factory, productivity has been increased by over 50 percent. The management intends to apply these same methods to office staff in order to reduce costs. Our company must adapt in a competitive world. We aim to find ways of avoiding unnecessary actions by all staff. We therefore propose to pay a month's extra salary to any person who in the management's opinion has put forward the more practical suggestion to improve a particular office routine. All suggestions should be sent to the Managing Director's office before the end of next month.

- 语篇2

New ideas are an old tradition at Siemens. The company that grew out of the original Siemens & Halske is today a highly innovative leader in the world electrical and electronics market. Composed of Siemens AG and an array of domestic and foreign subsidiaries, the contemporary Siemens organization continues to set milestones on the road to progress.

Siemens maintains its own production facilities in 35 countries and operates a world-wide sales network. With more than 300,000 employees, it is one of the largest companies in the world electrical/ electronics industry, having recorded annual sales of DM 54 billion in the 1986/ 87 fiscal year. Reliable and far-sighted management is united with the youthful dynamism and zest for innovation that typify the company.

- 语篇3

May 10,2000

Gentlemen,

Thank you for your order of May 6 for six hundred sets of "Peony" television sets, but since you make delivery before Christmas a firm condition, we deeply regret that we cannot supply you as we have done on so many occasions in the past.

The manufacturers are finding it impossible to meet current demand for this very popular set. We ourselves placed an order for twenty-four sets a month ago, but were informed that all orders are being met in strict rotation and that our own could not be dealt with before the beginning of February.

I gather from your telex received this morning that your customers are unwilling to consider other makes. May I suggest that you try China National Light Industrial Products Corporation in Beijing? They may be able to help you.

Sincerely yours

- 语篇4

The Ice Sculpture Festival in Harbin

Perhaps no other place equals or exceeds Harbin in terms of the bone-cutting cold in

January. But it does not mean that people here have to be confined to their homes all day. On the contrary, every year when Harbin is enveloped in thick ice and heavy snow, many people from all over the world would come to celebrate the annual Ice Sculpture Festival lasting from January 1 to February 25. During the Ice Sculpture Festival, sculptors from worldwide would make a contest for the Finest Ice-and-Snow Artwork Prize. Under the curtain of night, the illumination of thousands upon thousands of twinkling colorful lights makes the colorful ice sculptures more charming.

第八章 商务汉英语段语篇对比分析与翻译

1. 思考题(略)

2. 句子翻译

(1) A: Do they buy their drinks at the local supermarket?
B: No, but we do.

(2) Government, at the federal, state, and local level, seeks to promote the public security, assure fair competition, and provide a range of services believed to be better performed by public rather than private enterprises.

(3) In the event that a court of competent jurisdiction decides that any portion of this Loan Agreement is null and void or unenforceable, then the remaining parts of this Loan Agreement shall survive the invalidity of any other term of this Loan Agreement and shall remain valid and enforceable to the fullest extent permissible by law.

(4) If possible, ask her to lunch to learn more about her. Think of it as a job interview, because that is virtually what it is.

(5) Since then, I have written no fewer than four times to Mr. Perron, explaining that it is not at all convenient for me to travel two hundred miles in order to collect the necklace in person, and asking him to post it to me. I have received no reply to any of these letters. May I ask you to contact Mr. Perron and persuade him to send me my necklace as soon as possible?

(6) Hearing loss, which is typically prior to teenage years, progresses throughout one's lifetime. Although hearing loss is now the world's number-one health problem, nearly 90 percent of people suffering hearing loss choose the problem untreated. For many millions, treating hearing loss in a conventional way can involve numerous office visits, expensive testing and adjustments to fit your ear. Thanks to Crystal Ear, the "sound solution" is now convenient. Almost 90 percent of people with mild hearing loss, and millions more with just a little hearing drop-off, can be dramatically helped with Crystal Ear. Moreover, its superior design is energy-efficient, so batteries can

last months. Crystal Ear is now available to help these people treat hearing loss with a small hearing amplifier.

3. 语段语篇翻译

- 语篇 1

At some time, you will undoubtedly bring in new machines, substances and procedures which could lead to new hazards. If there is any significant change, you should take this into consideration. In any case, it is good practice to review your assessment from time to time. Don't amend your risk assessment for every trivial change or each new job; but if a new job introduces significant new hazards of its own, you will want to consider them in their own right and do whatever you need to keep the risks down.

- 语篇 2

Preeminence in R&D gives Lockheed advantages in aeronautics, missiles, space and military electronics. It makes us stronger competitors; better able to manage national priority programs and deliver technology that is both reliable and affordable. Just what you'd expect from a premier aerospace company. Just what you get from Lockheed.

- 语篇 3

Coca Cola's trick is the world's first three-dimensional commercial, and Coke will distribute some 40 million special viewing glasses nationwide through grocery stores and fast-food chains. Cleverness aside, some critics decry the offbeat offerings. Political columnist George Will grouses, "Trying too hard is the spirit of contemporary advertising." 3-D or not 3-D? That's the question for advertisers.

- 语篇 4

Hunting-and-gathering economies ruled for hundreds of thousands of years before they were overshadowed by agrarian economies, which ruled for about 10,000 years. Next came the industrial ones. The first began in Britain in the 1760s, and the first to finish started unwinding in the U.S. in the early 1950s. We are halfway through the information economy, and from start to finish, it will last 75 to 80 years, ending in the late 2020s. Then get ready for the next one: the bio-economy.

- 语篇 5

It's Not What You Are, It's Where You Are

Just as the world seems to be becoming more homogenized, with consumers finding it difficult to distinguish between myriad similar products and services, so corporate image is recognized as being an increasingly important way to win and retain.

However, opinions differ as to what exactly "image" entails. For some companies, it is limited to a recognizable logo and memorable slogan. For others, it has more far-reaching implications affecting everything from the choice of star endorsing their products, to the color of the wallpaper in the reception area, to the actual location of their offices. This last factor can say more about a company and its aspirations than might first appear. Consider for a moment the choices available and what each one might suggest to a potential client.

Do you want to be in an old style building in the city center, giving the air of a traditional, long established, but possibly rather conservative, establishment? Or do you underline your optimism, self-belief and modernity by moving into a specially designed building in the heart of the new, out of center, business development, alongside successful multinationals and, quite possibly, some of your competitors? Even having a modest office attached to a factory on the edge of a run-down industrial estate could be seen to reflect your company's work ethic and dedication to investing in essentials, rather than wasting money on such trivialities as a Miro or a Monet for the boardroom.

第九章 商务汉英文体对比分析与翻译

1. 思考题(略)
2. 句子翻译

(1) We have the honor to inform you of the dissolution of our partnership, and that, having let our former premises, we have taken for the receipt and payment of outstanding accounts, an office at No. 10, T. St.

(2) The samples submitted do not tempt us at the prices named; state the very lowest we can accept and we will wire you "yes" or "no".

(3) We have never received a bill of lading or invoice from you; and if any of your letters to us contained such documents, they must, in some way, have been miscarried.

(4) The price of $800 per set is acceptable, provided you increase the quantity of your order to 3,000 sets.

(5) After you ship the goods we ordered, you may draw upon us for the amount of the invoice.

(6) Cartons as a kind of packing container have been extensively used in international trade. Therefore, you need not worry about their seaworthiness.

(7) So far as we know, insurance companies accept goods packed in cartons to be insured against TPND. In case of theft and pilferage, you may be assured that you will get indemnification from the insurance company concerned.

(8) The traces of pilferage are easier to be found out for the goods packed in cartons

than in wooden cases. Therefore, they will help you to get compensation from the insurance company.

(9) The packing of our Men's Shirts is each in a poly-bag, 5 dozens to a carton lined with water-proof paper and bound with two iron straps outside.

(10) It is necessary to make transshipment at Hamburg for goods to be shipped to our port. Therefore, your packing must be seaworthy and can stand through handling during transit.

3. 语篇翻译
- 语篇1

Company Background

Shui On Properties Limited (SOP) was the property development arm of Shui On Group prior to the formation of Shui On Land Limited in 2004. SOP expanded its business into the Chinese Mainland in 1985 and built a sizable portfolio of property development and investment projects in the Mainland. Its prime developments in the Mainland have been injected into Shui On Land, the flagship property company of the Shui On Group. SOP now focuses on property investment with interests in Hong Kong, China, the Chinese Mainland and New York.

Shui On Properties' current property investment projects include:
* Shui On Plaza and City Hotel in Shanghai
* Shui On Centre in Hong Kong
* Riverside South Development in Manhattan, New York, the USA (20% interest)

- 语篇2

Employee Loyalty in Service Firm

Hotel, shop and restaurant chains, which employ thousands of people in low-paid, dead-end jobs, are discovering that high labor turnover rates resulting from the indiscriminate hiring of "cheap" workers can be extremely costly.

Cole National, a Cleveland-based firm which owns Child World, Things Remembered and other specialty shops, declared a "war for people" in an effort to recruit and keep better staff.

Employees were asked: What do you enjoy about working here? In the past year, have you thought about leaving? If so, why? How can we improve our company and create an even better place to work? Employees replied they wanted better training, better communications with their supervisors and, above all, wanted their bosses to "make me feel like I make a difference". Labor turnover declined by more than half; for full-time sales assistants, it declined by about a third.

Marriott Corporation, a hotels and restaurants group, has also decided to spend more money on retaining employees in the hope of spending less on finding and training new ones. In one year, it had to hire no fewer than 27,000 workers to fill 8,800 hourly-paid job slots.

To slow its labor turnover, Marriott had to get a simple message accepted throughout its operating divisions: loyal, well-motivated employees make customers happy and that, in turn, creates fatter profits and happier shareholders. Improved training of middle managers helped. So did a change in bonus arrangements.

At the same time, Marriott became more fussy about the people it recruited. It screened out job applicants motivated mainly by money: applicants which the company pejoratively described as "pay first people". Such people form a surprisingly small, though apparently disruptive, part of the service industry workforce. Marriott found in its employee-attitude surveys that only about 20% of its workers at Roy Rogers restaurants and about 30% of its workers at Marriott hotels regarded pay as their primary reason for working there.

Many middle managers in service industries are more comfortable coping with demands for more money than with demands for increased recognition and better communications. They will have to change their ways. Surveys say that when 13,000 employees in retail shops across America were asked to list in order the 18 reasons for working where they did, they ranked "good pay" third. In the first place was "appreciation of work done", with "respect for me as a person" second.

- 语篇3

MEMORANDUM

From: The Managing Director   **FOR**:   **PLEASE**:
To: Personnel Managers   Action   Display
Date: 18th March, 2020   Comment   File
                                         Information Discussion   Return
                                                            Pass To: _____

Subject: Installation of coffee machines

The board is thinking of installing automatic coffee machines in the offices of each division. Before we do this we need to know:

(1) how much use our staff will make of them;
(2) how many we would need;
(3) whether time now used for making coffee would be saved.

Can you provide us with your views on:

(1) how the staff will react to the idea;
(2) how we can deal with the union on the matter.

If possible, I would like to receive your report before the next board meeting on 1st April.

第十章　汉英商标对比分析与翻译

1. 思考题（略）

2. 句子翻译

(1) John will Buick to Vancouver from Seattle next weekend.

(2) Jack had the first chapter of the book, *The Story of the English*, Xeroxed and paid 4 dollars for it.

(3) Jane is Fording to Detroit while Jack is Chevying to Seattle.

3. 请判断以下汉英商标的翻译是否恰当并说明理由

(1) 恰当。Sailing 的音译为"席而灵"，意译为"航行"，因此作为旅行小闹钟的商标十分贴切。

(2) 不恰当。Fang 在英语里指（犬、狼等的）大牙或毒牙。这样的口红谁敢买？

(3) 恰当。汉语中"凤"和"龙"都是高贵、吉祥的象征，在西方"凤"也是吉利的，因为在西方神话中，Phoenix 与再生、复活有关。

(4) 恰当。STEPTWOLVES 使人联想起男子汉气概或男性的性格特征。

(5) 不恰当。英语里有短语 to show the white feather，意思是"软弱，临阵脱逃"，有侮辱人的意思。因此，在英语国家这种钢笔会备受冷落。

(6) 恰当。因为 Deer 在英语中没有歧义。

(7) 恰当。在英语中，Dalphne 曾是一个露珠女神的名字，她美丽优雅，用作女鞋的商标当然合适。

(8) 不恰当。在英语中 Cock 一词除了指代雄鸡外，还暗指人体某隐私部位。这样的商标品牌不仅有损于产品的形象和荣誉，而且能直接影响产品的销售，因此这种商品投放到英美市场以后，顾客会寥寥无几。

(9) 恰当。"旺德福"这三个字都寓意吉祥、生意兴隆，译为 WONDERFUL 后很好地转换了源语的美感。

(10) 恰当。原商标"回力"有"回天之力"之意，英译 Warrior 的发音与源语的发音最相似。英语译词所表达的"战士""勇士""武士""壮士"的意思很符合运动鞋商品的审美情趣。

第十一章　汉英商用名片对比分析与翻译

1. 思考题（略）

2. 名片中的地名和职务名称翻译

(1) 168 Century Avenue

(2) 5 Changshou Feeder Road

(3) Deputy Manager

(4) Vice Chairman

(5) Marketing Director

(6) Manager of Human Resources Department

(7) PR Manager

(8) CEO / Chief Executive Officer

(9) CFO / Chief Financial Officer

3. 名片翻译

(1)

Shanghai Foreign Language Edu. Press
Wang Qiang(Editor)
295 Zhongshan 1st Rd. Shanghai, 200083
FAX: 021-65425400   TEL: 021-65425300

(2)

China National Light Industrial Products Imp. & Exp. Corp
Li Weimin
Manager of Imp. Dept
82 Guangqumen Street, Dongcheng District,
Beijing, 100076
Fax: 021-65425400   Tel: 021-65425300

(3)

CHINA EASTERN AIRLINES
BEIJING BRANCH(OFFICE)
MA CHUN
General Manager
67 Wangfujing St.   Tel: 4665363
Beijing, China   Fax: 4082694

第十二章　商务汉英信函对比分析与翻译

1. 思考题(略)

2. 句子翻译

(1) We are interested in your men's shirts displayed in your showroom.

(2) Please send us 5 copies of your latest catalogs at your earliest convenience.

(3) If terms and delivery date are satisfactory, we should expect to place regular orders with you.

(4) We shall be obliged if you will send us some samples with the best terms at your earliest convenience.

(5) We thank you for your letter offering your services and should like to discuss the possibility of expanding trade with you.

(6) Please note that we can only accept payment by L/C in our business dealings with

the developing countries.

(7) We shall make delivery of the goods upon receipt of your order.

(8) As soon as we are able to say anything definite (give you further information) regarding our supply of compressors, we will cable you again.

(9) If you want to purchase this product, we are able to supply as much as you require.

(10) Payment by cash against documents is acceptable to us.

(11) The relative L/C will be established through the First National Bank, Jakarta. We thank you very much for your prompt arrangement of shipment upon receipt of it.

(12) We'll accept your price if you can meet our needs and make an earlier shipment.

(13) We are not in a position to entertain business at your price, since it is far below our cost.

(14) We will appreciate it if you replace the damaged goods.

3. 语篇翻译

• 语篇1

Gentlemen,

In regard to the first shipment against our Contract No. 1234, we wrote you on 7th instant that part of the goods was not in conformity with the contracted specifications. We requested you to give us explanations and advise us how you would deal with the matter, but up to now we have not yet received any reply.

So we regret to say that we cannot bind ourselves to accept the second lot of goods. We have to request that you should postpone the shipment of the goods for the time being. It goes without saying that we have no obligations whatever in this matter.

We are looking forward to your reply.

Yours faithfully

• 语篇2

September 18, 2019

Gentlemen,

Our Order No U89

The 100 coffee sets supplied to the above order were delivered yesterday, but we regret that 15 sets were badly damaged.

The packages containing the coffee sets appeared to be in good condition and we accepted and signed for them without question. We unpacked the coffee sets with great care and can only assume that the damage must be due to careless handling at some stage prior to packing.

We shall be glad if you will replace all 15 sets as soon as you can. Meanwhile, we have put the damaged coffee sets aside in case you need them to support a claim on your suppliers for compensation.

Yours sincerely

- 语篇 3

October 12, 2019

Gentlemen,

Here we venture to write and have a self-introduction to you. We are acting as the agent for the Ceramics Department of your Tianjin Office for some time and our efforts have proved mutually satisfactory. You may refer to them for this.

As we specialize in the trade of household and decorative wares, such as porcelain wares, lacquer ware and crystals, we are desirous to act as your exclusive agent for the promotion of sales of your products in Vancouver.

If you are agreeable to our proposal, please outline the terms on which you will be prepared to enter into an exclusive sales agreement with us.

Truly yours

第十三章 商务汉英合同对比分析与翻译

1. **思考题(略)**
2. **句子翻译**

(1) The contract is made out in English and Chinese languages in quadruplicate, both texts being equally authentic, and each Party shall hold two copies of each text.

(2) This contract is signed by the authorized representatives of both parties on Dec. 9, 2019. After signing the contract, both parties shall apply to their respective Government Authorities for ratification. The date of ratification last obtained shall be taken as the effective date of the contract. Both parties shall exert their utmost efforts to obtain the ratification within 60 days and shall advise the other party by telex and thereafter send a registered letter for confirmation.

(3) The contract shall be valid for 10 years from the effective date of the contract and on the expiry of the validity term of the contract, the contract shall automatically become null and void.

(4) The outstanding claims and liabilities existing between both parties on the expiry of the validity of the contract shall not be influenced by the expiration of this

contract. The debtor shall be kept liable until the debtor fully pays up his debts to the creditor.

(5) Any clause, covenant or agreement in a contract of carriage relieving the carrier or the ship from liability for loss or damage to, or in connection with, goods arising from negligence, fault or failure in duties and obligations provided in this article or lessening such liability otherwise than provided in these rules shall be null and void and no effect.

(6) The Contractor shall be responsible for the true and proper setting-out of the Works in relation to original points, lines and levels of reference given by the Engineer in writing and for the correctness, subject as above-mentioned, of the position, levels, dimensions and alignment of all parts of the Works and for the provision of all necessary instruments, appliances and labor in connection therewith.

(7) Upon successful completion of the tests the Purchaser shall sign a Plant Acceptance Certificate evidencing such completion and listing any agreed Deficiencies to be corrected by CAE within such period as may be agreed with the Purchaser.

(8) The Purchaser shall be able at all times to account for all copies of the Proprietary Software which are required to be made to permit its efficient use in its intended function.

(9) At all times during the performance of the works, the Subcontractor shall provide the Contractor with accurate and complete information with respect to the works already performed, the works in progress, the works scheduled and the events effecting the performance thereof and shall make available to the Contractor all relevant planning and reporting documents (daily, weekly and monthly progress reports, accident and security reports, payrolls, list of labor staff and expatriates).

(10) The distributor shall store and transport the products in conditions that will preserve the products in good condition and will comply with any reasonable requests made by the Supplier concerning the conditions in which the products are to be stored and transported.

3. 语篇翻译

● 语篇 1

SALES CONTRACT

Contract No.: _____

Date: _____

Signed at: _____

The Seller: _____

Address: _____

Tel: _____

Cable Address: _____

The Buyer: _____

Address: _____

Tel: _____

Cable Address: _____

(1) This Sales Contract is made by and between the Seller and the Buyer whereby the Seller agrees to sell and the Buyer agrees to buy the under-mentioned goods according to the terms and conditions stipulated below:

Name of Commodity, Specification & Packing	Quantity	Unit Price	Amount
Total Value:			

(With 5 % more or less allowed)

(2) Shipping Marks: To Be Designated by the Seller:

(3) Insurance: To be covered by the Seller for <u>110%</u> of the total invoice value against <u>All Risks</u> as per Ocean Marine Cargo Clause of the People's Insurance Company of China (excluding S. R. C. C.). Should the Buyer desire to cover other risks besides the afore-mentioned or for an amount exceeding the afore-mentioned limit, the Seller's approval must be obtained first and all additional premium charges incurred therewith shall be for the Buyer's account.

(4) Port of Shipment:

(5) Port of Destination:

(6) Time of Shipment:

---

(7) Terms of Payment: The Buyer shall establish Confirmed, Irrevocable, Transferable, Divisible and Without Recourses Letter of Credit in favor of the Seller for the full contracted value ..., payable at sight against presentation of the shipping documents, to the negotiating bank of China. The Letter of Credit must reach the Seller before ... and remain valid for negotiation in China till the 15th day after date of shipment.

(8) Inspection: The Certificate of Quality, Quantity/Weight issued by ... shall be taken as the basis of delivery.

(9) Force Majeure: The Seller shall not be held responsible, if the Seller, owing to Force Majeure cause or causes, fails to make delivery within the time stipulated in the Contract or cannot deliver the goods. However, in such cases, the Seller shall inform the Buyer immediately by cable and, if it is requested by the Buyer, shall also deliver to the Buyer by registered post, a certificate attesting the existence of such a cause or causes.

(10) Discrepancy and Claim: In case the Seller fails to ship the whole lot or part of the goods within the time stipulated in this Contract, the Buyer shall have the right to cancel the part of the Contract which has not been performed 20 days following the expiry of the stipulated time of shipment, unless there exists a Force Majeure cause or the Contract stipulation has been modified with the Buyer's consent. In case discrepancy on the quality of the goods is found by the Buyer after arrival of the goods at the port of destination, the Buyer may, within 30 days after arrival of the goods at the port of destination, lodge with the Seller a claim which should be supported by an Inspection Certificate issued by a public surveyor approved by the Seller. The Seller shall, on the merits of the claim, either make good the loss sustained by the Buyer or reject their claim. It is agreed that the Seller shall not be held responsible for any loss of losses due to natural causes of the Insurance Co.; in case the Letter of Credit does not correspond to the Contract terms and the Buyer fails to amend thereafter its terms in time, after receipt of Credit opened by the Buyer does not reach the Seller within the time stipulated in the Contract, the Seller shall have the right to cancel the Contract or to delay the delivery of the goods and shall have also the right to claim for compensation of losses against the Buyer.

(11) Arbitration: Any dispute arising from the execution of or in connection with this Contract, should be settled through negotiation. In case no settlement can be reached, the case shall then be submitted to the Foreign Trade Arbitration Commission of China Council for the Promotion of International Trade, Beijing, for settlement by arbitration in accordance with the Commission's Provisional Rules of Procedure. The award rendered by the Commission shall be final and binding on both parties.

(12) Obligations: Both the Signers of this Contract, i. e. the Seller and the Buyer as referred to above, shall assume full responsibilities in fulfilling their obligations as per the terms and conditions herein stipulated. Any dispute arising from the execution of or in connection with this Contract shall be settled in accordance with the terms stipulated above between the Signers of this Contract only, without involving any Third Party.

(13) Other Terms:

① The Seller reserves the option of shipping the indicated percentage more or less than the quantity hereby contracted, and the covering Letter of Credit shall be negotiated for the amount covering the value of quantity actually shipped.

② The contents of the covering Letter of Credit shall be in strict accordance with the stipulations of the Sales Contract. In case of any variation thereof necessitating amendment of the L/C, the Buyer shall bear expenses for effecting the amendment. The Seller shall not be held responsible for possible delay of shipment resulting from awaiting the amendment of the L/C, and reserves the right to claim with the Buyer for the losses resulting therefrom.

③ Except in cases where the insurance is covered by the Buyer as arranged, insurance is to be covered by the Seller with a Chinese insurance company. If insurance for additional amount and/or for other insurance terms is required by the Buyer, prior notice to this effect must reach the Seller before shipment and is subject to the Seller's agreement, and the extra insurance premium shall be for the Buyer's account.

④ The Buyer is requested to send to the Seller authentic copy of the License-application (endorsed by the relative bank) filed by the Buyer and telegraphically advise the Seller immediately when the said License is obtained. Should the Buyer intend to file reapplication for License in cases of rejection of the original application, the Buyer shall contact the Seller and obtain the latter's consent before filing the reapplication.

THE SELLER: THE BUYER:

One copy of this Contract is to be returned to the Seller by airmail after duly signed by the Buyer.

- 语篇2

**APPOINTMENT AS CONTRACT
FULL-TIME SENIOR CUSTOMS ADMINISTRATOR**

AN AGREEMENT FOR SERVICES made the 1st day of September, 2019 between Company A of Beijing, China (address) (hereinafter referred to as "the Company") as one part and Mr. Smith of London, the UK (address) (hereinafter referred to as the Contractor) of the other part.

WHEREBY IT IS AGREED AND DECLARED AS FOLLOWS:

(1) THAT the Company shall ...

(2) This agreement shall commence on ...

(3) ...
(4) ...
IN WITNESS WHEREOF, both parties set their hands on the date herein mentioned.
SIGNED BY (Name):
Designation:
For and on behalf of:(signature)
Contractor:
Designation:
For and on behalf of:(signature)

● 语篇3

CONTRACT

No.:
Date:

The Buyer: Anderson Trading Company, Denmark
The Seller: Guangdong Native Produce Imp. & Exp. Co.

This contract is made by and between the Buyer and the Seller, whereby the Buyer agrees to buy and the Sellers agrees to sell the under-mentioned goods according to the terms and conditions stipulated below:

(1) Commodity: Wuyi Peanuts

(2) Specifications: FAQ 2018 Crop

(3) Quantity: 100 m/t.

(4) Unit price: US $500.00 per m/t, CIF Aarhus Denmark

(5) Total value: US $50,000.00 (Say US dollars fifty thousand only)

(6) Packing: In 3-ply gunny sacks of 50kg each

(7) Shipping marks: ...

(8) Insurance: To be effected by the seller for 100% of invoice value plus 10% against All Risks

(9) Terms of shipment: During July, 2019 with transshipment at Copenhagen

(10) Port of shipment: Huangpu, China

(11) Port of destination: Aarhus, Denmark

(12) Terms of payment: By irrevocable L/C payable by draft at sight. The L/C should reach the seller 30 days before the time of shipment and to remain valid for negotiation in China until the 15th day after the day of shipment.

Done and signed in Guangzhou on this twentieth day of April, 2019.

The Buyer	The Seller
(Signature)	(Signature)
Title	Title

第十四章　汉英商业广告对比分析与翻译

1. 思考题(略)

2. 对比分析

　　因为《新闻周刊》是以普通大众为读者对象的,所以刊登在上面的广告的受话者或交际对象也是大众读者,因此信息的表达方式也必须是大众化的,所用词汇比较通俗,句式结构也较简单。同时,它采用了直接的方式来树立公司的品牌形象,比如,广告宣传他们的产品是"Known Worldwide for Quality Sound and State-of-the-Art Features",公司是"Big Name Recording Star"。

　　因为《音响评论》杂志有比较专业化的读者,所以美国AKAI公司采用了另一种劝说策略。它侧重于对受话者或交际对象的诉诸,通过与他们进行直接交流来赢得信任。广告的表达方式不仅劝说性强,而且很诙谐幽默,如head的双关用法。"It's a head that many audiophiles feel has set the industry's performance and durability standards."的言外之意是:《音响评论》杂志的读者也一定是音响爱好者,也一定会持同样的观点,所以也一定会认同我公司的品牌(胡曙中,2004)。

　　由于受话者不同,两则广告所用表达方式也随之发生了变化,这样的变化是很自然的。

3. 句子翻译

　　(1) Balloons. Easy on your feet. Easy on your pocket.

　　(2) Pepsi Cola. Taste that beats the other colds.

　　(3) The orangemostest drink.

　　(4) The driver is safer when the road is dry; the road is safer when the driver is dry.

　　(5) Only White Wings bring you mmmmmmoisture.

　　(6) Our aim: Mark a global hit—Shengjia Auto Electric.

　　(7) All through the night, Night of Olay enhances the natural regeneration of your skin by keeping it constantly moist, easing tiny wrinkles and making your skin softer and more delicate.

　　(8) Business success often means being in the right place at the right time. Be at the center of opportunities. Register as an exhibitor at **INNOVATION & DESIGN EXPO**!

　　(9) Marvels of the marvelous marble of Yixing.

　　(10) Our shoe polish is surely of the first rate; it shines your shoes and you look great.

　　(11) Applying "Dabao" morning and night, makes your skincare a real delight.

　　(12) It gives you joy. It gives you fun. It gives you beauty. It gives you love.

　　(13) A Special Cola. A Special Choice.

(14) We are ready.

4. 语篇翻译

- 语篇1

Somewhere in the world—in dense jungle, or basking desert, or polar wasteland—an explorer could even now be navigating by dead reckoning. For this task, an absolutely reliable time-piece is essential.

Ever since its introduction in 1926, the Rolex Oyster has been the choice of explorers and adventurers. The virtual indestructibility of the Oyster case and utter reliability of the movement it contains have ensured that countless oysters have accompanied their wearers into history books.

Yet the Rolex Oysters that have voyaged to the ends of the earth and depths of ocean are in every respect the same watches that you will find in any official Rolex jeweler.

Every single Rolex Oyster that leaves Geneva is capable of accompanying its owner wherever he or she cares to venture.

Where in the world will you be taking yours?

- 语篇2

"A bank is a place where they lend you an umbrella in fair weather, and ask for it back again when it rains."

The Northern Trust Company in Chicago is grateful we did not inspire that telling quotation from Robert Frost. Frost was a four-time recipient of the Pulitzer Prize for Poetry, and his remark demonstrates his crusty New England sense of satire.

For over 96 years we've been protecting people from a rainy day, and now we're serving today's generation. With personal banking products like our Equity Credit Line, it lets you use the roof over your head to gain a personal line of credit. We want to talk to you about it. And about all your banking needs.

If you don't want to get wet, give us a call.

(312)630-60000

Northern Trust Bank

We want to talk, and you can quote us.

- 语篇3

LIPTON "JIGGLES UP" HERBAL TEA

Herbal teas don't have to be dull.

Because now there's a delicious new range from Lipton.

Fruity, spicy, tangy ... but we'll let their names tell you how wonderful they taste.

Gentle Orange, Refreshing Mint, Lemon Soother, Quietly Chamomile and Cinnamon Apple.

And they're not only delicious, they're also caffeine free.

So you can jiggle a Lipton Herbal as often as you like.

Lipton

Herbal Tea

Caffeine Free

- 语篇 4

"Snow Mountain" Cashmere Sweaters are lustrous in color, and supple, light, warm and comfortable to wear. Owing to their fine quality, excellent workmanship, novel designs and style, and complete size range, they have gained popularity from consumers at home and abroad.

第十五章 汉英商业说明书对比分析与翻译

1. 思考题（略）

2. 句子翻译

(1) The rated voltage of the appliance is 220V alternating current and the rated frequency is 50Hz. It can vary from 180V to 220V.

(2) A nourishing beverage for all ages. An excellent gift in all seasons.

(3) This machine is equipped with a gear transmission mechanism, and its multi-dies are arranged in line. It can draw steel, aluminum, brass and other kinds of metal wires.

(4) Add sugar and milk to taste.

(5) Simple construction, easy operation and maintenance, and comparatively high productivity.

(6) Ingredients: fresh beef of high quality, sugar, chili oil, sesame oil, salt, condiments.

(7) You should complete this customs declaration in the English language. Another language may be added provided it is accepted in the country of destination; further information can be obtained at a post office.

(8) Do not spray over food or tableware. Do not use or store near fire. Do not strike. It should be kept in cool place and kept away from the children.

(9) To obtain the best performance and ensure years of trouble-free use, please read this instruction manual carefully.

(10) When operating the machine, don't put your foot on the pedal switch board

constantly in case you might accidentally step on the switch, resulting in an accident.

3. 语篇翻译

- 语篇1

Within warranty period, the consumer should show the valid purchase invoice of the appliance and other relevant guarantee documents defined by the manufacturer when asking for free of charge repair. Consumer should keep the warranty card and the purchase invoice properly and show them together when asking for free of charge repair. The warranty period starts from the invoice date. If the customer loses the invoice, it starts from the manufacturing date.

- 语篇2

Pantene PRO-V Treatment Shampoo

Pantene PRO-V gives you healthy, shiny hair. Pantene PRO-V Treatment Shampoo now contains even more Provitamin B5, which deeply penetrates your hair from root to tip, making it healthy and shiny. With a built-in conditioner, Treatment Shampoo cleans and conditions in one easy step.

Directions: Wet hair and lather. Rinse thoroughly. For extra moisturization to prevent split-ends, use regularly Pantene PRO-V Treatment Moisturizer.

- 语篇3

Beijing Quanjude Roast Duck Restaurant

Started in the third year of Tongzhi Reign (1864 A. D.) of the Qing Dynasty, Quanjude Roast Duck Restaurant, famous for its specialties both at home and abroad, has a history of more than one hundred and thirty years.

The restaurant specializes in roast duck and Shandong-style specialties, especially offering the unique "all-duck banquet". With high cooking techniques and a fine tradition, Quanjude boasts quite a number of renowned chefs.

Completed in 1979, the seven-story restaurant, located on the southeastern side of Hepingmen Ave. cross, covers a floor space of 15,000 square meters in all with forty and more dining rooms of all kinds. The greatest roast duck restaurant at home and abroad, it can receive two thousand guests at the same time in a most graceful, comfortable and magnificent environment.

With excellent service and rich regional flavors, all the staff members warmly welcome domestic and international customers to enjoy their best-known roast duck and Shandong-style delicacies.

- 语篇4

Zipper Lock Usage Instructions

The lock is set at the manufacturer to open at 000. You can keep it as your combination, or set a new one as following steps:

Firstly, push the button in the direction of the arrow and hold it, until completing the next step.

Secondly, turn the dials to your desired personal combination.

Thirdly, release the button and rotate the dials so that your three secret numbers can't be seen.

Fourthly, now your new personal code is set.

Fifthly, if you want to change to a new combination, repeat the steps.

参考文献

Ellis, M. & Johnson, C. 2002. *Teaching Business English* [M]. Oxford: Oxford University Press.

Gartside, L. 1989. *English Business Studies* [M]. Plymouth: Macdonald and Evans Ltd.

Grandy, R. E. 1987. In Defence of Semantic Fields [A]. In Lepore, E. *New Directions in Semantics* [C]. New York: Academic Press.

Grice, H. P. 1975. Logic and Conversation [A]. In Cole., P. & Morgan, J. *Syntax and Semantics 3: Speech Acts* [C]. New York: Academic Press.

Halliday, M. A. K. & Hasan, R. 1976. *Cohesion in English* [M]. London: Longman.

Halliday, M. A. K. 1973. *Exploration in the Functions of Language* [M]. London: Edward Arnold.

Happ, H. 1985. *"Paradigmatisch"—"Syntagmatisch"* [M]. Heidelberg: C. Winter.

Hatim, B. & Mason, I. 2001. *Discourse and the Translator* [M]. Essex: Longman Group UK Ltd.

Hofstede, G. 1998. *Masculinity and Femininity: The Taboo Dimension of National Cultures* [M]. Thousand Oaks, Calif.: Sage Publications.

Hutchinson, T. & Waters A. 1987. *English for Specific Purposes: A Learning-Centered Approach* [M]. Cambridge: Cambridge University Press.

Hutchinson, T. & Waters, A. 2002. *English for Specific Purpose* [M]. Shanghai: Shanghai Foreign Language Education Press.

Hymes, D. H. 1972. On Communicative Competence [A]. In Pride, J. B., Holmes, J. *Sociallinguistics* [C]. Harmondsworth: Penguin.

Jones, L. & Alexander, R. 1989. *International Business English Student's Book* [M]. Cambridge: Cambridge University Press.

Jordan, R. R. 1997. *English for Academic Purposes: A Guide and Resource Book for Teachers* [M]. Cambridge: Cambridge University Press.

Leech, G. 1981. *Semantics: The Study of Meaning* [M]. Secend ed.

Harmondsworth: Penguin Books Ltd.

Leech, G. & Svartvik, J. 1974. *A Communicative Grammar of English* [M]. London: Longman.

Newmark, P. 1988. *A Textbook of Translation* [M]. New York: Prentice Hall.

Newmark, P. 1991. *About Translation* [M]. Clevedon: Multilingual Matters.

Newmark, P. 2001. *Approaches to Translation* [M]. Shanghai: Shanghai Foreign Language Education Press.

Nida, E. A. 1964. *Toward a Science of Translating: With Special Reference to Principles and Procedures Involved in Bible Translation* [M]. Leiden: E. J. Brill.

Nida, E. A. 1993. *Language, Culture, and Translating* [M]. Shanghai: Shanghai Foreign Language Education Press.

Nida, E. A. 1998. *Language, Culture, and Translating* [M]. Huhehot: Inner Mongolia University Press.

Nida, E. A. 2001. *Language and Culture: Contexts in Translation* [M]. Shanghai: Shanghai Foreign Language Education Press.

Nida, E. A. & Taber, C. R. 1969. *The Theory and Practice of Translation* [M]. Leiden: Brill Academic Pub.

Nord, C. 1997. *Translating as Purposeful Activity* [M]. Manchester, UK: St. Jerome Publishing.

Palmer, L. R. 1936. *An Introduction to Modern Linguistics* [M]. London: MacMillan and Co., Ltd.

Potter, S. 1969. *Changing English* [M]. London: Deutsch.

Quirk, R., Greenbaum, S., Leech, G. et al. 1972. *A Grammar of Contemporary English* [M]. London: Longman.

Sapir, E. 1921. *Language: An Introduction to the Study of Speech* [M]. New York: Harcourt, Brace & Co.

Sapir, E. 1970. *Culture, Language and Personality* [M]. Berkeley: University of California Press.

Saussure, F. 1983. *Cours de linguistique générale* [M]. Paris: Payout.

Scollen, R. & Scollon, S. 2002. *Intercultural Communication: A Discourse Approach* [M]. Beijing: Foreign Language Teaching and Research Press.

Shaw, R. D. 1987. The Translation Context: Cultural Factors in Translation [J]. *Translation Review*, (23): 25-29.

Whorf, B. L. 1956. Grammatical Categories [A]. In Carroll, J. B. *Language,*

Thought and Reality: Selected Writings of Benjamin Lee Whorf［C］. Cambridge, Massachusetts：The MIT Press.

Wittgenstein, L. 1953. *Philosophical Investigations*［M］. Oxford：Blackwell；New York：Macmillan.

Wood, L., Sanderson, P., Williams, A. et al. 2002. *Pass Cambridge BEC Vantage (Student Book)*［M］. Beijing：Economics Science Press.

安亚中,张健.2008.汉英大词典[Z].北京:商务印书馆国际有限公司.

包惠南.2001.文化语境与语言翻译[M].北京:中国对外翻译出版公司.

蔡基刚.2003.英汉写作修辞对比[M].上海:复旦大学出版社.

曹志耘.1992.广告语言艺术[M].长沙:湖南师范大学出版社.

常玉田.2002.经贸汉译英教程[M].北京:对外经济贸易大学出版社.

陈望道.2006.修辞学发凡[M].上海:上海教育出版社.

成昭伟,周丽红.2011.英语语言文化导论[M].北京:国防工业出版社.

程镇球.2002.翻译论文集[M].北京:外语教学与研究出版社.

戴卫平,裴文斌.2008.英汉文化词语研究[M].北京:科学出版社.

方梦之.2003.实用文本汉译英[M].青岛:青岛出版社.

方梦之.2004.翻译新论与实践[M].青岛:青岛出版社.

冯克江.2010.说明书的文体特征与翻译[J].宜春学院学报,32(11):161-164.

冯庆华,刘全福.2011.英汉语言比较与翻译[M].北京:高等教育出版社.

冯志杰.1998.汉英科技翻译指要[M].北京:中国对外翻译出版公司.

傅敬民,张顺梅,薛清.2005.英汉翻译辨析[M].北京:中国对外翻译出版公司.

顾维勇.2005.实用文体翻译[M].北京:国防工业出版社.

何维湘.1997.商务英语应用文写作[M].广州:中山大学出版社.

恒齐,隋云.2003.商务应用文的英译应与国际接轨[J].中国翻译(3):74-77.

胡丽霞.2007.目的论指导下的商品说明书翻译[J].武汉科技学院学报(4):70-72.

胡曙中.1993.英汉修辞比较研究[M].上海:上海外语教育出版社.

胡曙中.2004.现代英语修辞学[M].上海:上海外语教育出版社.

胡亚红,李崇月.2009.从系统功能语言学角度研究商务合同的翻译[J].内蒙古农业大学学报(社会科学版)(3):354-371.

黄艺平.2010.从语用角度看商务翻译的礼貌性原则[J].中国科技翻译(4):34-37.

黄勇.2007.英汉语言文化比较[M].西安:西北工业大学出版社.

霍莉·罗迪克.2005.如何写出完美的商务英语信函[M].郁震,等,译.北京/西安:

世界图书出版公司.

贾文波.2004.应用翻译功能论[M].北京:中国对外翻译出版公司.

贾文波.2007.应用翻译:多元交际互动中的整体复杂行为[J].外语与翻译(4):32-39.

简·沃特森.2004.商务英语写作指南[M].鲁刚,译.上海:上海世界图书出版公司.

金惠康.2003.跨文化交际翻译[M].北京:中国对外翻译出版公司.

来东慧.2005.商务英语翻译中的跨文化因素[J].郑州航空工业管理学院学报(社会科学版),24(1):92-94.

黎运汉.2005.商务语言教程[M].广州:暨南大学出版社.

李彬.2003.符号透视:传播内容的本体诠释[M].上海:复旦大学出版社.

李长栓.2004.非文学翻译理论与实践[M].北京:中国对外翻译出版公司.

李发根.2004.语言理论与翻译研究[M].合肥:中国科学技术大学出版社.

李明.2006.英汉互动翻译教程[M].武汉:武汉大学出版社.

李明.2007.商务英语翻译:汉译英[M].北京:高等教育出版社.

李明清.2009.基于"变通"原则的商务英语翻译[J].外国语文(A1):117-120.

李运兴.2000.语篇翻译引论[M].北京:中国对外翻译出版公司.

连淑能.1993.英汉对比研究[M].北京:高等教育出版社.

连淑能.2002.论中西思维方式[J].外语与外语教学(2):40-46,F003-F004.

连先.2002.商务专题英文写作[M].北京:外文出版社.

梁玉茹,黄远鹏.2011.从合作原则的视角下探讨商务英语信函的翻译[J].内蒙古农业大学学报(社会科学版)(2):354-355,368.

刘重德.1979.试论翻译的原则[J].湖南师范大学社会科学学报(1):115-120.

刘法公.1999.商贸汉英翻译专论[M].重庆:重庆出版社.

刘法公.2002.商贸汉英翻译的原则探索[J].中国翻译(1):45-48.

刘法公.2004.商务汉英翻译评论[M].北京:外语教学与研究出版社.

刘继超,高月丽.2002.修辞的艺术[M].北京:石油工业出版社.

刘宓庆.1998.文体与翻译[M].北京:中国对外翻译出版公司.

刘宓庆.2001.翻译与语言哲学[M].中国对外翻译出版公司.

刘宓庆.2003.翻译教学:实务与理论[M].北京:中国对外翻译出版公司.

陆国强.1983.现代英语词汇学[M].上海:上海外语教育出版社.

罗健.2002.商务英语写作教学探新[J].外语界(6):45-48.

马会娟.2004.商务英语翻译教程(外经贸版)[M].北京:中国商务出版社.

马会娟.2005.论商务文本翻译标准的多元化[J].中国翻译(3):81-84.

孟广君.2009.商务文体翻译虚实语义语际比较分析[M].上海翻译(2):44-47.

潘红.2004.商务英语英汉翻译教程[M].北京:中国商务出版社.
潘文国.1997.汉英语对比纲要[M].北京:北京语言大学出版社.
潘月洲.2008.商务英语翻译教程[M].北京:北京交通大学出版社.
彭萍.2004.商务文本翻译尺度的探讨[J].上海科技翻译(1):19-22.
彭增安.1998.语用・修辞・文化[M].上海:学林出版社.
钱歌川.1978.英文疑难详解[M].香港:中外出版社.
秦秀白.1986.英语文体学入门[M].长沙:湖南教育出版社.
秦秀白.2002.英语语体与文体要略[M].上海:上海外语教育出版社.
琼斯(Jones, L.),亚历山大(Alexander, R.).2000.剑桥国际商务英语[M].北京:华夏出版社.
萨默斯.2004.朗文当代英语大辞典(英英・英汉双解)[Z].朱原,等译.北京:商务印书馆.
邵志洪.2005.汉英对比翻译导论[M].上海:华东理工大学出版社.
申小龙.2000.语言与文化的现代思考[M].郑州:河南人民出版社.
沈苏儒.1998.论信达雅——严复翻译理论研究[M].北京:商务印书馆.
石春让,白艳.2012.新世纪十年来商务英语翻译研究:回顾与前瞻[J].解放军外国语学院学报(1):80-85.
索绪尔.1980.普通语言学教程[M].高名凯,译.北京:商务印书馆.
谭硕.2008.涉外商务信函翻译策略初探[J].商业文化(学术版)(11):190.
谭卫国.2003.中西文化与广告语言[J].上海师范大学学报(哲学社会科学版)(2):107,111-112.
谭载喜.1997.翻译中的语义对比试析[A].//杨自俭,李瑞华.英汉对比研究论文集[C].上海:上海外语教育出版社.
谭载喜.2004.西方翻译简史[M].北京:商务印书馆.
汪榕培,卢晓娟.1997.英语词汇学教程[M].上海:上海外语教育出版社.
汪滔.2001.克服重重文化障碍——再谈涉外广告翻译[J].四川外语学院学报(6):87-88.
王垂基.2008.词文化源考[M].广州:中山大学出版社.
王大来.2005.商务英语形合与汉语意合对比研究[J].中国科技翻译(3):42.
王德春.1987.修辞学词典[Z].杭州:浙江教育出版社.
王德春,陈晨.2001.现代修辞学[M].上海:上海外语教育出版社.
王逢鑫.2001.英汉比较语义学[M].北京:外文出版社.
王虹力.2009.中国学生的商务信函语用失误[J].青年科学(9):221.
王力.1957.中国语法理论[M].北京:中华书局.

王立非,李琳.2011.商务外语的学科内涵及发展路径分析[J].外语界(6):6-14.

王兴孙.1997.对国际商务英语学科发展的探讨[C]//上海对外贸易学院国际商务外语学院.商务英语教学探索:全国高校第二届国际商务英语研讨会论文集.上海:上海交通大学出版社.

王盈秋.2001.商务合同翻译中汉英转换的语域视角[J].渤海大学学报(哲学社会科学版)(5):90-95.

王永泰.2002.翻译标准不宜苛求统一[Z].2002年10月于广东外语外贸大学召开的"第三届全国多语翻译理论研讨会"交流论文.

王月峰,胡登勇.2007.商务英语翻译中的文化差异[J].考试周刊(16):30.

王佐良,丁往道.1997.英语文体学引论[M].北京:外语教学与研究出版社.

危东亚.1997.汉英词典[Z].北京:外语教学与研究出版社.

威廉·冯·洪堡特.1997.论人类语言结构的差异及其对人类精神发展的影响[M].姚小平,译.北京:商务印书馆.

韦钦.2005.中英广告中的文化对比[J].广西右江民族师专学报(1):104.

文月娥.2008.功能主义目的论在中国的接受与研究[J].西南科技大学学报(哲学社会科学版)(4):91.

翁凤翔.2002.实用翻译[M].杭州:浙江大学出版社.

翁凤翔.2007a.简明商务英语词典[Z].上海:上海外语教育出版社.

翁凤翔.2007b.当代国际商务英语翻译[M].上海:上海交通大学出版社.

肖青云.2005.中美广告文化差异对比研究[J].惠州学院学报(社会科学版)(4):94-98.

谢建平.2008.功能语境与专门用途英语语篇翻译研究[M].杭州:浙江大学出版社.

谢金领.2007.世纪商务英语翻译教程[M].大连:大连理工大学出版社.

徐烈炯.1990.语义学[M].北京:语文出版社.

许建忠.2002.工商企业翻译实务[M].北京:中国对外翻译出版公司.

杨景萍.2011.语言相对论对跨文化交际的影响[J].鸡西大学学报(综合版)(8):118.

杨晓荣.2001.翻译批评标准的传统思路和现代视野[J].中国翻译(6):14.

杨一秋.2003.合同英语文体特点及翻译要点[J].中国科技翻译(4):40-42,111.

叶玉龙,王文翰,段云礼.1998.商务英语汉译教程[M].天津:南开大学出版社.

尹帮彦.2006.汉语熟语英译词典[Z].上海:上海外语教育出版社.

尤金·A.奈达.2001.语言文化与翻译[M].严久生,译;陈健康,校译.呼和浩特:内蒙古大学出版社.

余富林,王占斌,岳福新,等.2003.商务英语翻译(英译汉)[M].北京:中国商务出版社.

袁建军,梁道华.2009.国际经贸英文合同的语言特征与翻译[J].重庆交通大学学报(社会科学版)(5):127.

张传彪.2012.变通乃翻译基本属性[J].中国科技翻译,25(2):41-44.

张春柏.2009.英语笔译实务(三级)[M].北京:外文出版社.

张会森.2003.修辞学通论[M].上海:上海外语教育出版社.

张敬.2009.汉英对比与广告翻译策略[J].外语教学研究(16):219-221.

张新红,李明,李克兴,等.2003.商务英语翻译:英译汉[M].北京:高等教育出版社.

赵彦春.2005.翻译学归结论[M].上海:上海外语教育出版社.

周锡卿.1987.英语谚语词典[Z].北京:北京出版社.

周晓,周怡.1998.现代英语广告[M].上海:上海外语教育出版社.

朱永生,严世清,苗兴伟.2004.功能语言学导论[M].上海:上海外语教育出版社.

邹海峰,赵耀,(美)Manvel Lunes.2004.国际商务信函与合同模板手册[M].北京:中国商务出版社.

邹力.2005.商务英语翻译教程(笔译)[M].北京:中国水利水电出版社.